Designing World Language Curriculum for Intercultural Communicative Competence

Also Available from Bloomsbury

Using Literature in English Language Education, edited by *Janice Bland* Teaching Beginner Level English Language Learners, *Lesley Painter-Farrell* and *Gabriel Diaz Maggioli*

Process Drama for Second Language Teaching and Learning, *Patrice Baldwin* and *Alicja Galazka*

Performative Language Teaching in Early Education, *Joe Winston*

Language Education in the School Curriculum, *Ken Cruickshank, Stephen Black, Honglin Chen, Linda Tsung* and *Jan Wright*

TESOL and Sustainability, edited by *Jason Goulah* and *John Katunich*

Teaching English-Medium Instruction Courses in Higher Education, *Ruth Breeze* and *Carmen Sancho Guinda*

Essentials for Successful English Language Teaching, 2nd edition, *Thomas S. C. Farrell* and *George M. Jacobs*

Teaching Literature in Modern Foreign Languages, edited by *Fotini Diamantidaki*

Designing World Language Curriculum for Intercultural Communicative Competence

Jennifer Eddy

BLOOMSBURY ACADEMIC
LONDON • NEW YORK • OXFORD • NEW DELHI • SYDNEY

BLOOMSBURY ACADEMIC
Bloomsbury Publishing Plc
50 Bedford Square, London, WC1B 3DP, UK
1385 Broadway, New York, NY 10018, USA
29 Earlsfort Terrace, Dublin 2, Ireland

BLOOMSBURY, BLOOMSBURY ACADEMIC and the Diana logo are
trademarks of Bloomsbury Publishing Plc

First published in Great Britain 2022

Copyright © Jennifer Eddy, 2022

Jennifer Eddy has asserted her right under the Copyright, Designs and
Patents Act, 1988, to be identified as Author of this work.

For legal purposes the Acknowledgements on pp. xxii–xxiii constitute an
extension of this copyright page.

Cover design: Charlotte James
Cover image © melita/Alamy Stock Photo and hudiemm/Getty Images

All rights reserved. No part of this publication may be reproduced or transmitted
in any form or by any means, electronic or mechanical, including photocopying,
recording, or any information storage or retrieval system, without
prior permission in writing from the publishers.

Bloomsbury Publishing Plc does not have any control over, or responsibility for, any third-
party websites referred to or in this book. All internet addresses given in this book were
correct at the time of going to press. The author and publisher regret any inconvenience
caused if addresses have changed or sites have ceased to exist, but can accept no
responsibility for any such changes.

A catalogue record for this book is available from the British Library.

A catalog record for this book is available from the Library of Congress.

ISBN: HB: 978-1-3501-8067-3
PB: 978-1-3501-8066-6
ePDF: 978-1-3501-8069-7
eBook: 978-1-3501-8068-0

Typeset by Integra Software Services Pvt. Ltd.
Printed and bound in Great Britain

To find out more about our authors and books visit www.bloomsbury.com
and sign up for our newsletters.

To my mother; you gave me love, music, theatre, wisdom and encouragement at times of extreme adversity

To Brian, Maria, Ann and Flori; you gave me loyalty, care, kindness and trust when all around me there was none

To all my students, past, present and future; you are the best teachers I could ever have.

Contents

	List of Figures	viii
	List of Tables	ix
	List of Appendices	xi
	Preface	xiii
	Foreword	xxi
	Acknowledgements	xxii
1	Unfolding Curriculum with No End in Mind	1
2	(Re) Imagining Curriculum to Reveal the Cultural Story	37
3	From Coverage without Pity to Designing with Performance for Transfer: Make It New Everyday	75
4	Designing for Interpretive Goals: Exploring Meaning for Mediation	117
5	Designing for the Interpersonal Goal: Consensus on Meaning for Mediation	163
6	Designing for Presentational Goals: Creating Meaning for Mediation	197
7	Putting It Together for Articulation and Transfer	239
	Appendices	273
	Glossary	318
	References	321
	Index	338

Figures

1.1	Intercultural Curriculum Aligns Novel Assessment Design Articulated Performance and Transfer (ICANADAPT)	9
1.2	ICANADAPT Template Stage 1	10
1.3	ICANADAPT Template Stages 2 & 3	11
1.4	AATT Template	12
2.1	ICANADAPT Concept Map	67
3.1	Understanding Begins with Creative Transfer	83
3.2	Complexity, Autonomy, Novelty for Mediation and Transfer	97
3.3	Georges Seurat. A Sunday on La Grande Jatte – 1884. 1884/86. The Art Institute of Chicago. CC0 Public Domain Designation	112
3.4	AATT Leisure in 1884 and Today	113
7.1	ICANADAPT Concept Map Health	257

Tables

1.1	Traditional and Articulated Curriculum Compared	8
1.2	Articulated Assessment Transfer Task (AATT) Viva la Vida	28
1.3	AATT Sana, Sana	32
2.1	From Culture on the Margin of Curriculum to Centre Stage	45
2.2	AATT Axe Porridge	49
2.3	AATT Inside-Outside Spaces	56
2.4	AATT Capoeira: The Symbol of Resistance	63
2.5	Enduring Understandings and Objective Statements Compared	69
3.1	Turnarounds for Transfer	85
3.2	AATT The Wounded Lion Still Knows How to Roar	91
3.3	AATT Lockdown Yoga	99
3.4	Stages of Language Assessment Transfer Examples	104
3.5	AATT Made in Italy	106
4.1	What Interpretive-Receptive Is and Is Not	125
4.2	Cultural Community Authentic Texts	131
4.3	Questioning in the Interpretive Mode	134
4.4	AATT *The PaperBoy*: Story of Identity and Hope	138
4.5	AATT *Takiwātanga*: My/His/Her Own Time and Space	143
4.6	AATT Arirang: The Song of the People	148
4.7	AATT Child Labour	152
4.8	Interpretive Mode Task Sampler across Three Levels	156
4.9	Listening with Visuals Sampler across Three Levels	157
5.1	What Interpersonal-Interactive Is and Is Not	168
5.2	AATT One Lucky Day	174
5.3	Interpersonal Mode Sampler	179
5.4	AATT Social Justice: Bullying, Human Rights, Racism	182

5.5	AATT Celebration of Eid	186
5.6	Collaboration Sampler	189
5.7	AATT Chanson Pour Haiti	191
6.1	What Presentational-Productive Is and Is Not	202
6.2	Presentational Task Products	204
6.3	Presentational Task Sampler	204
6.4	AATT Wedding Celebration of the Yorùbá People	208
6.5	AATT Diverse Families in the German-speaking World	214
6.6	AATT THE Food City	219
6.7	AATT Gender-Based Violence	225
6.8	AATT in Xochitl, in Cuicatl	232
7.1	Summative and Formative Assessment	243
7.2	None to Nigh to Near to Novel Transfer Annotated	245
7.3	AATT School and Education	247
7.4	Stage Three Unit Guide Sample	251
7.5	AATT Our Lives, Our Homes	253
7.6	Lesson Plan	258

Appendices

Appendix A		Stage One and Stage Three at a Glance	273
Appendix B		Intercultural Transfer Targets Articulation Chart	274
Appendix C		ICANADAPT Unit Sample Viva la Vida	275
Appendix D		Perspectives, Practices and Products Inventory	279
Appendix E		Bridge to Design Axe Porridge	281
Appendix F		OSEE for Intercultural Performance Assessment	283
Appendix G	Website	Bridge to Design Inside-Outside Spaces	
Appendix H		Layers, Lifespan and Level	284
Appendix I	Website	Bridge to Design Capoeira: The Symbol of Resistance	
Appendix J		Side by Side	285
Appendix K		AATT Review Criteria and AATT Design Rubric	286
Appendix L	Website	Bridge to Design the Wounded Lion Still Knows How to Roar	
Appendix M	Website	Bridge to Design Lockdown Yoga	
Appendix N		Assessment for Transfer Inventory	290
Appendix O	Website	Bridge to Design Made in Italy	
Appendix P		Bridge to Design Leisure in 1884 and Today	291
Appendix Q	Website	Bridge to Design the Paper Boy: Story of Identity and Hope	
Appendix R	Website	Bridge to Design Takiwātanga: My/His/Her Own Time and Space	
Appendix S	Website	Bridge to Design Child Labour	
Appendix T	Website	Bridge to Design Child Labour	
Appendix U	Website	Bridge to Design One Lucky Day	
Appendix V	Website	Bridge to Design Social Justice: Bullying, Human Rights, Racism	

Appendix W	Website	Bridge to Design Celebration of Eid	
Appendix X	Website	Bridge to Design Chanson pour Haiti	
Appendix Y	Website	Bridge to Design Wedding Celebration among the Yorùbá People	
Appendix Z	Website	Bridge to Design Diverse Families in the German-speaking World	
Appendix AA	Website	Bridge to Design THE Food City	
Appendix BB	Website	Bridge to Design Gender-Based Violence	
Appendix CC	Website	Bridge to Design In Xochitl, In Cuicatl	
Appendix DD		Full Unit Sample	293
Appendix EE	Website	Bridge to Design School and Education	
Appendix FF	Website	Home Unit	
Appendix GG	Website	Bridge to Design Our Lives, Our Homes	
Appendix HH		Axe Unit	303
Appendix II	Website	Axe Lesson Plans and Presentational Rubric	
Appendix JJ	Website	Child Labour Unit	
Appendix KK	Website	Lockdown Yoga Unit	
Appendix LL	Website	Gender-Based Violence Unit	
Appendix MM		Unit Plan Guide	309
Appendix NN		Master List Mode Tasks	311
Appendix OO		ICANADAPT Template	314
	Website	ICANADAPT, AATT, Lesson Plan Fillable Templates	
Appendix PP		Tool for Articulation with the Seven Guiding Principles for World Language Curriculum Design	316

Preface

We need to prepare language learners for the inevitable unexpected

For over fifteen years, world language educators said I needed to write this book. They became familiar with my work at Queens College and at numerous national and state conferences including AATSP, ACTFL, FLENJ, MaFLA, NCOLCTL, NECTFL, NYSAFLT and STARTALK, in publications and for local district, state and university professional development initiatives. At Queens College, City University of New York, I have the honour to work with the most dedicated teacher candidates and faculty, as well as with educators across the United States and internationally who have attended my workshops and lectures and implemented the design framework and principles in this book. As programme director and associate professor of world language education with a background in music, drama and theatre, I research and prepare teachers on creative design for curriculum and assessment. In 2005, I directed workshops on Understanding by Design (UbD) for K-12 teachers and university faculty with *Authentic Education*, a cohort of professional development educators led by Grant Wiggins. In 2006, I published *Sonidos, Sabores, y Palabras* (Eddy, Heinle/Cengage), which aligned backward design/UbD principles with the National Standards for foreign language learning in the twenty-first century (NSFLEP, 1999/2006). *Sonidos* was the first book of its kind to address world language performance task design with Enduring Understandings and Essential Questions aligned to each song track, using overarching intercultural themes within the lyrics as authentic texts. I called this framework UC:ADAPT, Uncovering Culture: Assessment Design Aligning Performance and Transfer. In order to plan performance assessment for articulation across levels, I developed the AATTs: Articulated Assessment Transfer Tasks. Over the years through practice with educators, the design has evolved to the model in this book, Intercultural Curriculum Aligns Novel Assessment Design Articulated Performance and Transfer, *ICANADAPT*. This acronym aptly describes what the self-directed learner does, when creating new products and solving problems in the language to foster mediation and make languages and cultures accessible to others.

Designing World Language Curriculum for Intercultural Communicative Competence engages the teacher as designer of creative, novel performance tasks along a spiral, articulated curriculum for transfer and language learner autonomy. The book aligns the theoretical framework with extensive practical features for revising, designing and unfolding bespoke curricula through recursive intercultural themes coupled with novel tasks that transfer language learning from the classroom to community to develop communicative competence over the life-span.

This curriculum design asks educators and learners to develop questions, evaluate and use authentic text evidence to communicate information, come to a consensus and conclusion. This inquiry then guides learners in experiential tasks and key performance assessments that develop and connect critical thinking, problem-solving, mediation and collaborative skills needed for community and workplace engagement. With the framework outlined in this book, teachers and learners not only examine how other cultures present themselves through texts, but see themselves as a social agent (COE, 2001) to contribute and co-construct meaning from these texts, create new works and participate with confidence using the language they own right now.

Language is creativity by design.

Creativity is our reaction, our response to a situation or context. Because we are all different, each act of communication is distinctive, every instance often unanticipated. Whatever we see, read, hear, or watch, produces a unique reaction from us. We respond both in the moment and with time to think and refine, but when we do engage, the interaction always comes from a place of reform, variation and revision. We make language new. Therefore, practice at this unpredictable art is best served by novelty in tasks and constant adjustment and adaptation on what is reclaimed for that moment. Unpredictability teaches us flexibility.

What is truly relevant is what our learners can do with the language when they are out there, how they can participate in the language within community, work and world. This includes participation in neighbourhoods, groups and organizations. School administrators tell me it is what they look at when making decisions about our programmes against an investment of four or more years. This requires flexible use of language from performance tasks which practise adaptability, a habit best accomplished early and often. The only thing predictable about life in the language realm is how unpredictable it really is.

World Language Education curricula have been typically organized by coverage of grammar rather than focusing on performance task design for use in intercultural contexts. Even in light of efforts to sequence by proficiency goals indicated by CEFR and ACTFL, there is a dearth of materials for language instructors and departments at all levels of instruction on curriculum design of key performance tasks. Fixed and static textbook tasks and linguistic components in isolation cannot prepare the learner for the inevitable unpredictability and flexibility necessary for authentic communication. This book guides instructors and teacher educators on revision design of MFL/EFL language curricula by unfolding intercultural perspectives through articulated tasks, which reprise over the span of a spiralled programme between levels, schools, and university. Whether your programme goals look towards the Seal of Biliteracy, NCSSFL-ACTFL, the CEFR, or Key Stages Three (7, 8, 9), Four (10 and 11 the GCSE years), straight through to A level and university, the exemplars and strategies in this book will guide educators in creative, novel tasks and curriculum design. Secondary and post-secondary programmes alike often lament on the lack of articulation between programmes. In countries where universities grant credit to courses taught at the secondary level, this poses an even larger problem. Universities with these agreements will certainly find the book useful to developing collaborative programmes with partnership schools.

Designing Articulated Assessment Transfer Tasks (AATTs) and ICANADAPT exemplars

The twenty-four exemplars in this book represent all levels of instruction, authored by talented teaching artists and educators from kindergarten to university. They hail from public and private schools and universities, large and small, from the following languages and cultures: Arabic, Chinese, Èdè Yorùbá, French, German, Hindi, Italian, Japanese, Korean, Ladino, Nahuatl, Portuguese, Russian, Spanish, Te Reo Māori and Urdu. Each chapter features their AATT exemplars with templates and strategies for designing custom, bespoke curricula and performance assessments. Exemplars are in English so that all instructors may explore them, adapt and swap the tasks, integrate ideas and concepts and make comparisons and connections with the languages and cultures they teach as they design. Links to additional authentic multimedia texts in the languages represented in the exemplars with additional resources are located on the Companion Website.

I invite you to learn from a diverse group of teachers, department chairs, district supervisors, university professors, administrative directors and disciplined experts in their field as they share their thought process as designers with their articulated task and unit exemplars. Their exemplars unfold intercultural and transdisciplinary themes of time and space, bullying, home and belonging, ingenuity, health practices and perspectives, identity, world cuisine and food piracy, autism, child labour, irony, honour, beauty, resistance and resilience, gender-based violence, education, celebration and leisure, diverse families, balance, creativity, survival and independence.

Designing World Language Curriculum for Intercultural Communicative Competence is intended for

- pre-service training and certification programmes for K-12 World Language, KS2/KS3/KS4/KS5, and A1-C2 Modern Foreign Languages as well as for in-service educator professional learning/PDC at any level of instruction
- teachers who never had curriculum and assessment design courses and are now tasked with that responsibility in their school
- programmes faced with performance goals in mind but found those efforts are still taking a back seat to grammar, topics and functions as the initial reach for many colleagues
- all language disciplines. Post-secondary faculty at many universities have redesigned or refreshed their majors using these tools as well.

By working together using the exemplars and tasks in this book, teacher candidates, trainees and in-service teachers see how collaborative inquiry facilitates articulated or linked design for a more cohesive programme and department, rather than siloed in solitary work patterns by separate language or level.

This book and Companion Website resources:

✔ Identify and outline theoretical framework of curriculum design for teacher preparation and language programme development

✔ Explain and apply intercultural perspectives for articulation and transfer tasks

✔ Demonstrate and provide strategies, templates and exemplars for curricular units, schemes of work and performance assessment design.

Design Features

The book models for educators the process and many of the same design features, practices and components as recommended for curriculum and assessment design with our learners. This scheme aims to guide educators in shifts outlined in throughout the chapters and meet them wherever their prior knowledge or experience may be as designers.

Enduring Understandings and Essential Questions

These are presented for each chapter. These present concepts of curriculum and assessment design for this framework, intended for teachers to continue the inquiry throughout their preparation and for self-directed professional learning goals.

Key Terms and Concepts

New terms, concepts, as well as familiar topics relevant to each chapter are listed, then presented and explained in context.

Research in Practice

This section provides teachers with brief annotated applications from selected researchers and practitioners on a particular area of inquiry which are further explored throughout the chapters. Although this list is not intended to be exhaustive, it provides teachers with a great place to start as well as expand their pedagogical content knowledge of the profession. This feature is particularly useful for seasoned teacher educators seeking to guide instructional decisions with research and sound practices. Many elementary and secondary schools and districts require a professional learning plan each year with goals for the educator. Even as live and virtual professional learning communities and PDC opportunities abound, teachers are not always aware of ways to connect and implement educational theory and practice to second language instruction (Eddy, forthcoming). Teachers may also find this feature helpful when discussing curricular decisions with an administrator or parent, since curriculum and assessment design has become the responsibility of the teacher collective rather than of one department chair or administrator. Many teacher education programmes use a portfolio system with performances and artefacts from teaching as a capstone requirement for licensure or certificate. They are required to align researchers with practice within reflective written pieces for this portfolio as annotation for lessons and units. This section will prove invaluable for this purpose as they construct these reflections.

Pause to Ponder

This activity at the onset of each chapter asks educators to consider an issue or its implications with colleagues, by prompting or eliciting their background knowledge or their current understanding about a concept in world language curriculum and assessment.

Check for Learning

These formative tasks engage educators on steps to design either alone or with colleagues, to model the Gradual Release of Responsibility (GRR) of *I do, we do, you do* (Fisher & Frey, 2006; Pierson & Gallagher, 1983).

Teacher as Designer

This section introduces the AATT exemplar with some background on the design thinking as well as 'look-fors' that show evidence of articulation between levels, task type and strategies used for design and implementation of these Key Performance Assessment Tasks.

Voices from the Field

In the words of the authors and artists who inspired the AATT exemplars, these educators speak about their design process and particular features about their work. They share why the sequence of tasks is important and why the concept or theme is essential to revisit and reprise within a spiral curriculum.

Articulated Assessment Transfer Task (AATT) exemplar

A selection of AATT exemplars is featured in each chapter, curated for its content and relevance to the concepts discussed. They are presented in their entirety, even though the chapter may engage educators to design in a particular communicative mode. It is important to see how the entire AATT functions and the interdependence of all parts of this cohort model performance assessment design.

Bridge to Design

These 'near transfer' tasks found on the Companion Website as Appendices function as part of the 'we do' in GRR, where we analyse the exemplar together to reflect and reveal key features, components and noticings. Each AATT exemplar has a companion *Bridge to Design*. This feature poses questions to ourselves and our colleagues, then clarifies and elaborates for further suggestions on follow-up tasks. These tasks invite you to delve more deeply into each exemplar, reveal intercultural threads and connect to their own spiral design process. They also ask you to envision 'before and after' the AATT tasks, engaging you to design a novel one. This models the process your own learners will do. Finally, you are asked to pose a question to the author of the exemplar.

Each *Bridge to Design* includes Research in the Practice Redux, to bring us back to what informs the exemplar and connects us with other researchers and practitioners that the methods instructor may incorporate throughout a course or seminar. The *Bridge* models collaborative mediation techniques and strategies for working together in a community of practice.

Collaboration for Articulation

These questions or short tasks are designed for new and experienced practitioners to do together as a step towards collaborative curriculum development. Many teachers I work with never designed articulated curricula before, and they always appreciated time together to share ideas and their own change within the process.

Design for Transfer

These are Key Performance Tasks to close each chapter on design components of ICANADAPT or AATTs for articulated curricula and assessments. These tasks are recommended for methods or curriculum/assessment course syllabus for faculty incorporating the principles and examples in this book. These Key Performances also guide teachers in writing reflective commentaries or providing evidence as for an in-service teacher professional goals report or student teacher portfolio assessment. A master list anthology or catalogue of these Key Performance Tasks is given at the close of Chapter 7.

Discuss the Issues

Each chapter has discussion questions or statement prompts based on the exemplars and concepts within the chapters which relate to shifts in instructional practice. These engage educators in inquiry and lively professional debate and are meant to provoke more questions and ideas for further exploration or action research.

Reflect and Revisit

A reprise of concepts and application questions, designed to circle back towards refining curricular decisions or assessment task design.

Companion Website

The Companion website provides methods instructors and educators with useful ancillaries: the AATT and ICANADAPT exemplars with live links to authentic, cultural community materials, Chapter PowerPoints, Infographics and PDF Appendices, blank templates and other tools for the methods course or for curriculum and assessment design initiatives in a school or department.

Let's Begin

I hope this book inspires you to become co-designers with your learners, to instill in them that language is an act that expects creativity and validates imperfection because communication happens. It is always new. Give learners the confidence to use what language they have with others and to continue creating language without us, by making new meaning every day. Value and respect the inevitable unexpected with novelty.

Foreword

Designing World Language Curriculum for Intercultural Communicative Competence

by Jay McTighe, Educational Author and Consultant
Co-author of *Understanding by Design*®

Why do we teach anything? What are the long-term aims of language instruction? Arguably, the ultimate goal of schooling is to prepare learners to use their learning; i.e. to be able to transfer specific knowledge and skills to a variety of real-world situations. To this end, Dr Eddy notes that 'language is creativity by design', and that phrase sums up the essence of this book. Unlike the conventional approach to language teaching featuring rote learning of vocabulary and grammatical rules, Eddy reminds teachers to always keep the 'end in mind' and emphasize language in use for effective communication, aligned appropriately with culture and context. Accordingly, her pedagogical approach is inherently performance-based, focused around the design and use of authentic communication tasks that call for learners to transfer their emerging language skills in varied cultural contexts.

The book's uniqueness and value stem in large measure from its blending of the theoretical with the practical. Dr Eddy combines the authority of an academic researcher with the pragmatism of a veteran educator to produce this timely and valuable resource. Readers are presented with a variety of usable language tasks along with numerous curriculum/assessment design tools – all anchored by a rich, conceptual system reflecting best practices for language learning. Her approach to language instruction is brought to life through an impressive set of illustrative exemplars, reflecting the full range of grades, languages and inter-cultural contexts. In sum, this book offers something for everyone involved in developing real-world language capabilities.

As Grant Wiggins, co-author of Understanding by Design, reminds us, 'The point of school is not to get good at school but to effectively parlay what we learned in school in other learning and in life.' This book is dedicated to this aim, and your language learners will thank you for heeding its advice.

Acknowledgements

The AATT and ICANADAPT exemplars in this book are written by educators, artists and leaders in their profession who believe in this project and my work. My deepest appreciation to you for your care, intention, time and expertise in designing your exemplars with me. It is truly an honour to work with all of you. They are listed here in order of appearance in the chapters.

Dr Victoria Gilbert	Spanish
Ekaterina Kalmanson	Russian
Shiyo Kuo-Flynn	Japanese
Dr Célia Bianconi	Portuguese
Sarah Aroeste	Ladino
Bhavya Singh	Hindi
Antonino Bonanno	Italian
Dr Gabriela Nik Ilieva	Hindi
Keri Opai	Te Reo Māori
Soojin Choi Kim	Korean
Gina Durand	Spanish
Dr Patricia Lennon	Spanish
Romeena Kureishy	Urdu
Dr Elcie Douce	French
Dr Kazeem Kẹ́hìndé Sanuth	Èdè Yorùbá
Dr Paul Garcia	German
Mike McCloskey	German
Dr Ida D'Ugo	Spanish
Irwin Sánchez	Nahuatl
LingLing Xie	Chinese
Susan Hanna-Wicht	Arabic

To Marissa Coulehan, my graphic designer and project assistant: Her expertise with technology in our profession as a Spanish teacher, along with keen eyes,

Acknowledgements

ears and patience, provided revised graphics and designed many new images that matched my conceptual vision for this book. Thank you, Marissa!

Thank you, Queens College, my department chair, Dr Eleanor Armour-Thomas and the Department of Secondary Education and Youth Services for supporting my work and our programmes in World Language Education.

Thank you to Modern Foreign Language and World Language colleagues at all levels of instruction, for making languages and cultures accessible, rewarding and relevant to our learners. In this book, I have made every effort to ensure accuracy, acknowledgment, attribution and inclusion; any errors or omissions are not intentional. My sincere thanks to all the researchers and practitioners who have contributed to our profession and inspired my journey in it.

Chapter 1

Unfolding Curriculum with No End in Mind

Enduring Understandings

- ∞ Intercultural transferable goals focus and unfold vertically articulated or linked curriculum.
- ∞ Curriculum and assessment are planned backward from these concepts and inform key performance assessments with transdisciplinary visibility.
- ∞ Using a language appropriately within any culture requires high adaptability and tolerance of new situations.
- ∞ Evidence is determined by the extent to which we can manage incomplete information and solve problems without cues or extensive support.
- ∞ Curriculum and assessment design goals focus on mediation between and across cultures.
- ∞ Creativity for language learning is a tool as well as a goal.
- ∞ Teaching and learning happen within unique and shared social, cultural and historical contexts.

Essential Questions

- Q What does it mean for learners to be ready for a world they haven't yet experienced?
- Q To what extent are relevance and applicability inherent qualities of curriculum and assessment?
- Q What is the role of the instructor as designer?
- Q What does vertical articulation look like in language curriculum design?
- Q How does unpredictability teach flexibility?
- Q What is the value of poise over perfection?

Key Terms and Concepts

Articulation	Mediation for Transfer
AATT	Articulation Spiral Points
ICANADAPT	Aesthetic Education
Transfer	Drama Pedagogy
Autonomy	Transdisciplinary

Research in Practice

The work of the following researchers and practitioners will guide you to cite sources which inform your planning, assessment and instructional decisions in pre-service portfolio assessments or in-service professional learning plans.

ACTFL, 2012 Adair-Hauck, Glisan, Koda, Swender & Sandrock, 2006 NCSSFL, 2017 Sandrock, 2015	NCSSFL-ACTFL Can-Do Statements align with the ACTFL Proficiency Guidelines, the ACTFL Performance Descriptors for Language Learners and the three modes of communication
Bräuer, 2002 Greene, 1995, 2001 Heathcote & Bolton, 1995 Kao & O'Neill 1998	Aesthetic Education and Drama Pedagogy strategies support performance assessment, improvisation and intercultural competence
Bruner, 1960, 1996 Bower, Coyle, Cross, & Chambers, 2020 Coyle, Bower, Foley & Hancock, 2021	Do not postpone important concepts; anything can be taught effectively on a spiral curriculum. We make meaning by understanding intercultural response to various disciplines

Byram, 1997, 2009; Byram & Wagner, 2018 Byram & Fleming, 1998	Intercultural communicative competence as interaction with others to understand, contribute and mediate between languages and cultures. Drama facilitates meaning-making, improvisation and intercultural awareness
Byrnes, 1990, 2008	Need for vertical articulation and transition at all levels of MFL/world language instruction
Council of Europe, 1998, 2001, 2020	Learners are 'social agents' who develop competence through action, situation and performance rather than mechanized practice
Eddy, 2006a/b, 2007a/d/e, 2015a/c, 2016b, 2017	Cultural perspectives unfolding articulated curriculum design with key performance transfer tasks
Kramsch, 2006, 2009, 2011	Social and cultural symbols facilitate meaning and mediation
Liddicoat 2002 Liddicoat, et al., 2003	Acquisition of culture is cyclical and constant across a curriculum, focusing on action and understanding rather than information and facts
Lamb, 2000, 2008, 2017 Little, 2003, 2009a/b, 2011, 2012	Teacher and learner autonomy; self-reflection tools with the European Language Portfolio
McTighe & Silver, 2020	Learners engage in key performances aligned with long-term transfer goals across the curriculum; these demonstrate understanding rather than recall and application only in the way it was learned.
National Standards in Foreign Language Education Project, 1996, 2006 National Standards Collaborative Board, 2015	Standards for Foreign Language Learning in the twenty-first century World Readiness Standards for Learning Languages
North, 1992, 2000 North & Piccardo, 2016, 2019 Piccardo, 2013; Piccardo & North, 2019	Co-constructing and facilitating meaning for mediation with others in plurilingual and pluricultural space

Vygotzky, 1962, 1997	We create our own knowledge by asking questions and exploring what we know Use drama and art as mediator to negotiate everyday life in social settings
Wiggins & Mc Tighe, 2005, 2013	Curriculum is designed backward, first from disciplined concepts as desired results; key performance assessments next, which inform knowledge, skills and instructional decisions last

I can

- Define articulation and its role in developing intercultural curriculum and assessment
- Identify components and principles of Articulated Assessment Transfer Tasks and ICANADAPT design framework
- Explain the role of teacher as designer for learner autonomy

> **Rewind**
>
> Which ideas stand out for you after reading the Preface?
>
> Ask your colleague three questions based on the Preface.
>
> What do you think an articulated curriculum for world language/MFL looks like?
>
> Explain your experience with learning and/or teaching a language.
>
> What are you looking forward to learning about in this book that will benefit your work?

Overview

This chapter engages World Language/MFL teachers to think as designers. The premise of starting with the end in mind shifts design thinking from a single course or key stage/target, to what the learner understands and is able to do by the end of the programme, to continued community engagement without the teacher present. In this model, key concepts and must-have themes are uncovered which reprise and resurface not only in classroom instruction but throughout life in literature, arts, cultural history and all disciplines we encounter in daily life. This framework and articulated assessment system enable creative, intercultural language curricula with no end by design. Teachers and learners are often put in the role of passive consumer rather than active participant. They are hesitant to use language in new contexts and instead maintain an illusion of rules and finite predictability that is passed down to the next group of learners. This chapter defines and justifies the shift to make the case that articulated curricula and tasks designed for innovation and unpredictability create active language learners as agents for intercultural collaboration across their lifespan. Design with no end in mind.

Examining Dissonance in the Profession

In Paulo Freire's work, *Pedagogy of the Oppressed* (2018), 'Knowledge emerges only through invention and re-invention, through the restless, impatient, continuing, hopeful inquiry human beings pursue in the world, with the world, and with each other' (Freire, 71–72). For far too long and in spite of flickers of reform, modern/world language learning still largely operates under the banking model of teaching and learning that Freire denounces in his book. In that model, Freire spoke of the learner as a passive spectator and advocated for the learner to be a re-creator. For Modern Foreign Languages (MFL)/World Languages (WL), the banking model subordinates teachers as transmitters, reducing learners as the depository of cultural facts and grammatical forms, through artificial manipulation by textbooks or digital worksheets serving the curricular buffet. There is a decline in the uptake of MFL/WL in many countries and states, past the basic requirement if indeed there is one. The attrition or elimination of language offerings causes many in our profession to search for answers. More than ever, our profession needs to question, examine and promote relevance and applicability not only for the relatively short moments our learners are with us, but for their entire lives.

Learners cannot be limited to receiving, sorting and answering items from a repository. This shift starts with Teacher as Designer and further recognition of the issue, first with policy makers at all levels of instruction, then with MFL/World Language teacher education programmes. Teacher *autonomy* then, in turn, can facilitate the shift towards learner autonomy (Holec, 1988; Lamb, 2000, 2008, 2017; Little, 1995, 2007, 2009b, 2012). The framework presented in this book withdraws the banking model in exchange for teacher and learner to lean and push inquiry as co-investigators with each other and in extension as self-directed language users within their communities. As questions are uncovered and learners discover more about themselves and other cultures, there are greater opportunities for deep learning and invention through novel products and performances that matter within cultures. It is not enough for teachers to tell and for learners to copy and echo. Our curriculum design should focus on learner autonomy: what learners do which is new, so that they can continue to do it without us.

What truly matters is what we can do and accomplish flexibly and securely within a range of cultures when we are out there in the world; how we can adapt and thrive for community, career, relationship and world readiness. School administrators tell me it is what they look for when making decisions about our language programmes: relevance and applicability. Standards reforms with enhanced requirements may be welcome news; however, our profession experiences ever-increasing marginalization. Not all districts, states, countries and independent schools have a minimum language study requirement, but even in those that do, our field has incurred retrenchment of languages, diluted content, outsourced instruction and reduction in language choice. Uptake in languages continues to decline in secondary programmes (ACIE, 2017; Hagger-Vaughn, 2016), and post-secondary registrations report less students taking languages other than English even with the increased need for language skills in the workforce (Looney & Lusin, 2018). For many schools, it becomes a matter of marketing and investment. Administrators consider a limited budget against a time investment of four-plus years of language learning and often only see a decontextualized curriculum that is not applicable or relevant to other disciplines and expectations of twenty-first-century life. Even with district, state or national curricula in place, teachers lament the lack of collaboration for articulation and transition between levels, buildings and schools. When teachers are isolated to only the level they teach and not involved in what occurs before and after their own course, schemes of work and material are often retaught or reviewed with learners not going beyond novice level (Byrnes, 1990, 2008). Grammar forms and vocabulary lists in isolation and classroom exercises disconnected from life issues, interactions, activities, demands and concerns do not help learners to use the language for long-term goals (Stoller, 2006). Programmes are downsized or language choices reduced or eliminated because administrators, parents and other stakeholders do not see how language classes prepare learners for civic, career, life-skill and global readiness.

Using a language appropriately in any given culture requires high adaptability, tolerance of new situations, dealing with incomplete information and problem-solving without cues (Eddy, 2017). Our lives are anything but predictable but rather steeped in diversion, adjustment and flux. The design outlined in this book encourages tolerance of ambiguity and adaptability by engaging in varied language and cultural contexts with novelty of task, context and audience instead of expected routine. The amazing thing about language and consequently its most daunting prospect is that we really don't know what is going to happen after we say something to someone else. We can't be entirely sure of their reaction to us and then our retort. We don't know how the scene is going to play out. This requires adaptation, which comes only from practice at both flexibility and agility, early and often. The only thing predictable about thriving in the language is how unpredictable it really is. To fully understand, flourish and thrive within language and cultures, it is not through rules remembered and lines rehearsed. It is through exploration, participation, creation and reflection, via varied and novel interactions of intercultural experience along the lifespan.

When intercultural concepts and practices are the framer and curricular hook, the learner is not only engaged for that time but will recognize them within their interactions long after they left your programme. You want to design for intercultural competence revealed over the course of the curriculum but, more importantly, for continued engagement without a teacher present. These concepts and perspectives unfold through key tasks, from situations one may encounter in daily life within cultures to exploring concepts and needs learners understand but may not have all the language for just yet. Most importantly, these tasks allow them to apply concepts, practices, knowledge and skills to new situations they will encounter, with the tools to manage and mediate communication with others.

Pause to Ponder

Table 1.1. depicts features of a grammar or topic coverage model next to those practices aligned with articulated design, introduced thus far and to be uncovered further in this book. What are some of the features you want to see or believe you will encounter in this framework? Which framework is more familiar to you in your experience as a second language learner? As a second language teacher? Can you give any examples that demonstrate any of the features below?

Table 1.1 Traditional and Articulated Curriculum Compared

Traditional grammar or topic coverage model	Practices aligned with articulated intercultural transfer design
Learner as passive, dependent and reliant.	Learner as active, independent and autonomous.
The textbook as curriculum.	Curriculum uses authentic transdisciplinary resources for intercultural transfer goals.
Units and schemes of work focus on drill and mechanical practice.	Relevant and applicable contexts and key performances frame curriculum, schemes of work and units.
Assessment is most often paper-pencil; grammar in isolation.	Key transfer tasks and formative performance assessments prevail within a variety of assessment evidence.
Learning about the language as four skills is the goal.	Learners use language to appraise, evaluate, critique and create culture, language and content.
Topics, themes or subjects are distributed or allocated by proficiency or performance target level.	Concepts of value in cultures inform all disciplines. These concepts and tasks appear at all levels for participation at any level of learner engagement.
Grammar is the topic of units or schemes of work.	Grammar required is selected after the task is designed to support it and is not the topic of the unit, lesson or scheme of work.
Learner receives isolated cultural facts that are fixed and static.	Learners engage in mediation strategies to bridge, exchange and clarify language between intercultural perspectives with the practices and products they reveal.
Teacher is a passive transmitter of information.	Teacher is an active co-creator of transformative learning.

Framing the Reinvention

The design framework *Intercultural Curriculum Aligns Novel Assessment Design Articulated Performance and Transfer* (*ICANADAPT*) and the *Articulated Assessment Transfer Tasks* (*AATT*) (Eddy, 2006b, 2007g, 2015c, 2017, 2019a) provide the curriculum and assessment system for the exemplars, implementation material and design tools in these chapters. ICANADAPT (see Figure 1.1) is a revision of the model *Uncovering Content: Assessment Design aligning Performance and Transfer* (UC:ADAPT) (Eddy, 2006a, 2007a/c, 2009b,

2010a), used to prepare World Language/MFL teachers at Queens College, City University of New York, as well as engage in-service teachers in design at professional development sessions and conferences since 2006. The design framework applied and integrated Backward Design (Mc Tighe & Wiggins, 2004; Wiggins & McTighe, 2005, 2007, 2011) principles to the Standards for foreign language learning in the twenty-first century (National Standards in Foreign Language Education Project, 1996/2006) revised as the World-Readiness Standards for Learning (National Standards Collaborative Board, 2015). These standards are composed of goal areas known as the 'five Cs': Communication, Cultures, Connections, Comparisons and Communities. The summary document states:

> The five 'C' goal areas (Communication, Cultures, Connections, Comparisons, and Communities) stress the application of learning a language beyond the instructional setting. The goal is to prepare learners to apply the skills and understandings measured by the Standards, to bring a global competence to their future careers and experiences. (National Standards Collaborative Board, 2015)

ICANADAPT (see Figure 1.2) continues to place the Cultures goal area first as linchpin for transferable concepts and goals, which *drives* the intercultural curriculum (Eddy, 2007a, 2010d, 2017). These concepts become vertical articulation paths for sustained inquiry. To identify intercultural transferable goals

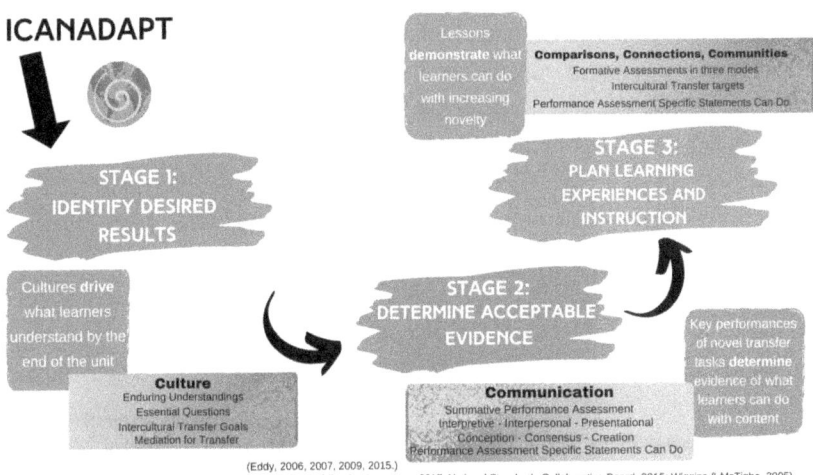

Figure 1.1 Intercultural Curriculum Aligns Novel Assessment Design Articulated Performance and Transfer (ICANADAPT)

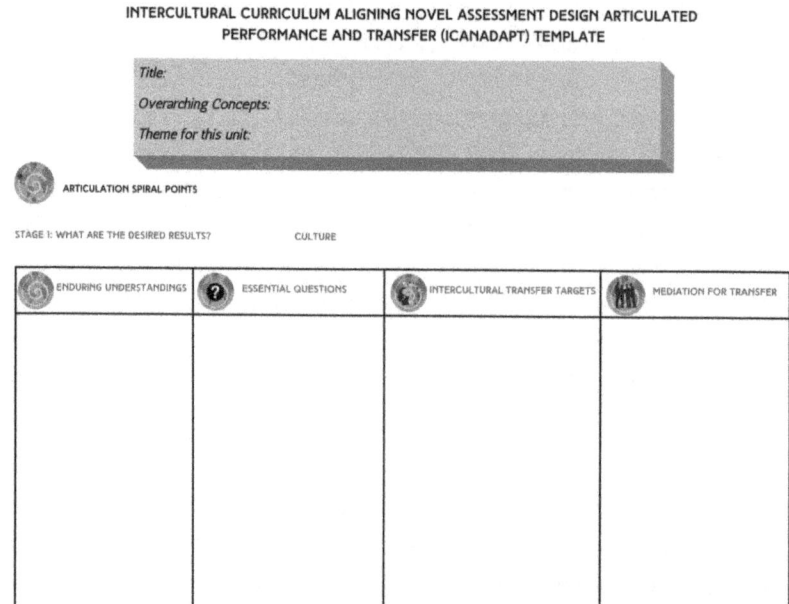

Figure 1.2 ICANADAPT Template Stage 1

in Stage One, Enduring Understandings and Essential Questions (EUs and EQs) (McTighe & Wiggins, 2004; Wiggins & McTighe, 2005) are developed through the lens of cultural perspectives, cultural history and transdisciplinary content. *Transdisciplinary* concepts spiral well for us because they cut through subject matter silos, emphasize their unifying concepts and facilitate new meaning-making within real-world themes, contexts and issues (Scarino & Liddicoat, 2016). This way of thinking helps construct new knowledge and skills. We want learners to interact with texts and think like the historian, writer or artist from an intercultural point of view. What do you want the learner to remember about the cultures? What matters most? How does a culture or cultures respond to these ideas, themes or content? If this were a story our cultures could tell, what would be the moral or proverb of that story? We refocus the line of inquiry from facts to cultural practices and perspectives, present across disciplines and recursive throughout the lifespan. To unfold cultures' story, we examine the many ways cultures think, feel or respond to a concept or idea in any discipline. The teacher focuses on what is truly worthy of understanding, e.g. the concepts, the 'moral' of the story, allowing for careful decisions on assessments that will demonstrate that understanding. The enduring understandings and essential questions have tremendous implications for assessment and also function like a curricular filter or sieve for content. Not everything has the same worth, particularly factual content that is easily accessed online. The burden of coverage is relieved when one realizes all similar verbs need not be taught during the same unit, for example, so that one can choose only what is relevant and required to do the performance assessment task in question.

Even after many years since its inception, the Communication goal area still tends to be misunderstood as linguistic forms and lexical content: practice in disconnected four skills with grammar and vocabulary. The four skills (Lado, 1961) are an artificial classroom construct; its assessment system presents isolated components, enabling a deficit model of grading with an unrealistic and unproductive emphasis on accuracy. The inefficiency of the 'four skills drill' does not support the goals of real language use – a developmental, experiential, integrated, creative and social act. The Interpretive, Interpersonal and Presentational modes of communication (Glisan, Adair-Hauck, Koda, Sandrock & Swender, 2003) function best as integrated performance assessments (IPA) (Adair-Hauck, Glisan, Koda, Swender & Sandrock, 2006) rather than separate receptive, interactive and productive modalities. The communication standard

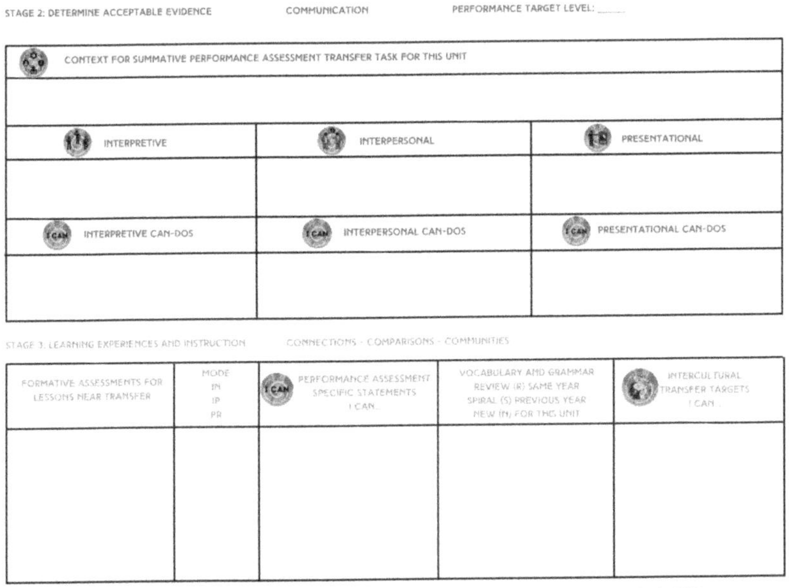

Adapted with permission from Eddy, J. 2017. "Unpacking the Standards for Transfer: Intercultural Competence by Design." from the Northeast Conference on the Teaching of Foreign Languages and the Editor of the NECTFL Review (Council of Europe, 2020); National Council of State Supervisors of Foreign Language, 2017; National Standards Collaborative Board, 2015; Wiggins & McTighe, 2005).

Figure 1.3 ICANADAPT Template Stages 2 & 3

ARTICULATED ASSESSMENT TRANSFER TASK (AATT) TEMPLATE

- ENDURING UNDERSTANDINGS
- ESSENTIAL QUESTIONS
- CONTEXT
- ARTICULATION SPIRAL POINTS
- INTERCULTURAL TRANSFER TARGETS
- MEDIATION FOR TRANSFER

	PERFORMANCE TARGET LEVEL	PERFORMANCE TARGET LEVEL	PERFORMANCE TARGET LEVEL
	AUTHENTIC MATERIAL DESCRIPTIONS	AUTHENTIC MATERIAL DESCRIPTIONS	AUTHENTIC MATERIAL DESCRIPTIONS
INTERPRETIVE TASK (I CAN)			
INTERPERSONAL TASK (I CAN)			
PRESENTATIONAL TASK (I CAN)			

Figure 1.4 AATT Template

determines our assessment system in Stage Two (Eddy, 2007d, 2017) (see Figure 1.3). Within the ICANADAPT framework are the Articulated Assessment Transfer Tasks (AATT) (see Figure 1.4) (Eddy, 2007a/2009a, 2015d, 2017, 2019a) which feature key performance assessments presented across three selected levels of learner engagement. The AATTs are framed with Enduring Understandings and Essential Questions and a common Context intended for all three levels. Learners can do the tasks collaboratively with all levels working simultaneously towards this context as a language cohort, as differentiated multi-levels in one classroom or even between levels, buildings or schools. The three tasks work in concert as Transfer tasks, to build the deliverable for this overarching Context and specific audience, reflecting the manner in which we use the language in the real world. All levels of learners can solve the novel problem posed in the context and create the product or deliverable according to their level of engagement. The AATTs also derive specific Mediation (COE, 1998, 2001, 2020) tools, called *Mediation for Transfer*. These are identified strategies within transfer tasks to clarify, compare, elaborate, facilitate, revise, reconstruct and collaborate with others to move both plurilingual and pluricultural space forward and make new language and cultural contexts within reach. In this way, Mediation for Transfer facilitates assessment as learning (Dann, 2014; Earl, 2003). Many teachers use the AATTs as summative assessments of learning, but they also can be used as formative assessments for learning to give feedback along the course of the unit (Hattie, 2012). Most important is that this stage *determines* the extent of transfer evidence, the application of repertoire for the novel task and autonomy of learner performance, a task done by themselves and beyond themselves. The AATTs engage teachers as designers with learners as active contributors, in response to a social and purposeful context for visible, vertical articulation across levels.

As teachers design the summative assessment first, they become more selective on what knowledge and skills are required for that task, thus reducing the amount of unrelated material (Wiggins & McTighe, 2005). The vocabulary and grammar are there, but they have been carefully chosen to move the learner closer to understanding intercultural concepts and realizing performance goals. The problem of excess coverage goes away. The learner now assigns purpose and coherence to the knowledge and skills needed for the assessment, rather than trying to recall skills in isolation and excessive drills that are not transferable to actual language use in daily life.

In Stage Three (see Figure 1.3), teachers plan formative assessments and instructional strategies for lessons. This comes last in Backward Design (Wiggins & McTighe, 2005) and is the opposite of typical practice. This is the stage most teachers associate with objectives and focus questions. These reside at lesson level, not to be confused with Enduring Understandings and Essential Questions developed at programme level in Stage One. In our courses and professional learning sessions, it was important to differentiate these and helpful to see Stage One and Stage Three *At a Glance* (see Appendix A), so teachers can see their distinctive characteristics side by side. As stated, we use recursive concepts and themes to design EUs and EQs; lesson content, skills and facts for recall tend to present in the objectives and focus questions. The latter tend to be self-limiting, finite and fixed, answerable by the end of a class period or two. In Stage Three, learners further engage the standards of Comparison, Communities and Connections in formative assessments which *demonstrate* increasing autonomy within varied intercultural contexts. Cultural practices, products and the perspectives that created them are revealed in lessons here, allowing for comparisons of cultures and application of this transdisciplinary content to real-life contexts. This is where the selection of relevant grammar and vocabulary occurs, which also works in concert with any curricula indicating these items or lists at set points, intervals or years. Teachers indicate grammar and vocabulary content essential for the tasks as Review, Spiral or New, further facilitating vertical articulation and transition between years, levels, key stages, buildings and schools.

The *NCSSFL-ACTFL can-do statements* (National Council of State Supervisors of Foreign Language, 2014/2017) were inspired by the European Language Portfolio (Little, 2003, 2009a, 2011, 2012; Little & Perclová, 2001; North, 1992). These provide self-reflection tools across performance targets and are useful to plan course, programme and benchmark targets. Teachers design performance assessment specific statements for ICANADAPT and AATTs, derived from the task itself and composed only after the task is written. This process makes sure the takeaway aligns only with that task and those skills therein. The process is repeated for formative tasks in Stage Three, to eliminate any deadwood and the risk of returning to the habit of surplus coverage not found in the tasks. The Intercultural Transfer Targets focus on perspectives, practices, comparisons, transdisciplinary connections and community engagement, designed for utility beyond the classroom. The National Curriculum of England states that 'A high-quality languages education should foster pupils' curiosity and deepen their understanding of the world' and 'provide opportunities for them to communicate for practical purposes, learn new ways of thinking' and 'provide the foundation for learning further languages, equipping pupils to study and work in other countries' (DfE, 2013). The ITT articulation chart shows a sample of two concepts with the statements across three levels of engagement (see Appendix B).

ICANADAPT and AATTs support principles within The Common European Framework of Reference for Languages: Learning, Teaching, Assessment (CEFR) (COE, 2001). These documents provide guidelines for curriculum, assessment and instructional materials against the backdrop of plurilingualism and pluricultural competence (CEFR Section 6.1.3, Council of Europe 2001:133–5). The CEFR initiated the concept of language competence and facility with a plurilingual repertoire to meet the developing and expanding needs of people in their daily lives. Thus, these materials signified a shift away from traditional language learning as a cloistered classroom exercise in linguistic forms to one of an active, action-oriented 'social agent', constructing meaning with others to do real-life tasks (Byram, 1997, 2009; Byram & Wagner, 2018; Piccardo, 2013; Piccardo & North (2019).

The Companion Volume (COE, 2018, 2020) added descriptors for aspects of mediation, online interaction and pluricultural competence. These materials add to the existing can-do descriptors to emphasize how and to what extent the speaker clarifies, compares, explains and bridges ideas from known to new. In addition, it facilitates the learner on a non-linear, creative course of action with language, who is not only tolerant of ambiguity but also has the tools to thrive flexibly in ever-changing linguistic and cultural environments.

These chapters contain ICANADAPT and AATT exemplars representing many languages, cultures and transdisciplinary content. These designs represent a shift from the 'one size fits all fact and forms depository' which renders the learner passive, dependent and reliant. ICANADAPT/AATT is a bespoke, spiral K-16 curriculum framework that encourages inquiry, meaning making, transferable concepts and new deliverables for an active, independent and autonomous learner for life.

> ### Collaboration for Articulation
> With colleagues, read the seven guiding principles below. Before reading further, pose questions with your colleagues about each principle. Discuss how these principles align or differ with practices you currently see in classrooms. How might these principles impact world language programme, unit and lesson design? In what ways could they impact student learning?

Seven guiding principles for world language curriculum design

1. Intercultural perspectives and transdisciplinary content unfold articulated curriculum and scaffold key tasks of meaningful performance.
2. Learners acquire and own language not by linear and predictable memorization of functions, structures and forms but through creative, unpredictable interaction in tasks using transdisciplinary content in texts.
3. Key Performance Tasks are designed for transfer to novel contexts, situations or audiences.
4. Complexity differentiates tasks, not topics, themes or texts.
5. Learners are active social agents co-constructing meaning through mediation and complex tasks across languages and cultures.
6. Tasks solve problems and create products relevant to college, community, work and world.
7. Learners take risks to apply their repertoire flexibly but not with native-like accuracy.

> **1** Intercultural perspectives and transdisciplinary content unfold articulated curriculum and scaffold key tasks of meaningful performance.
>
> Vertical Articulation between levels, buildings and schools
> Concepts and content for disciplined thinking
> Key Performance Tasks as Articulation Spiral Points

As curricula and schemes of work change in response to curriculum requirements or initiatives, now more than ever will be a need to develop articulated programmes with a conceptual framework. World Language *articulation* defined for this book is an intentional, collaborative design of intercultural curriculum, with transdisciplinary performance assessments as evidence of learner progress between levels and buildings, in order to thrive as language users beyond school.

Articulation is most often associated with horizontal and vertical articulation. Many classroom teachers are familiar with horizontal articulation, or a continuity of materials, methods, strategies and expectations across the same level with similar goals (Lange, 1982). Horizontal articulation is important for sure, but when considering proficiency with disciplined goals, we must plan with vertical articulation in mind. The profession has explored articulation with fair frequency, but lingering issues still remain (Byrnes, 1990, 2008; Couet, et al., 2008; Lange, 1982, 1988; Pesola, 1988), and the reasons for that are many. The requirements of an individual state or country vary. World Language learners may begin instruction at different entry and exit points with varying amounts of instructional time, either weekly or per class period. Coupled with that are diverse frameworks in place that may not recognize or implement a spiral and cyclical curriculum of language in tandem with culture (Liddicoat, et al., 2003). Liddicoat views cultural understanding not by mastery of information but by action, negotiation of meaning and reflection. This requires a process of revisiting and revealing cultures with one's own relationship to what they think, do and create, progressively over time with a framework that enables that. Many world language classroom teachers are accustomed to planning only for the content in the level they teach and are responsible for only their assigned courses. They often do not have opportunities to work with colleagues at other levels. This results in misunderstanding vertical articulation, its direct relationship to well-designed assessments and that relationship to curriculum design. Vertical articulation focuses on transition and forward motion between levels, buildings and schools but is designed backward from final goals for your whole programme. This tells you what those Key Performances should look like. It is important that teachers of all levels know and can design for evidence at that target goal, even if they teach novice levels. It makes it easier then to design assessments for each level preceding it and to understand the transition backward from the target.

Vertical articulation ensures realistic yet challenging expectations. It facilitates world language programme development and revision because it is intentional and collaborative. Teachers know what comes before and after the level they teach. Designing with colleagues is a way to ensure continuous progress for our learners.

We must reconceive, reorganize and market our profession not as deliverers of skills and subject matter from ready-made scripts or worksheet packets but as co-creators of content with learners in order to develop disciplinary thinking and innovation. This creativity is what people have done and continue to do every day. It is only within the classroom that subject matter tends to be compartmentalized, presented as facts and delivered as subject matter to be collected, sorted, memorized and returned verbatim as indication of learning (Gardner, 1999, 2006). To understand the diverse ways in which we respond and make meaning of the world, learners need to uncover ways of thinking, feeling and reacting within cultures and the disciplines in tandem with teachers (Bruner, 1996; Coyle, D., Bower, K., Foley, Y. & Hancock, J., 2021). These inform and reveal the contexts in which we live and work with each other. For many in our field, this may be a new way of looking at our profession, but it is necessary for relevance, applicability, visibility and viability. This means response and reflection upon what we know from diverse disciplines. People naturally draw upon a wide knowledge base via different cultural contributions and varied contexts. They use language to comment, reflect and adapt to them. In this curriculum design, learners make meaning of these contributions while simultaneously understanding the people who create them. In an articulated programme, they can see a concept in a discipline unfold from the onset, giving them the means to interpret evidence, pose questions and be ready to participate in a world they cannot anticipate.

Our ICANADAPT curriculum design and AATTs ask learners to interpret, respond, reflect, reorganize, revise, create and share content, on their own, with others and in relation to them. We take content we understand, transform it and create anew. The practice of separating disciplined concepts from personal and shared cultures is artificial. When units and schemes of work isolate language learning from disciplinary thinking, it is one reason why language learning is often perceived solely as classroom-confined skill exercises. Language departments are often not included in school or district curricular initiatives. For that reason, articulated programmes cannot merely sequence language levels with culture as add-on from publisher ancillaries but instead must reveal disciplined concepts that invoke intercultural response which matter to people. Across our articulated curriculum design, this intercultural, transdisciplinary channel becomes the conduit for meaningful language tasks along different levels of engagement. These key tasks become *Articulation Spiral Points*, tangible evidence of concepts, integrated perspectives, novel performances and products.

> **2** Learners acquire and own language not by linear and predictable memorization of functions, structures and forms but through creative, unpredictable interaction in tasks with transdisciplinary content in texts.
>
> Shift from coverage, drill and predictable items of passive learning
> Novel tasks for unpredictable and interactive learning
> Authentic community texts for complex tasks and common practices

Drills of most sorts usually separate a piece of knowledge or skill artificially from its whole and repeat the piece in isolation of its context (Van Patten, 2003, 2004, 2010; VanPatten & Rothman 2015). The AATTs demonstrate use of language for a real, authentic purpose and represent key performances in this design. There is often a misconception that classroom tasks called 'performances' are repetition and predictable memorization of grammar forms, facts, phrases or even entire dialogues. Those expectations will yield a passive learner that is not able to handle the complexity, variation and creativity insisted by real-world tasks with realities in flux and unforeseeable. The tasks and experiences we design must not promote a fixed and tidy predictable package but one more in keeping with what we inevitably face, at home or abroad. The exemplars throughout these chapters indicate a key shift away from coverage and repetition of item types to performances in a range of contexts that test interaction and flexibility.

Anaïs Nin is quoted to say, 'We don't see things as they are, we see things as we are.' We use our languages and cultures to access all other content disciplines, interpret content, exchange information about it and then inherently about ourselves (Bower, Coyle, Cross & Chambers, 2020; Coyle, 2007; Liddicoat & Scarino, 2013; Scarino, 2014; Scarino & Liddicoat, 2016; Swaffar &

Arens, 2005). Our learners must develop a facility with transdisciplinary texts and make meaning with what we see, hear, read and experience. These texts, verbal or image, whether written, visual, audio or tactile, are authentic and represent collective thought both complex and commonplace. Vygotsky (1962) believed that all works of art enhance the capacity of the learner to construct meaning. Kramsch (2006) supported visual arts to develop symbolic competence, particularly around a collaborative exchange of emotional reactions to works of art. The Queens College programme adopted the principles of *Aesthetic Education* (Greene, 1995, 2001) to examine a variety of texts and works of art through lines of inquiry, prior to using these materials for designing curricular units and lessons. Aesthetic education is defined by Maxine Greene (2001) as "an intentional undertaking designed to nurture appreciative, reflective, cultural, participatory engagements with the arts by enabling learners to notice what is there to be noticed, and to lend works of art their lives in such a way that they can achieve them as variously meaningful" (p.6). Perspectives and ideas essential to a culture can be uncovered and prompt further inquiry. Dr Greene believed imagination is released and infinite through our personal encounters with works of art: poetry, theatre, dance, music, fiction and visual arts. For those exemplars in this book, the modes of communication are supported by the Lincoln Center Education's Capacities for Imaginative Learning (Holzer, 2007). Through imagining, reworking and adaptation, the learner explores ideas through multiple points of view and learns to expect unknowns, tolerate ambiguities and be flexible to them. These are practices well placed in support of the adaptable and self-directed language learner.

Pause to Ponder

- Consider a concept, theme, idea or practice for any culture(s). How does the culture think, feel, behave, participate or *respond* to this theme?
- What do you want learners to understand and *remember* about the culture through Key Performance Tasks?
- Can you think of cultural perspectives you want learners to revisit and *reprise* throughout your curriculum?

> **3** Key Performance Tasks are designed for transfer to novel contexts, situations or audiences.
>
> Use differently from how it was originally learned
> On one's own, solve a novel challenge using language repertoire
> Creative, unpredictable interactions with more novelty over time

We need to prepare learners for the inevitable unexpected (Eddy, 2016a). We want our learners to chase unpredictability and be able to handle the highest order of ambiguity in any context. They must lay claim to it, make it their own as mercurial as it is and tame the beast. At least, make it work for them and those around them. *Transfer* is the ability to use knowledge and skills in a different context, setting or situation from how it was originally learned, with few to no cues or supports (Wiggins and McTighe, 2005). It requires that skills reside on worthy goals; principles, transferable concepts, enduring understandings and essential questions that will enable pupils to apply what they learned in meaningful and authentic ways. For World Languages/MFL, those worthy goals reside with cultural perspectives and practices for intercultural and transdisciplinary competence. Tasks that assess for transfer encourage creativity to emerge, whether alone or in groups, lending itself well to the types of spontaneous, unpredictable interactions we will encounter in any real-world situation.

Jay McTighe (2014) wrote that a transfer goal for world languages is to 'effectively communicate with varied audiences and for varied purposes while displaying appropriate cultural understanding'. It is precisely this flexibility and adaptability that is required when faced with different contexts, audiences and new situations found within all cultures. Therefore, transfer tasks are not repeated drill or duplication of subject matter as it was delivered from the teacher to the learner. Our performance tasks must provide for renovation of material in the mind of the learner (Johnstone, 1997). If we want our learners to move forward in proficiency, they must use their repertoire to solve a novel challenge or create a product using their repertoire, with increasing novelty and complexity.

> **4** Complexity differentiates tasks, not topics, themes or texts.
>
> All concepts are possible on spiral curriculum
> Topic and text do not determine the level; the task you design for it does
> Earlier and later learning become clear with onset creativity

Bruner (1960, 1996) said anything can be learned at any level in a spiral curriculum. Learners need to reprise and revisit concepts, perspectives and practice relevant to our cultures at all levels of engagement. This means that no concept, topic or perspective should be postponed until a higher level of proficiency; no theme is off the table. Learners should build a concept and vocabulary base early. Novice-level learners can identify words and images, make lists, indicate agreement or disagreement, and make sense of concepts in other simple binary terms (ACTFL, 2012; COE, 2009; Tschirner & Bärenfänger, 2012). Our learners are also familiar with topics and concepts from other content areas and the world around them. Texts, themes and topics do not establish the level. The target level is determined by the task you design (Shrum & Glisan, 2016). In our field, this means that we must not delay the ability to use the language until mastery of the whole system has been accomplished. Self-expression, creativity and exploration of cultures and their contributions must be there at the onset throughout and for all learners, even if they do not have all the language yet. They can do with what they have now and begin practice in mediation by doing so.

The ability to use the language is as important as knowledge of the language. The ICANADAPT and AATT exemplars examine perspectives that may be advanced but are still understood by tasks designed at their level of engagement. Tasks which encourage transfer show what pupils can do right now and improve the range, spontaneity, sophistication and coherence in which they do it.

> **5** Learners are active social agents co-constructing meaning through mediation and complex tasks across languages and cultures.
>
> Learners help construct, clarify, bridge and exchange
> meaning with and for others
> Novel tasks provide opportunities to collaborate and create new meaning
> Learners can mediate at all levels of engagement,
> starting with visuals and single words

As a profession, we should want learners to thrive and accomplish tasks in various situations to the best extent they can when they are out and about, with language they can use now. This is why their experience with us cannot be passive, receiving information and repeating what is told. The AATT and ICANADAPT exemplars in this book are designed for learners to co-construct meaning and facilitate communication with others to solve a problem, clarify items, elaborate and make comparisons from known to new. These strategies help enable the shift from passive to active through *Mediation*.

North and Piccardo (2016) state that 'Mediation involves the use of language in creating the space and conditions for communication and/or learning, in constructing and co-constructing new meaning, and/or in facilitating understanding by simplifying, elaborating, illustrating or otherwise adapting the original' (p. 87). The Common European Framework of Reference (CEFR) Companion Volume (2018) provided extensive examples at all levels of proficiency and added descriptors for different contexts in which mediation occurs, including plurilingual/pluricultural competence (2020). In this book, mediation is presented concurrently with each mode of communication: Interpretive/Receptive, Interactive/Interpersonal and Productive/Presentational. Effective meaning making and active mediation happen when tasks are structured with consistent and new opportunities to make meaning and apply it to novel situations in collaboration with others. Task-specific mediation strategies for the AATTs are presented as *Mediation for Transfer*, which identify task elements to bridge, extend and create meaning between the individual and others, enabling transfer for unanticipated opportunities which can arise.

The practice of keeping language fixed and same does not lend itself to be shared, negotiated or changed. Even in light of the shift from four skills to three integrated modes, we often still see four isolated skills in play and language learning appearing as a solitary act rather than interactive across varied contexts. 'Mediation is the process which connects the social and the individual' (Swain, Kinnear & Steinman 2015. P151). In facilitating meaning and clarifying social and cultural symbols, we see language emerge in a multimodal and interactive manner (Garcia & Wei, 2014; Kramsch, 2006, 2011). Novice-level pupils can point to images and single words on a street sign or pamphlet and convey new meaning to someone; it is what they can do now for someone else. Mediation strategies are the key to the other modes functioning properly with action and interaction and not just as a new name for an old practice. Stoller (2009) defines 'the zone of innovation', in which she asserts that 'teachers are less likely to shift and adopt novelty if it appears the same as what they currently do and thus, not worth the time to adjust' (Eddy & Bustamante, 2020. p. 637). Mediation strategies within transfer tasks facilitate that shift both within and outside the classroom for the learner, because of value added: revision, reconstruction and creation of new meaning. Novel transfer tasks mirror the unfamiliar and unpredictable, providing tools to make language situations manageable for someone else. Mediation for transfer is conveyed with another person's needs in mind. It is about access, solving a problem and giving them the means to do so in an often unpredictable and dynamic pluricultural space.

Within this design framework, *Drama Pedagogy* is the intentional yet improvised, unscripted response to relationships, perspectives, emotions and challenges to make meaning of text, contexts and symbols around us. We apply key elements of this collaborative process to facilitate this unpredictable space where every outcome is unique (Bräuer, 2002; Byram & Fleming, 1998; Eddy, 2019b; Fels & McGivern, 2002; Heathcote & Bolton, 1994; Kao & O'Neill, 1998; Liu, 2002; O'Neill, 1995; Schewe & Shaw, 1993; Van Lier, 2010). These experiences are just for ourselves; our learners are participants within the process itself, not as actors for stage production. To clarify further, these pedagogical strategies are different from theatre, which is scripted, performed and communicated with an external audience in mind. The DICE Consortium (2010) explains drama and theatre as 'a continuum, with process at one end, moving on through exploring, sharing, crafting, presenting, and assessing, toward performance at the other. The fundamental difference between the two ends of the spectrum is the difference between process and product' (p. 16). For drama pedagogy, the teacher can be 'in role' with pupils or not, but always is a facilitator and guide for learning. Within a fictional time, place and context, these strategies cultivate listening, improvisational speaking and collaboration. For AATT exemplars using these strategies, they can function as short drama workshops within an interactive, cultural design space: exploring relationships, sound, movement, mood and meaning (Eddy, 2006b, 2019b; Haseman & O'Toole, 1987). They help us solve a problem, however small or large, while also discovering things about ourselves and others. When learners develop confidence 'in role', it helps them to express their ideas, emotions, and those of other people. These are effective qualities when we need to clarify, relay or collaborate to negotiate meaning with others for mediation. Through this process, mediation for transfer can occur in different forms to develop empathy, tolerance of ambiguity, flexibility, improvisation and learner autonomy (Lamb, 2000, 2008, 2017; Little, 1995, 2007, 2009a/b, 2012), attributes that memorized, predictable practice cannot do.

---

6 Tasks solve problems and create products relevant to college, community, work and world

> Our identities, cultural response and contributions
> are found in every discipline
> Relevance and applicability to the learner must lie
> in what they see in daily life
> Learner autonomy can occur via tasks that emphasize
> novelty and value beyond the classroom

As language teachers, we must truly rethink the purpose of our field if we want it to remain solvent, relevant and meaningful for learners and, in turn, to improve and support the perception of our profession at large. I believe it is this: We are preparing pupils to pursue language and intercultural learning for their own use, with language and culture as interdependent and equal players in that inquiry. Transdisciplinary substance is the visible construct on which they reside. Our identities and cultural contributions are in every subject and discipline: the arts, science, literature, business, health, family and nature. Every piece of text that we ask our learners to respond to is connected to another discipline domain, one where students find themselves in school, after school and most certainly after they leave us. It is for this reason that our relevance and applicability to the learner must lie in what they see in their daily lives, because our cultures evolve with the thoughts and creativity that we pursue every day.

Some colleagues in the profession believe we are teaching World Languages so that our pupils will become language teachers. Indeed, if our learners want to join our profession, we would be delighted, but that has been and continues to be a small minority. Even if it were the case, our marketing strategy would need to change. Our curriculum cannot be a linguistics course. Those who wish to study that field or join ours will seek us out; they always have. K-12 teachers are not preparing linguists or even teachers in training. We do hope they elect to continue MFL courses in schools and university for whatever reason or pursuits they choose. Therefore, our programmes and curricula must focus on useful purposes, encouraging the extent in which they can use language right now and in ways they see played out in everyday life.

While it is understood that languages are useful for business, civic life or issues of national security, it is not enough to craft curricula and language programmes solely around college, career or wider world interests (Taylor & Mardsen, 2014). Our learners must experience languages and cultures as being valuable to themselves, not only just for now, but with frameworks that extend inquiry beyond the school building. We want learners to continue this inquiry, build relationships with people, reflect on their own identity and to do so with confidence, albeit not perfection and *without us*. I say without us because our goal is to prepare a flexible, self-directed, autonomous communicator. Learner autonomy happens through tasks that emphasize novelty and rely less on supports and rehashing everything learned before in the same way, yet again.

> **7** Learners take risks to apply their repertoire flexibly but not with native-like accuracy.
>
> The goal is to communicate within and between cultures
> with self-reliance, poise but not perfection.
> Design meaningful tasks first,
> then determine the grammar and vocabulary needed to do them.
> Challenge the risk-averse with tasks on what people think, do and create.

The issue of communicating with self-reliance and poise without perfection is key here and should not be a debate. We will communicate, make and extend meaning, create new and do so in spite of a textbook or classroom sequence of grammar (Van Patten, 2003, 2004, 2010, 2013). Grammatical forms and syntax are outcomes or corollary to acquisition. It is not that grammar has no place in this curriculum design; it just should be one of the last planning steps in design. Rather than grammar framing and naming a unit or lesson, the conceptual intent, content and key performance tasks do.

This is not to say that grammar and vocabulary are not important to know and assess. They should just not be the first thing or even the second items considered in design. They work together better with greater intention and purpose. In this framework after designing the tasks, instructors will notice and become quite selective on the forms, syntax and vocabulary learners need to do the tasks. The tasks will determine the specific grammar and lexicon needed. They also show that not every form is needed at the same time, in the same unit or lesson. The key takeaway is that grammar helps us to avoid misunderstanding, refine and polish communication, not for creating it in the first place.

The perception and practice of our profession cannot be reliant on fixed sets of rules, functions, facts and vocabulary lists that only have relevance in a classroom, with tasks that require perfection. As long as our programmes, assessments, materials and instruction are presented and marketed this way, our results fall short of what our discipline is truly about, along with its purpose and relevance. Liddicoat advocates not for native-like objectives but 'an intermediate intercultural "third place" developed between the sets of practices in the first and second language' (2002, p. 11). Our field needs to present language acquisition and intercultural competence as interdependent, not mutually exclusive, integrated and spiralled in programme curricula and assessment. Both should value skills on meaning making and mediation with real-life tasks designed first, which then indicate the structures and vocabulary necessary with which to do them. These tasks centre on people and their daily lives. They pose a challenge for learners to reflect on informational, literary and artistic texts in concert with acquiring the language. This is not about learning static facts; those are easily obtained online, and we hardly need classrooms for those now. What we do need is curricula that prime the learner to notice and react, improvise and respond, reflect on the unique and familiar and to solve problems and create products of value beyond the classroom.

It has been said often in our profession that our learners should be risk takers with the language. To make that happen, we need to do that ourselves, and they will take their cue from us (Brantmeier, 2013). The mixed message learners often receive is the expectation to give back exactly what was taught to them. These assessments lull the learner into a false reality of predictability and a demand for more of the same. Risk taking and preparing for the inevitable unexpected releases creativity. What we know is without this, there is nothing original. There is an inherent beauty in trial and error, give and take and negotiation of meaning in language. Drama pedagogy and Aesthetic Education strategies focus on reaction in the moment and guide learners to improvisation, so that language at whatever level can be used flexibly and with confidence. This collaborative process supports the learner beyond the classroom. These strategies in tasks allow learners to experience themselves in a new language, not residing only in texts, but through interaction as embodied practice (Byram & Fleming, 1998). One of our goals at Queens College is to engage teachers in these strategies with different texts to connect experiences and link relationships to it. The tasks create encounters with the text similar to an artist design process as they create works of art and help the learner to construct meaning (Holzer & Noppe-Brandon, 2005). Creative performance tasks extend the text and deepen inquiry into what people think, what people do and what they create. This process allows the teacher and subsequently the language learner to explore ideas collaboratively through multiple points of view (Holzer, 2005), adapt to unknowns and be flexible to them, thus gently challenging the risk-averse.

Pause to Ponder

- How can learners solve a problem or create a product for an audience beyond self and classroom?
- How can all learners engage and understand the concept and prepare a deliverable according to their level of engagement?
- How can learners demonstrate Complexity, Autonomy and Novelty?

Teacher as Designer

These two exemplars examine health perspectives and practices across three levels of learner engagement (see Tables 1.2 and 1.3). As with all the AATTs in this book, they are designed to be done collaboratively as a language cohort, between levels, buildings and schools. They also can take place within one classroom where there is differentiation within the same course. The Enduring Understandings and Essential Questions are for health at the programme level, addressed with varied key assessments throughout the curriculum. Thus, they are not 'one and done' with this assessment. These assessment tasks are unfolded vertically with increasing depth and complexity through the tasks. The three vertical spiral points for this AATT indicate performance deliverables and evidence at the pupil's level. It is important to note the shift from self-interests to others; healthy school meals to dietary needs of others; then finally to changes in cultural practices past to present. The latter reinforces the use of time frames in order to do the tasks. Intermediate-high performance tasks need to include those features targeted at advanced low (ACTFL, 2012). The expectation is that pupils can engage in different time frames albeit not consistently on all topics yet. We will notice at each level that the AATT tasks incline into and favour the next level criteria.

Mediation strategies examine facilitation of meaning for others who may not understand the language and culture. At any level, language users can place themselves as social mediators, even to identify *remedios caseros* such as herbs and preparations with an image or gesture to help someone. The deliverables in this exemplar solve the problem in the context and develop products that may be of value to someone else, beyond the confines of the classroom. AATTs can be summative assessments of learning at the end of a unit or formative checks for learning. To see additional formative assessments for one level, see the ICANADAPT template for Health (see Appendix C).

Voices from the Field

Every culture has its home remedies, its *remedios caseros*. In Mexico, like so many things it is taken to the level of an art form. The Enduring Understanding, 'Health and wellness integrate mind, body and spirit' is one that could be unfolded over curricula for intercultural competence. No matter what language a pupil takes at your school, they will come away with transferable concepts and practices from these EUs and EQs. When a programme develops EUs and EQs in common across language offerings, there are even more opportunities for collaborative inquiry.

What can we learn about how different countries support health and diet? Does a campaign to eliminate *comida chatarra* (junk food) from school lunches work? How does accessibility to fresh food or natural medicine in urban and rural areas play a role? How has cultural history influenced diet? What are 'must have' wellness perspectives that stand the test of time in the cultures you teach? How have traditions changed, and why? Let learners do their own investigation as a transfer task.

One day when I was cooking in Mexico and learning to prepare chiles, despite careful handwashing, I missed a spot. I had touched my face and my eye was on fire. The señora calmly took a lock of my long hair and folded it in a loop. She gently touched my eye in the corners and on the lashes with the loop of hair and calmly told me to open it. I did cautiously and to my amazement, the burn was almost gone. She had me close again and after a few more dabs with the lock of hair, the pain had disappeared. She showed me how her family used the dry hair to draw out the volatile oils from the eyes, saying, "If you love our food, don't cut your hair too short; you may need it again." Thank you, Ana, for sharing all your *remedios caseros* with me and caring for my mind, body and spirit while I lived with you and your loving family.

Dr Jennifer Eddy, Queens College, City University of New York

Table 1.2

Articulated Assessment Transfer Task   Viva la Vida

Dr Jennifer Eddy   **Spanish**

Table 1.2 Articulated Assessment Transfer Task (AATT) Viva la Vida

Enduring Understandings
* Health practices and perspectives vary across cultures.
* Health and wellness integrate mind, body and spirit.
* Socio-political, media and environmental factors play a role in healthcare.
* Health depends on many factors, including our diet, culture and lifestyle.

Essential Questions
? In what ways do media and socio-political issues affect our health and lifestyle?
? To what extent does culture inform our health and wellness practices?
? How do we talk about our health with others in my family and community?

Context
Viva la Vida! is looking for episode content with a focus on healthy lifestyles.

Articulation Spiral Points
@ Identify health practices across cultures.
@ Prepare meal plans and multimedia informational content.
@ Select foods based on different dietary needs.
@ Explain changes over time in health practices for different communities.

Intercultural Transfer Targets	Mediation for Transfer
• I can identify and compare health practices and food products to help me understand perspectives. • I can choose and design health-conscious meal options with community needs in mind. • I can identify school foods served in different countries. • I can suggest healthy food choices for stores in my community.	• Bridge and exchange ideas and concepts on diet and wellness to others. • Compare health examples to what others already know. • Indicate healthy or unhealthy food choices from images to others unfamiliar with the cuisine. • Collaborate to clarify health concerns or issues. • Paraphrase main points and details on remedios caseros.

Novice High	Intermediate Mid	Intermediate High
Interpretive Task Descriptions		
Pupils watch videos on meals from different Spanish-speaking cultures and view infographics on diet to select and list which popular foods are healthy or not.	Pupils examine a variety of infographics and videos from Spanish-speaking cultures; identify diet concerns; and categorize food items with high sugar, salt, fat and carbs. Pupils write three questions about the foods.	Pupils read articles and watch videos on remedios caseros to compare indigenous and conventional practices for diet and health issues that have changed over time. They compare these with home remedies from their own cultures.

Can Dos		
I can identify healthier food options from various cultures.	I can categorize foods across cultures. I can pose questions from diet information and concerns.	I can compare intercultural health practices, their changes and influences.
Interpersonal Task Descriptions		
Learners decide which meals from different cultural communities are best for a healthy lunch.	With a partner, ask your questions and come to consensus on which food items to include on a diet for people with different health needs and goals.	Learners discuss the pros and cons of remedios caseros for various health concerns and decide which ones to include in the Good Life! episode.
Can Dos		
I can select healthy options from a variety of cuisines with a partner.	I can choose the proper foods depending on someone's dietary needs.	I can discuss and choose traditional cultural remedies with a partner.
Presentational Task Descriptions		
Learners present a school meal plan for the Viva la Vida! episode on healthy school food.	Viva la Vida! is focusing one week on diabetes. Create a multimedia presentation on healthy lifestyle choices to address this issue.	Viva la Vida! Presents Los Remedios Caseros: Ayer y Hoy, focusing on how these remedies are valued and may have changed over time depending on the needs of the community.
Can Dos		
I can present a healthy school menu featuring popular dishes from many communities.	I can make a presentation with facts and suggestions on a local and global health concern.	I can explain health trends across various cultural communities then and now.

Teacher as Designer

Dr Victoria Gilbert carries the articulation of health and wellbeing back to young learners with *Sana, Sana*. In this AATT, her learners share ways to mediate and demonstrate care and concern between cultures, this time at a level meaningful for children. Heritage learners at this age can also examine remedios caseros and health concerns. Each level calls for a unique contribution or deliverable for the context audience. The overarching message and understanding of cultural perspectives and home remedies resonates with learners of all cultures. As this theme unfolds in the curriculum, they will be able to recognize these practices and values when they see them, adding to their intercultural repertoire within this discipline.

Voices from the Field

Health and well-being are an essential concern in many cultures. My experience as a child in Spain whenever I injured myself or felt sick was that I received the appropriate concern as well as a "remedy" that would help me to deal with the difficulty. It might be the boo-boo refrain, "*Sana, sana*" or a quick knot with my hair and some glue to avoid having to give me stitches for a cut in my head. This practical and careful approach to a child's typical injuries also included teas and salves for upset tummy or coughs. Being able to understand this type of reference, response and its origin to alleviate children's worries would support intercultural competence in these scenarios.

Accessing this knowledge and approach would help learners to navigate and understand what they, or their friends, might experience in the target culture. When hurt, we are often at our most vulnerable – it can be comforting to know about the value of care in the target culture by playing at these responses and exploring them.

In designing this exemplar, I thought of what type of experience a child might have while visiting a native Spanish speaker's home if they lost a tooth, became ill or had a fall in a play area. Stories help us to make meaning from unknowns and I find that children can relate to characters in a story setting. Young novices love to act out role-plays, "comfort a friend that fell" or share a story about what happens with a rite of passage like losing a baby tooth and *El Ratoncito Perez*. Older novices can inject humour by poking fun of some of the past stages of their lives with a meme, or do research and present solutions they have acquired by examining traditions in other cultures.

This series of performance tasks situates pupils in various scenarios where they would encounter a health challenge appropriate to their age group (a boo, boo, a loose tooth, an upset tummy) and provide advice based on the cultural context. By engaging pupils with the products and practices as they relate to childhood health issues, pupils can develop intercultural communicative competence by increasing their curiosity and ability to navigate and mediate different approaches and scenarios. Ultimately, they can create a story with a solution to share with others.

Designing curriculum thematically across multiple proficiency levels is a way of making sure all students are invited into learning. Because one's health is an essential subject for communication, the approach to health and wellbeing in a culture returns in a spiral form throughout the curriculum. This AATT illustrates how concern for others' health and well-being is common to all cultures and yet may be expressed in different ways.

Dr Victoria Gilbert, Spanish teacher and department chair, Saint David's School.

Table 1.3 Articulated Assessment Transfer Task   Sana, Sana

Victoria Gilbert, Ed.D., Chair Modern Languages, Saint David's School, New York
Enduring Understandings ∗ Health practices and perspectives vary across cultures. ∗ Health and Wellness integrates mind, body and spirit.
Essential Questions ? What happens when something hurts? ? How can I help a friend or family member deal with a health concern?
Context The *Viva La Vida!* Channel is looking for new content on healthy living ideas for all ages in the community.

Articulation Spiral Points
@ Link gestures with meaning of song lyrics.
@ Sequence steps or preparations.
@ Create memes.
@ Explain childhood character.
@ Share concerns and remedies.

Intercultural Transfer Targets	Mediation for Transfer
• I can sing to comfort a friend • I can compare childhood cultural symbols, icons and memes • I can identify home remedies in my own and other cultures	• Bridge and exchange ideas and concepts of response and solutions to health and wellness across the lifespan • Use simple words and non-verbal gestures for meaning • Compare a known concept or practice to a new one in another culture • Explain steps for remedies to people from other cultures

Novice Mid-High	Intermediate Low-Mid	Intermediate High
Sana ranita, sana Robleda, M.	"news" about Ratoncito Perez during quarantine	Cómo tratar las lesiones y evitar cicatrices Posturas sanas, tratamiento para dolores de estómago, tratamiento de depresión o tristeza tos
Interpretive Task Descriptions		
Students will listen to a pattern story or song about a child getting a boo-boo and use gestures aligned to the lyrics.	Students will read/view a story about *Ratoncito Perez*, the Spanish equivalent of our tooth fairy and answer questions. Older students examine a collection of memes about "*El Ratoncito Perez*" to determine their favourite and make up their own.	Younger heritage speaker students with advanced proficiency listen to native speakers about favourite home remedies or view videos on remedios caseros. They sequence the preparations step-by-step and paraphrase the home remedies.

\multicolumn{3}{c}{**Can Dos**}
I can use gestures in the song or story to get help for a boo-boo.	I can answer true-false questions about Ratoncito Perez and losing teeth.	I can identify ingredients in home remedies. I can sequence steps to prepare some basic home remedies.
\multicolumn{3}{c}{**Interpersonal Task Descriptions**}
Students will survey their friends' preferred method to cure a boo-boo or cut.	Students will compare *Ratoncito Perez* and the Tooth Fairy, then survey friends about which character they prefer to leave their tooth for, which is their favourite meme and why.	Students will view videos in each of the areas, survey friends to find out what health concerns are a priority for them and why. They will use this information to compose new materials and a story.
\multicolumn{3}{c}{**Can Dos**}
I can find out what my friends think is the best way to treat a cut.	I can find out what character my friends prefer and why. I can find out which meme they prefer and why.	I can find out what my classmates' health concerns are and why.
\multicolumn{3}{c}{**Presentational Task Descriptions**}
Students will sing the song to their partner who pretends to have a boo-boo. Older students examine the memes and create their own.	Students will narrate the steps involved in losing a tooth… with *Ratoncito Perez*. Older students can create a meme to show humour.	Students will prepare a story or design a PSA poster to share an approach to address a health concern.
\multicolumn{3}{c}{**Can Dos**}
I can recite ways to treat a cut and sing to distract a friend from a hurt body part.	I can explain who *Ratoncito Perez* is to others. I can create a meme that plays with the story of *Ratoncito Perez* in a humorous way.	I can compose informational materials and share possible solutions to health concerns.

Check for Learning

Do you see evidence of the seven guiding principles for world language curriculum design in the exemplars *Sana, Sana* and *Viva la Vida*?

How are these exemplars different from the grammar- or topic-based curriculum from the table above?

Bridge to Design

1 What cultural perspectives do Drs Gilbert and Eddy want pupils to understand from these exemplars?

2 Review the Presentational mode tasks from either *Sana, Sana* or *Viva la Vida* again. From what you already understand thus far, what can the student do as a result of these tasks? Can you think of other presentations or products for the *Viva la Vida* channel?

3 Which researchers and practitioners do you think may have guided the authors on these exemplars?

4 How are learners developing mediation strategies with these tasks? Give examples where you notice they are facilitating new meaning and concepts to others.

5 Is there a design feature that calls out to you? Share with colleagues.

Design for Transfer

With the language and culture(s) you are teaching in mind…

Consider a concept or perspective that you envision can be unfolded throughout your curriculum.

Consider a possible task that could solve a problem or create products of value to the community.

Discuss the Issues

1 Our curriculum should give learners the tools to continue creating language without us. Discuss.
2 The topic doesn't determine the level; the task you design for it does. Discuss.
3 How do we promote and support a self-directed learner who communicates with poise but not perfection? Why does it matter?
4 What are some of the challenges and benefits of vertical articulation?
5 Why are novel tasks key evidence of intercultural communicative competence?
6 Transfer does not happen by chance. Discuss
7 Learners often take their cue from the teacher. Explain the shift of language teacher as designer to challenge the risk-averse.

Reflect and Revisit

1 How does unpredictability teach flexibility?
2 Why do we want a curriculum that lasts over the lifespan of the learner?
3 Why might horizontal articulation be easier than vertical articulation?
4 Explain how the "four skills" is an artificial classroom construct. What does language look and sound like in real life?
5 How do Aesthetic Education and Drama Pedagogy help the learner construct meaning?
6 Explain Mediation and why it is important for preparing an autonomous language learner.
7 Explain the common context for all three levels of learner engagement in the AATT. Which feature of the AATT is the most compelling for you?

Chapter 2

(Re) Imagining Curriculum to Reveal the Cultural Story

Enduring Understandings

- ∞ The story of our cultures reveals both visible and invisible features.
- ∞ Invisible perspectives create, influence and inform the visible practices and products.
- ∞ Cultural universals unite us as humans, even though they manifest differently.
- ∞ Cultural histories both reveal and refute points of view for us to practice meaning-making.

Essential Questions

- Q How can world language curricula tell the story of cultures?
- Q What is going on? What are many ways to notice?
- Q How do cultural perspectives and contexts play a role in revealing these stories?
- Q What should learners revisit and remember?

Key Terms and Concepts

Intercultural Communicative Competence	Intercultural Transfer Targets
Intercultural Transferable Goals	Cultural Perspectives, Practices and Products
Enduring Understandings	Authentic Texts
Essential Questions	Layers, Lifespan, Level

Research in Practice

The work of the following researchers and practitioners will guide you to cite sources which inform planning, assessment and instructional decisions for use in pre-service portfolios or in-service professional learning plans.

Bennett, 1986, 1993, 2004, 2008	Learners communicate effectively in cross-cultural situations in a variety of cultural contexts.
Bräuer, 2002	Learners develop intercultural competence through drama pedagogy techniques.
Byram, 1997, 2008, 2011 Byram, Gribkova & Starkey, 2002	Learners develop critical thinking skills with independent inquiry to thrive flexibly in another culture rather than merely survive error free.
Byrnes, 2002, 2010	Integration of culture, content and language.
Cunico, 2005	Drama for intercultural competence.
Deardorff, 2006, 2008, 2009, 2011	Learners achieve effective behaviour and communication through a lifelong process of intentional tasks in a variety of intercultural contexts.

Eddy, 2006a/b/c, 2007a/f/g, 2009a/b, 2010a/b/c, 2011, 2015a/c, 2016b, 2017	Learners solve problems and create novel products in curriculum designed from cultural perspectives, themes and intercultural competence goals transferable to real world contexts.
Egan, 1989, 1992, 2005	Learners make sense of their world first through moral and emotional categories, then with concepts, perspectives and practices connected to familiar, big ideas.
Kearney, 2010	Learners should be immersed in a variety of texts that represent all stories, symbols and diverse perspectives that confirm, dispute and compete through recurring themes to make their own meaning.
Kramsch, 1993, 2006, 2011, 2013	Learners develop awareness about their own culture to explore, describe and interpret beyond words and actions to understand varied, changing and conflicting contexts.
Moeller & Nugent, 2014	Learners present communicative competence in that language as well as particular skills, attitudes, values and knowledge about a culture. The language classroom should not be just to transmit cultural facts and knowledge.
Liddicoat and Scarino, 2010, 2013	Learners engage in performance tasks and reflection within meaningful cultural contexts and practices from daily life.
Risager, 2007	Learners should explore culture beyond national and ethnic boundaries in a 'transnational and global context'.

I can

- Identify 'must-have', transferable cultural perspectives that matter
- Recognize cultural perspectives and concepts within texts and their practices as the bridge to disciplines that created them

- Select concepts that recur over the vertical articulation spiral
- Develop Enduring Understandings and Essential Questions
- Reveal the story of the culture(s) as Intercultural Transferable Goals

Rewind

Which key terms or concepts stand out for you from the last chapter, *Unfolding curriculum with no end in mind*?

Ask your colleague three questions based on the content from the last chapter.

Explain the most compelling idea from the previous chapter in your own words.

How is this concept or practice the same, similar or different to what you know or do?

Which concept or practice from *Unfolding Curriculum* do you think will have the greatest impact on your teaching? Why?

Overview

In the previous chapter, we examined the teacher as designer of curriculum, shifting from passive consumer of information to transmit, to one of active creator or co-creator to transform and transfer in tandem with the learner. We see that designing for vertical articulation permits the unfolding of curriculum as 'better backward' from transferable goals and key tasks which, in turn, allow all key stakeholders in a department to be part of the process. In this chapter, we discuss what those transferable goals are and how you will discover them in your curriculum. What does intercultural competence look like for you, not only for the classroom but within daily life? Are there cultural perspectives so integral to the culture and its people that we must understand in order to thrive? If our cultures could tell a story about how the people think, behave, respond and participate in any given context, what would be the moral of that story? How do these perspectives repeat along the lifespan? How and where do we see them resurface? What is our response and reflection?

Michael Byram (1997) defined Intercultural Competence (IC) as someone's 'ability to interact in their own language with the people from another country and culture'. He leans into language learning to define *Intercultural Communicative Competence* (ICC) as 'the ability to interact with people from another country and culture in a foreign language' (p. 71). Fantini and Tirmizi (2006) state it is 'a complex of abilities needed to perform *effectively* and *appropriately* when interacting with others who are linguistically and culturally different from oneself' (p. 12, emphasis in original). Byram explains that ICC considers another person's needs and views with a desire not only to understand different cultures but also to contribute to these relationships and mediate communication between languages and cultures. These definitions are supported by the CEFR (2001), the World Readiness Standards (2006/2015) and the NCSSFL-ACTFL Can Do Statements (2017). The CEFR Companion Volume (2020) provides comprehensive descriptors for mediation, building relationships and collaboration, all with the goal of plurilingual/pluricultural competence. Even with repeated calls to integrate language and culture in professional literature (Byrnes, 2002, 2010; Kramsch, 1993; Lange & Paige, 2000; Moeller & Nugent, 2014; Sinicrope, Norris & Watanabe, 2007), we still see detached and often superficial content, often delivered as facts and forms. Language and culture are interdependent, interactive and reciprocal (Byram, 1997; Kramsch, 1993, 1995; Liddicoat, Papademetre, Scarino & Kohler, 2003; Wagner & Byram, 2015). The space we create for learners must operationalize these qualities. As a profession we need to facilitate a collaborative, improvisational intercultural design space (Eddy, 2016b/c/d) in which learners can explore and connect concepts with their own practices to solve problems and create products with the needs of others in mind.

These statements on ICC outline the need for a notable shift in curriculum and assessment design which diffuses and neutralizes the notion of flawless grammar highly prized in the classroom, to the promotion of meaning, negotiation and creativity outside of it. Unlike paradigms that emphasize native-like speaking as a goal, our focus instead needs to be on key tasks for learners to discover perspectives from others and about themselves (Sercu, 2006). Byram, Gribkova and Starkey (2002) encourage classrooms that are learner-centred and interactive, questioning their ideas through reflection, comparison and collaboration. Liddicoat and Scarino (2013) explain it as 'an understanding of culture as facts, artefacts, information and social practices, as well as an understanding of culture as the lens through which people mutually interpret and communicate meaning' (p. 46). Bennett (1993) describes a developmental process and transition from denial, defence and minimization of cultural difference (ethnocentric stages) to acceptance, adaptation and integration of differences (ethno-relative stages). He also steps away from learning discrete facts about a culture and more towards developing generalizable, intercultural skills learned via focused and purposeful tasks about a culture through language. In the Process Model of Intercultural Competence, Deardorff (2006, 2008, 2009, 2011) reinforces the notion of *effective* and *appropriate* via intentional tasks in a variety of intercultural contexts or situations to assess Intercultural Communicative Competence. In order to design these tasks and move from knowing about a language to participation with other people, we must consider the role of intentional curriculum design through transferable goals inherent to and between cultures.

Transferable Goals for Intercultural Communicative Competence

The Council of Europe and NCSSFL-ACTFL advocate the shift from a fixed, static progression of grammar, vocabulary and facts about culture to a curriculum suitable for a flexible, adaptable learner-in-society. The Standards for Foreign Language Learning (National Standards in Foreign Language Education Project, 1999) stated that 'the true content of the foreign language course is not the grammar and the vocabulary of the language, but the cultures expressed through that language' (p. 43). The revised World-Readiness Standards for Learning Languages (National Standards Collaborative Board, 2015) then emphasized application of language learning beyond the classroom. The Council of Europe's Guide for the Development and Implementation of Curricula for Plurilingual and Intercultural Education states, 'Intercultural competence, for its part, is the ability to experience otherness and cultural diversity, to analyse that experience and to derive benefit from it' (Beacco, Byram, Cavalli, Coste, Cuenat, Goullier & Panthier, 2016, p. 10). This means we must examine culture with intention, not only practices and products both domestic and international, but also the perspectives that inform and create them. The National Curriculum for Languages states that 'learning a foreign language is a liberation from insularity and provides an opening to other cultures' (DfE, 2013). Our ability to communicate in culturally appropriate contexts within new spaces, teams, partnerships and organizations is essential to live and work within our communities and beyond. This depends upon how we respond, mediate, identify and connect with our own and other cultures within a diverse set of perspectives and concepts. For that reason, MFL curriculum design must be framed with Intercultural Transferable Goals.

Intercultural Transferable Goals represent concepts of mind and perspectives within a culture or cultures that inherently matter so much that they resurface and reprise in many contexts and disciplinary texts to experience anew. In *Beyond Culture*, Hall (1976) first presented the iceberg model which has had many visual renditions and is quite familiar to our profession. This visual depicts tangible aspects of the culture which are visible and easily taught, with values, beliefs, mindsets and perspectives invisibly but deeply anchoring and informing what we do and create. How our cultures treat elders, share meals, handle conflict and manage time all deeply matter and resurface in cultural history, practices and products over time. When we critically examine cultural histories, we recognize that its interpretation comes from all the people who influenced them: their perspectives, attitudes and points of view. These perspectives reprise and can change. They oblige us to question and be responsive to those perspectives that may differ from current thinking but nevertheless continue to shape and inform what people think, do and create today. These are so compelling that they recur and transfer for reinterpretation and are again relevant in our many facets of daily life. This is why the curriculum must be framed with these reprising transferable goals. They stand the test of time with lasting value. These concepts should inform, emerge and become visible via tasks in class, because they will re-present in life long after pupils have left your classroom or school. These overarching perspectives advance performance assessment design for transfer moving the learner to solve novel problems and create products in novel situations with value beyond the classroom (Eddy, 2009a, 2017; McTighe & Wiggins, 2004; Wiggins, & McTighe, 2005). Byram, Gribkova and Starkey (2002) describe culture as a dynamic, changing force, and thus these qualities suggest a curricular design of constant engagement, curiosity and inquiry (Council of Europe, 2001). The transferable goals reprise and reside within Key Performance Tasks for a unit or scheme of work and become Articulation Spiral Points. As presented earlier, these represent novel performances that solve problems or create products with increased complexity in the curriculum. These tasks help pupils cope with inevitable changes, challenges and diverse contexts to become self-directed, autonomous learners for life.

As teachers, we also need to understand how perspectives are reflected in cultural practices and the related products people make. We need to know how cultures inform different content areas and respond to subjects as their people go about their daily lives (Coyle, 2007; Jourdain, 2008). This is not about reaching across the hallway to a colleague from another subject. This is how to identify values, themes, beliefs, ideas, practices and viewpoints representing many disciplinary fields within different texts: informational, literary, art, film, music, media, just about anything that people within the culture use or create. Consistent investigation of texts coupled with meaningful tasks allows both the teacher and learners to widen intercultural repertoire and see culture as the living, dynamic system it is, not portrayed as a fixed, static, relic found in some textbooks. As we work with learners to reveal and interpret perspectives and practices, they learn to relate to others as well as adapt to inevitable change. Rather than expecting sameness and then experiencing disappointment when faced with flux and ambiguity, learners will understand the value of adaptation, variation and change as the more predictable reality.

Pause to Ponder

Why is it important to learn adaptation and tolerance of ambiguity? Discuss with a colleague.

A Shift from Culture on the Margin of Curriculum

If you experienced learning a second language in a classroom setting, was culture fully integrated within content and language or merely added on, peripheral or detached? Long after researchers indicated a need for this separation to cease (Kramsch, 1993, 2013; Magnan, 2008; Omaggio-Hadley, 2001), the disconnect continues to exist in the world languages profession. Even in light of the World Readiness Standards (2015), Intercultural Competence Can-Do Statements (NCSSFL-ACTFL, 2017) and extensive effort and intention within the profession (Byram, 1997; Bower, et. al., 2020; Coyle, 2007; Deardorff, 2006; Moeller & Nugent, 2014; Wagner, Perugini & Byram, 2018) to promote Intercultural Communicative Competence (ICC), there still is evidence that the profession at large needs more support, models and examples to realize its goals (Chen & Yang, 2015). Textbooks tend to deliberately instruct and explain culture, while teachers often present it as facts. These snippets are relegated to the 'little blue box' located literally and figuratively on the margin of curriculum. It is why many language learners experience a superficial treatment of culture or it is not integrated as it appears naturally within disciplines we see and encounter every day. If cultural practices and products are merely presented as cursory knowledge of facts within our units and lessons, these remain cloistered in the limited context of how they were taught.

Table 2.1 From Culture on the Margin of Curriculum to Centre Stage

Preparing learner as error free to merely survive	Adaptable communicator intended to thrive
Fixed, static set of information to recall	Dynamic, process of engagement
Teaching 'objective culture'; the cultural products (literature, music, food) and practices as activities	Teaching 'subjective culture' (the exploration of underlying cultural values) and beliefs as channel to critical reflection on practices and related products
Passive receptor with facts about culture	Responsive actor for exploration, participation, creation, experience through disciplinary tasks

Check for Learning

Table 2.1 represents a shift from cultures on the margin or periphery of curriculum to cultures as the centre, a channel for interaction and critical reflection.

1   Give an example in your learning experience of culture on the margin of curriculum.
2   If you could choose one 'must-have' perspective and practice of the culture(s) you teach, what would you want us to understand?
3   Is it necessary to be error free in order to communicate? Discuss.

From Transmit to Transform

Our life experiences consist of concepts, themes and lessons which resurface, reprise and repeat. These experiences allow us to apply them to different contexts and situations with flexibility and adjustment. As you may recall your own language learning experience, flexibility and adaptability were essential when faced with new situations. Our focus must shift from the image of an ideal speaker without error who can survive in another culture to one who communicates flexibly, progressively yet securely so that they can thrive within any culture (Council of Europe, 2001, 2020). Culture transmitted as facts and information for recall does not allow for active engagement by the learner. Many teachers are concerned they do not know enough about the culture to be able to teach it thoroughly; they still are working within the mindset of mere transmission of information. Instead, the process given here transforms the learner to become active in their world and allows teachers to be co-creators in learning, where culture is the framer for exchanging all meaning, solving problems and creating products we see every day. This is why the vision and objectives of standards and frameworks in our profession can be accomplished only by engaging instructors themselves in the process of designing bespoke curriculum, with ICC articulated via embedded transferable goals. Through intentionally designed curricula, schemes of work, units and transfer tasks, our learners will consider their own perspectives and those of other cultures. They will refocus and shift continuously via novel tasks to learn not only practices and products, but also the context and approach that people employ to make sense of their world.

In order for us to mediate communication between others successfully, it means that skills must reside on worthy goals; transferable concepts, contexts, approaches, with Enduring Understandings, Essential Questions and tasks that will enable students to apply what they learned in new, meaningful and authentic ways. For Modern World Languages, we can examine *Perspectives, Practices, and Products* for what people think, what people do and what they create.

With technological advances, our world, its citizens, practices and products have become more accessible to all of us. The cultures standard (National Standards Collaborative Board, 2015) is composed of products, practices and the perspectives that created them. Cultural Products are both tangible and intangible *benefits* required, desired or justified by the perspectives, beliefs and values of that culture: what people make. Practices are the *behaviours*, social interactions accepted by a culture. These are generally what people do and are more visible. Perspectives are *beliefs,* invisible concepts which illustrate our cultures' views of the world, including meanings, attitudes, values and ideas. These are responsible for creating the practices and products: what people think. What are the beliefs, behaviours and benefits that our diverse cultures maintain and which matter most to them?

Check for Learning

How do language and culture work together for us to interpret, exchange and create meaning? How can we guide learners to build pluricultural repertoire, facilitate pluricultural space and mediate with progression towards higher levels of engagement? (COE, 2001). Let's first identify some Cultural Perspectives, Practices and Products so that we know them when we encounter them. Let's recognize these and then discuss specific examples within our own cultures.

(See Appendix D)

The Curriculum Unfolds the Cultural Story

Daniel Pink (2006) said, 'Stories are easier to remember because stories are how we remember' (p. 101). Most of our experiences and our knowledge are organized as stories in our minds. It is our way of looking into the future, reaching back into the past, planning and explaining (Armstrong, Connolly & Saville, 1994). Kieran Egan (1992, 2005) explains learner development based on how the learner accesses and engages with the world. Pupils under the age of ten seek moral and emotional categories to make sense of their world. Adolescents learn best when new concepts, perspectives and practices are connected to familiar ideas from other contexts and disciplines. Our world tosses concepts at us in a transdisciplinary way, creating the story of our cultures as we process them. Just as it unfolds, so does articulated curriculum over the lifespan of the learner through more opportunities to interact within cultures. The story of a culture unfolds information and knowledge but does so with context, perspectives and emotion.

Intercultural competence, like the Enduring Understandings and Essential Questions designed for it, is never finished but continually in progress in response to new experiences and reflection upon actions. That is why our curriculum is designed with no end in mind, to develop learner autonomy (Lamb, 2017) with the tools to always find and see more. These diverse experiences inform how learners understand what is valuable. This is why it is best not to present cultural content as lists of facts. Whereas in the past, facts were hard to come by, confined in libraries. Now facts are free and available to us at lightning speed. When one can access facts so quickly, they lose value. What really matters now is how to use information in different contexts, adapt and share them in a way that matters to the recipient. This is done through mediation, communication, actions, problem-solving and deliverables that meet the needs of individuals or a community.

Some educators might ask, shouldn't one hold some concepts back until learners can express all the cultural comparisons, explanations and reflections completely in the target language? That answer is no; our learners need to see concepts and perspectives early and often and the ability to understand them is not linked to how well one can speak the language. This happens as a result of tasks that practice transfer, novelty and adaptability at all levels of instruction.

> **Collaboration for Articulation**
>
> Discuss the value of 'all topics, all levels' with your colleagues. How can we unfold any theme, concept or topic for any level of instruction? What determines complexity? Why is it important to start building the scaffolds early and connect concepts and knowledge from other disciplines? How does this facilitate vertical articulation rather than restricting a topic to a level?

Teacher as Designer

Ms Kalmanson shares the Russian cultural perspective of *Smekalka*, the quick-witted ingenuity with thinking out of the box to solve problems. She pairs this with *Khlebosolstvo*, where literal bread and salt transform to become the figurative word for *Hospitality*. Both are embedded and ingrained in Russian folklore, behaviours, practices and products while at the same time are intercultural transfer concepts. Let's see how she unfolds these two concepts through articulated tasks across levels (see Table 2.2). Her learners will understand these concepts with increasing complexity before completing the Russian programme. Ms Kalmanson incorporates drama pedagogy in this exemplar. How do the pupil's actions 'in role' as described in the context enable their work throughout the tasks? What truths can we learn from fiction? What do patterns in cultural history teach us today?

> ## Voices from the Field
>
> Folk tales are an absolutely invaluable and inexhaustible resource for world language teachers. As little children acquire culture and language from the folktales, our learners can have incredible hands-on cultural and language experiences.
>
> The Axe Porridge seems to be a simple story about a greedy Old Lady and a Soldier but has a great number of cultural layers and concepts. This story teaches us kindness, sharing, patience and forgiveness; it teaches us that the smartest

person is not the one who has the most, but the one who is willing to share or can make others want to share voluntarily. One of the most important cultural perspectives of the Axe Porridge is the complex concept of *smekalka*, which is not only an ability to get what we want using the means handy, an ingenious mind, but an ability to cope with a difficult situation or crisis and act effectively.

Even our novice learners, thanks to distilled language present in the tale and task, will easily and interactively acquire centuries-old wisdom, life lessons, connect them to their own experiences, and, possibly, differentiate their own values. Paraphrasing a well-known Russian aphorism, we all came out of folktales.

Ms Ekaterina Kalmanson, Russian teacher, James Madison High School, Brooklyn, New York.

Table 2.2 Axe Porridge   Russian

Articulated Assessment Transfer Task	Ekaterina Kalmanson
Enduring Understandings * There are differences and similarities between how people value and demonstrate hospitality. * Clever improvisation and 'Thinking outside the box' are shared intercultural perspectives.	
Essential Questions ? What is *hospitality*? ? How do we think 'outside the box' and handle problems creatively? ? How do we emerge from a difficult situation with no support or resources? ? Do some perspectives belong to one culture and others to many?	
Context This is the first day of detective school. The students are mystified by an anonymous letter. The letter states that Russian people have *smekalka* and every Russian can make porridge from an axe. Even though the author of this mysterious letter states that Russian people are kind and hospitable, the students are perplexed. They begin an independent investigation on this mystery of *smekalka*. To find out the axe porridge recipe, they go to the library. They learn that there is no axe porridge recipe, but a book called *Axe Porridge*. The Russian language and culture expert agrees to tell them the story. After finding out what *Axe Porridge* is, our young detectives find out more about Russian people, their values, *smekalka* and ways to show hospitality. To celebrate that *smekalka* is a universal quality, students organize the *Smekalka* Fair with Russian hospitality traditions.	

Articulation Spiral Points
- Integrate *smekalka* and hospitality examples.
- Recreate story for modern audiences.
- Debate changes in values.
- Compose video.

Intercultural Transfer Targets	Mediation for Transfer
• I can recognize Russian culture values and beliefs. • I can identify ways Russian people show their hospitality to someone unfamiliar with the culture. • I can show hospitality in a culturally appropriate manner. • I can compare Russian *smekalka* and hospitality with that of my own culture.	• Bridge and exchange ideas and concepts of hospitality and creative problem-solving. • Identify visuals, symbols and memes to explain concepts applicable to real-life context. • Explain information on an infographic or chart to someone. • Recognize words to indicate concepts in proverbs. • Compare practices and cultural norms around hospitality and problem-solving.

Novice High	Intermediate High	Advanced Mid
~ Axe Porridge – an interesting and very instructive everyday fairy tale. A resourceful and savvy soldier offered to cook up porridge from an axe. The soldier lures valuable food from the hostess, which she would never voluntarily share with the poor person. ~ Russian Artifice and Smekalka Museum celebrating ingenuity and improvised, creative solutions.		
Interpretive Task Descriptions		
Axe porridge is a symbol of Russian *smekalka*. Virtually investigate the Russian Artifice and Smekalka Museum and find evidence of Russian *smekalka* and hospitality.	In order to prepare for the upcoming meeting on Russian *smekalka*, Russian people values and beliefs, you need to virtually investigate the Russian Artifice and Smekalka Museum and streets around it. Fill out an official report answering the following questions:	Virtually investigate the Russian Artifice and *Smekalka* Museum, take notes to get ready to give exact directives to the group of detectives that gets ready to visit Russia in order to investigate Russian *smekalka* and artifice. What objects are symbolic of Russian Artifice?

Write down the information we need to know about this museum (address, hours, rules and regulations). If you like what you see, mark it with +; if you do not like it, mark it with -. Remember our detective school values each student's opinion.	What city is this museum located in? Are tourists allowed to take pictures there or do they need to do it secretly? What objects did you find? Do these objects reflect Russian Artifice or *smekalka*? Is there an axe porridge in the museum? Are Russians hospitable? Students write three questions to ask another detective's opinion.	What exhibits demonstrate Russian *smekalka*? What will detectives eat and where? Will they be served axe porridge? What can they expect from locals in hospitality? What are their beliefs and values? Has anything changed over the years in Russian culture and their own? We are sure that you have many more questions to ask. Pose questions to discuss and clarify with your peers later.
Can Dos		
I can identify the signs of Russian *smekalka* with visuals. I can find information about museum. I can differentiate between *smekalka* and artifice.	I can find the information I need using the Russian website. I can understand the difference between Russian *smekalka* and artifice. I can identify how Russians show their hospitality. I can distinguish Russian people's beliefs and values.	I can retrieve key information from the Russian website. I know what to expect from Russian people in terms of their hospitality traditions. I can understand the difference between *smekalka* and artifice. I can distinguish Russian people's beliefs and values.

Interpersonal Task Descriptions		
Discuss with your classmates your findings and opinions. As you match information or opinions, put a check mark. What is your conclusion? Do only Russians have *smekalka*? Are they hospitable? Decide together on *smekalka* for Russian and other cultures.	There is an emergency meeting in the detective school. Ask your questions with your fellow detectives. Discuss what axe porridge and *smekalka* are, and if Russian people are hospitable. Is *smekalka* only a Russian trait? What are the values and beliefs of Russian people? Support your opinion with evidence from the virtual investigation.	Participate in a meeting dedicated to developing a set of rules for detectives investigating in Russia. What are do's and don'ts for the group of detectives? What can we expect from Russians in how they show their hospitality? What are their values and beliefs? Are Russians ingenious people? Are they the only people who have *smekalka*? Debate and support your opinion with evidence from the virtual museum investigation.
Can Dos		
I can exchange information on museum exhibits. I can offer opinions about Russian hospitality and *smekalka*. I can decide on information to include about Russian people beliefs and values.	I can compare information about Russian *smekalka* and evidence from my own culture. I can ask questions about ways Russian show their hospitality. I can exchange opinions about Russian people's beliefs and values.	I can exchange information and ideas about *smekalka* from Russian culture and my own. I can exchange information and ideas about the Russian people's traditions, values, and beliefs.

Presentational Task Descriptions		
Students will create a flyer about the 'Russian Artifice and Smekalka Museum' or Russian hospitality traditions or Axe Porridge infographic recipe to hand out at the Fair.	Students will present their own *smekalka* examples of ingenuity and improvisation from their cultures and recreate the axe porridge story in modern times to present at the Fair.	Students will create an interactive video for the Fair, 'Russian *smekalka*, hospitality, values, and beliefs' for first-time Russian visitors (NearPod-based) or Create a graphic novel/comic book on how to emerge from difficult situations with quick resourcefulness.
Can Dos		
I can recreate an axe porridge recipe. I can design a flyer about the Russian Artifice and Smekalka Museum and Russian hospitality traditions	I can present examples of *smekalka* from my own culture. I can create a story about *smekalka* and present it. I can recreate Russian hospitality traditions.	I can deliver a presentation or write a comic book on Russian *smekalka*, hospitality, values, and beliefs.

Bridge to Design

Let's go deeper into Ms Kalmanson's design process and collaborate with colleagues for additional ideas and reflection on this exemplar before working on your own design.

(See Appendix E.)

Concepts through images: Give us more to see

Visual thinking (Morain, 1997; Yenawine, 2013) and Aesthetic Education (Greene, 2001; Holzer, 2005) allows learners to meet the intangible by connecting concepts with images and works of art. Images help us understand complex subject matter for which we may not have words yet, or ever. Genelle Morain (1997) explained that images grant you access, to be part of that culture and see things as they do. An image is a cultural contribution. The image also is the means by which you can experience and interpret something the way that culture does. Images stir and inspire emotions, helping us to visualize vocabulary and concepts within the cultural contexts and perspectives that created them. Images tell stories about a culture and in turn about others, when we connect to them and recreate a new one. In *Thinking in Pictures*, Temple Grandin (2006) says categories are the beginning of concept formation. We can do this first and more readily with images, which communicate meaning more readily than print. We do not need to have perfection in language form; we can use images to rouse curiosity and tell a story with the small amount of language we have. A lot of cultural information is offered to us through images: people, interaction, rituals, space. These all become easy 'reads' or 'tells' when we become aware of their relevance. Single images become words to a poem, a song, to an entire film, play, or novel when artists perform creative transfer. What themes or concepts come from an image? What do we see?

Check for Learning

OSEE for Intercultural Performance Assessment

In order to engage our learners to investigate and guide their progress towards ICC, as educators we need to experience and model this ourselves. The OSEE tool (Berardo & Deardorff (eds.) 2012; Deardorff, 2009) helps us analyse our ideas or preconceived notions about cultural practices and products by interpreting authentic material, to then uncover the perspectives that created them. The four steps to the OSEE process are: *Observe, State, Explore, Evaluate*. Our programme aligned these with the modes of communication (Glisan et al., 2003). Now this InterCultural Performance Assessment (ICPA) could also be adapted to use with pupils.

Your instructor selects one of the following culturally authentic texts: film clip, images, photographs, objects. For this activity, try to select one which is unknown to the class. Alternatively, everyone in a class or department can bring in an image or object and do this as a gallery walk activity.

Interpretive:
O – Observe: Watch the video carefully or observe the image, photograph or object closely.
S – State impartially and objectively what you see and hear, without giving personal opinions or assumptions. Write two questions by yourself.

Interpersonal:
E– Explore possible explanations regarding the products or practices in the video, image, photo or object within your small group. Gather more information with others. Ask your two questions. Come to consensus.

Presentational:
E – Evaluate these explanations and the perspectives responsible for the products and practices you see.
  Connect with new authentic text of similar themes from the culture(s) you teach. Compare with those Perspectives, Practices and Products.
  Develop and present findings.
  Write three intercultural transfer targets. These statements start with I can…
Based on Berardo and Deardorff (eds.) 2012; Deardorff, 2009. (See Appendix F.)

Teacher as designer

Ms Kuo-Flynn and her learners examine the concept of space and the Japanese cultural perspective of inside-outside space. We will see how she unfolds this concept over a curriculum with the tasks for extending information, starting with this Intercultural transferable goal in Japanese culture (see Table 2.3). The distinction of *uchi* and *soto*, inside and outside, respectively, is present throughout Japanese culture. *Uchi* is the inside, the familiar, the home. *Soto* is the outside, the unknown and unfamiliar. The concept extends beyond physical places to groups and social dynamics. It is so important that it is revisited throughout the Japanese curriculum. When pupils finish the programme, they will understand this concept, see evidence of it in many texts and will recognize it throughout interactions in daily life. As you review the exemplar and the **Bridge to Design** questions later, can you think of examples of *uchi* and *soto* in other cultures? How are they the same or different? Has this concept and practice changed?

Voices from the Field

My Articulated Assessment Transfer Task exemplar addresses intercultural competence by introducing the concept of *Uchi* (Inside) and *Soto* (Outside) distinction that are highly valued in Japanese culture. Students are introduced to this cultural concept by exploring the domestic space of Japanese-style hotels called *Ryokan*.

This exemplar describes the importance of understanding the clear distinction between inside and outside space within public areas. In Japanese culture, such distinction is even more explicit in the area of hotel accommodation. Other cultures should understand that the concept of inside-outside distinction can sometimes be unique; they can connect with it by reflecting on how a personal and public space is distinguished at their local hotels. With my exemplar, even a novice learner can unpack this concept by watching an authentic video of Japanese-style hotels and by talking about the tangible objects that are typically used inside each hotel, since the concept of inside and outside space is well reflected in those objects. Designing this exemplar has helped my teaching and student learning to be more culturally authentic with a clear learning goal in our mind.

What I like most about designing the AATT exemplars is that it allows teachers to transform their classrooms into an authentic cultural environment for students to communicate with one another in the target language. The AATTs also enable teachers to organize their pedagogical ideas and unit goals in a comprehensive manner. I notice that my students are perceiving themselves as active language speakers rather than as passive language learners when they do these tasks.

Shiyo Kuo-Flynn, Japanese instructor, Japanese Dual Language Program, PS 147, Brooklyn, New York.

Table 2.3 Inside-Outside Spaces   Japanese

Articulated Assessment Transfer Task	Shiyo Kuo-Flynn
Enduring Understandings	
* Cultural perspectives and practices regarding inside-outside distinction influence the way we live.	

Essential Questions
? What does inside-outside distinction in our home space tell us about our lifestyle?
? To what extent does our personal space change from one culture to another?

Context
For this year's Japan Day at Central Park, you have been asked to volunteer at the tourism booth for educating visitors about the customs of a Japanese-style inn.

Articulation Spiral Points
@ Describe concepts with visual supports in an infographic.
@ Offer practical information for different needs with a brochure.
@ Justify opinions on inside-outside space in a video presentation.

Intercultural Transfer Targets	Mediation for Transfer
• I can recognize features of Japanese living spaces. • I can organize descriptions of a Japanese inn. • I can share characteristics of Japanese practices. • I can compare Japanese living spaces with those of my own culture.	• Bridge and exchange ideas and concepts of inside outside spaces. • Identify visuals, objects, and examples. • Explain features of Japanese spaces. • Compare and contrast characteristics of Japanese and Western living space.

Novice High	Intermediate Mid	Advanced Low
Webpage of Japanese inn	Inn and hotel finder	Article on Japanese and Western-style inns
Interpretive Task Descriptions		
Students watch a video on a Japanese-style inn, identify objects and form three questions about the video.	Students visit a Japanese-style inn reservation website to select three different inns from different parts of Japan. Students pose three questions and write a brief description for each inn that they selected.	Students read the online article on Japanese-style inn vs. Western-style hotel and summarize their findings by comparing and contrasting the two different types of hotel accommodation.

Can Dos		
I can identify and recognize the objects used inside a Japanese-style inn.	I can organize the descriptions given for each Japanese-style inn. I can write a description of each inn.	I can summarize differences and details between the Japanese-style inn and Western-style hotel and their significance.
Interpersonal Task Descriptions		
Students select one item that attracted their attention the most from the video and describe it for their peers.	Students select one inn from the website, share it with their peers and ask and answer their questions about the inns. They can discuss which inn seems more attractive to tourists with different needs.	Students exchange their summaries, decide and agree on which summaries to include in the presentation for the tourism booth.
Can Dos		
I can share and talk about the item that I liked with my peers after watching a video.	I can exchange information, ask questions and discuss the Japanese style-inn with my peers.	I can read and provide my peers with feedback for the summary related to the different types of hotel accommodation in Japan.
Presentational Task Descriptions		
Students design an infographic of what is inside a Japanese style inn.	Students create a brochure that introduces the Japanese-style inn they selected for different groups of tourists.	Students prepare a video to show at the tourism booth on Japanese-style inn vs. Western-style hotel and present advantages and disadvantages of each type of hotel accommodation.

Can Dos		
I can design an infographic with simple words and features of a Japanese inn.	I can present information related to the Japanese style-inn and explain to others in the class.	I can express opinions on hotel accommodation in Japan and support my position using authentic resources.

Bridge to Design

Let's get closer to Ms Kuo-Flynn's design process and collaborate with colleagues for additional ideas and questions to guide your design work.

(See Appendix G. in Companion Website Chapter 2.)

Swaffar and Arens (2005) define language as 'a set of culture-based performances, situated in various public, private, and disciplinary contexts' (p. 20). Our learners can explore and attain disciplinary literacies (National Literacy Trust, 2020) in their own and other languages and cultures. Intercultural language use is shaped by all kinds of variables, usually occurring through participation and interaction with others. Transfer depends upon understanding the intercultural transferable goals, the perspectives that connect otherwise isolated facts, skills and experiences. We need to co-create these culture-based performances with learners so they can extend themselves through creative transfer and experience the intercultural in yet another way. These transfer tasks become Articulated Spiral Points of performance within the larger curricular story. With these tasks, pupils can demonstrate a sharper understanding of an intercultural concept by creating it in the context of something else or for someone else (Eddy, 2017).

These concepts are your lens for prioritizing what really matters, the organizer for connecting skills and actions. For Ms Kalmanson, one of them for Russian is *smekalka*. For Ms Kuo-Flynn, it is *Uchi* and *Soto*. These teachers do not want any pupil leaving their programmes not understanding those well or not able to interact appropriately within that context. These concepts give purpose to the skills, grammar and vocabulary. These concepts transfer to other contexts and have lasting value beyond the classroom. They require "uncoverage" over time. They are not "covered" in a lesson, a few class periods or mastered in secondary school, never to be needed again. Understanding these concepts is a process that lasts the lifespan. Most importantly, these are ideas and concepts deeply embedded in the culture that you want learners to remember and revisit, throughout your course, their time at your school, throughout their lives.

As instructors, we design tasks for learners to observe or experience language and culture, then to compare and reflect with their home language and culture. These tasks comprise the intercultural transferable goals that will serve us well when working with others in community, work and world. After students leave a language programme and continue to engage with different cultures in life and work, they will be able to hook their new experiences onto the ever-expanding intercultural story.

To further help identify perspectives and transferable goals as well as craft EUs and EQs for Stage One within this model, consider the following indicators as a litmus test: *Layers, Lifespan and Level* (Eddy, 2010c, 2015c, 2016d, 2017). *Layers*: Does the learner have to return to this intercultural concept often, going deeper with these perspectives through different performance assessments? Are we likely to be reminded of this concept, does it reappear albeit in different settings? *Lifespan*: Could we change our minds about the importance of this concept for ourselves over our lifespan? *Level*: Do you really need to know all about it to really understand it? Can it also be understood by anyone even on a surface level? Even as a child? If you can say 'yes' to these questions when considering an intercultural perspective and concept, then it represents a "must-have or non-negotiable" transferable for the culture or between cultures. These are so inherently important to a culture that although they may be invisible, when an error is made, people notice and it matters. Let's consider pupils or university students studying abroad and someone is invited to a party by a host family. Upon arriving, she or he is shocked that aunts, uncles, grandparents and other elders are at this party. In that culture, parties have guests of every age in attendance, unlike other cultures where 'party' may mean only those in a common age group. The concept of leisure time as spent with people of all ages together is an important cultural perspective. It would be a failure on the part of a programme not to instil this concept early and often, through authentic materials and tasks exploring other values concerning leisure and intergenerational social participation in the target culture.

Some educators may say cultural perspectives are too abstract, yet we know that young learners are quite adept at metaphor and abstract ideas (Egan, 1989). For example, there are concepts that even novice learners and young children can understand, even though they cannot yet explain it fully in the target language. If the concept can be understood at a basic level, then it is probably a concept that intercultural perspectives have informed, shaped, and will continue to do so. *Smekalka* and *Uchi/Soto* are examples that meet the criteria for Layers, Lifespan and Level. These allow someone to look at culture across various settings, such as business, health, arts and social interaction, so that learners see these concepts revealed in multiple contexts. These patterns arise from daily social learning ingrained over lifetimes. Another excellent example is the concept of time; how a culture values and organizes time, is it fluid or rigid? Must you be prompt or is lateness acceptable or even expected? Is there a start and stop time on your party invitations? Would that be rude or insensitive? What does that mean for you?

For the previous Check for Learning tasks, you identified perspectives, practices and products and then examined an authentic text to discover those behaviours, beliefs and any products or benefits embedded in that text. Now let us shift to the culture or cultures you teach.

Check for Learning

Layers, Lifespan and Level

Let's consider the above criteria and choose those concepts, perspectives and practices that matter to the culture you are teaching. To arrange your thoughts, you can use the graphic organizer.

(See Appendix H.)

Teacher as Designer

In the exemplar below (see Table 2.4), Dr Célia Bianconi places the recurring theme of resistance and resilience in the curriculum within the shifting presence of Capoeira as key to understanding the Afro-cultural history of Brazil.

"Capoeira traveled through history until it was recognized as cultural patrimony of Brazil in 2007. Today Capoeira attracts adepts in many parts of the world. The Brazilian martial arts are not only teaching movements; it represents the history and culture of Brazil. Capoeira teaches discipline, empowerment and collaboration within a synthesis of rhythm and music. More than a practice exercise, it is a community of practice and part of history. Capoeira represents resilience. Once a forbidden and marginalized practice, now you see it taught and performed all over the world. Capoeira is one of the voices of our national culture. Capoeira represents the resiliency of enslaved African people and then of Brazilians throughout their history" explains Dr Bianconi.

Voices from the Field

The link between language and culture is an essential part of the foreign language acquisition process in the classroom setting and beyond. The introduction of intercultural themes, such as the ones that promote critical thinking and the understanding of an unfamiliar reality, equips learners with repertoire to draw comparison from their own reality. Starting with the historical information and further exploring patterns of a cultural product (e.g. music or books) allow students to explore the relation among cultural practice (social interactions) and perspectives (values and meanings).

Teaching different levels can be challenging, as it requires special attention on how to present the topic as well as to determine achievable expectations, objectives and outcomes accordingly. For example, a novice may need to learn more vocabulary and images in order to fully understand the material, while intermediate and advanced learners can go beyond word level by contributing to discussion and expressing ideas, even if production takes place through pre-defined structures and language chunks. Preparing a lesson for different levels demands my full consideration and planning of all the steps for a continuous growth of proficiency, where I must place the students in the centre of the learning.

Dr Célia Bianconi, Master Lecturer of Portuguese, Boston University.

Table 2.4 Capoeira: The Symbol of Resistance   Portuguese

Articulated Assessment Transfer Task	Célia Bianconi
Enduring Understandings * Music and dance help us express ourselves when other ways are restricted, silenced, or forbidden. * Performing arts often serve as symbols of resistance and visibility across cultures. * Unpredictability trains us for flexibility. * Art represents layers of social history and culture. * Different art forms have been banned throughout history.	
Essential Questions ? Why would art be prohibited? ? Why do we persevere in the face of resistance? ? Why are singing, clapping, drumming and body movements part of Capoeira? ? How do different art forms influence each other? ? What do we learn from our perseverance and resilience? ? How do Capoeira and other art forms overcome a marginalized image and become an important part of cultural history? ? What can Capoeira tell us about community and social practices?	
Context Your local community wants to feature Capoeira at the international dance festival and also offer classes in the school district to promote physical education. They need informational materials to present, promote and support this curricular initiative.	
Articulation Spiral Points @ Identify musical instruments, sounds, and movements with interactive displays. @ Explain changing status throughout cultural history. @ Justify inclusion in schools via blogs and written proposals. @ Synthesize information and concepts of Capoeira for community engagement in a video.	

Intercultural Transfer Targets	Mediation for Transfer
• I can identify instruments and movements of Capoeira. • I can ask questions on the role of Capoeira in the community and cultural history. • I can explain and compare examples of discipline and a community of practice from my own culture. • I can discuss Capoeira as a symbol of resiliency and power.	• Bridge and exchange ideas and concepts of Capoeira discipline, collaboration, and resilience. • Explain instruments and movements of Capoeira to guide in comparisons with forms from other cultures. • Use visuals of Capoeira at different time periods, colonial time to present, to show its presence and change over time. • Summarize information on Capoeira to clarify its role in physical education.

Novice High	Intermediate High	Advanced Mid
Images and text on capoeira instruments Cartoon about Capoeira Documentary	Documentary Reading on Capoeira History with video	Documentary Article: CAPOEIRA: A HISTÓRIA E TRAJETÓRIA DE UM PATRIMÔNIO CULTURAL DO BRASIL
Interpretive Task Descriptions		
Students will watch videos on Capoeira, see images, listen to the music and learn about the music instruments of capoeira. Students will make a list with the names of the instruments, match instruments to body movements, and identify them when played on the graphic organizer. Students prepare questions for the Capoeira performers about instruments, movements and general inquiries about the practice.	Students read about the history, music and role of capoeira in physical education and write five questions related to the article and video. Students compare Capoeira with other dance and physical education practices with those of their culture using a Venn Diagram and Frayer Model. Students prepare questions for the Capoeira performers on the history of the practice, the motivation behind the art form, and a comparison of this dance with other forms in different cultures.	Students read about the history of capoeira and write from the perspective of social justice and inclusion. Then write a summary to synthesize ideas and the shifting role of Capoeira over time. Students prepare questions for the Capoeira performers on the role of Capoeira over time and what it represents throughout changes in cultural history of Brazil.

(Re) Imagining Curriculum to Reveal the Cultural Story

Can Dos		
I can recognize the music of Capoeira and name the musical instruments. I can prepare questions for performers about the practice.	I can pose questions and make inferences on the cultural history of Capoeira, its role in the community and compare these movements with those from my culture.	I can explain and retell Capoeira's history and transformation from symbol of resistance to cultural patrimony. I can pose questions for performers on the role of Capoeira and its changes over time.
Interpersonal Task Descriptions		
Students share their likes and dislikes about the sounds of the instruments and will compare with familiar sounds and instruments of their own culture to choose content for their informational poster. Students ask the performers questions on the instruments, sounds and spoken words of Capoeira.	Students will ask their questions to peers and performers, to come to a consensus on the historical context of Capoeira, cultural comparisons and its importance in the community.	Students discuss with performers and each other how Capoeira's image has changed over the years throughout the history of Brazil. Students make comparisons between this example and a significant shift over time of a tradition from their own culture.
Can Dos		
I can share and talk about Capoeira instruments	I can ask and answer questions and decide key details about Capoeira with a partner.	I can discuss Capoeira as a community practice as well as part of social justice and make comparisons with other cultural practices and their changing role in cultural history.

Presentational Task Descriptions		
Students will create their own posters about Capoeira for the festival and school board.	Students will work in groups to present a video about Capoeira and its importance as community practice.	Students will write a blog about Capoeira to present their ideas to the festival organizers and compose a persuasive proposal with suggestions on how to incorporate the practice of Capoeira in the school curriculum.
Can Dos		
I can design an interactive poster display to describe Capoeira and the musical instruments used to accompany its body movements.	I can develop a video and discuss the importance of capoeira as a community practice.	I can explain the importance of Capoeira as an important practice and persuade others to include it in community activities and school physical education programmes.

Bridge to Design

Let's go deeper into Dr Bianconi's design process and collaborate with colleagues before working on your own design.

(See Appendix I in Companion Website Chapter 2.)

Check for Learning

Develop a Concept Map

The ICANADAPT Concept Map helps you make a visual representation of one recurring concept or theme for our articulated curriculum. Start developing your map now with components you have learned thus far. As you move forward in these chapters, you will add more to your map and edit as you go along. (see Figure 2.1)

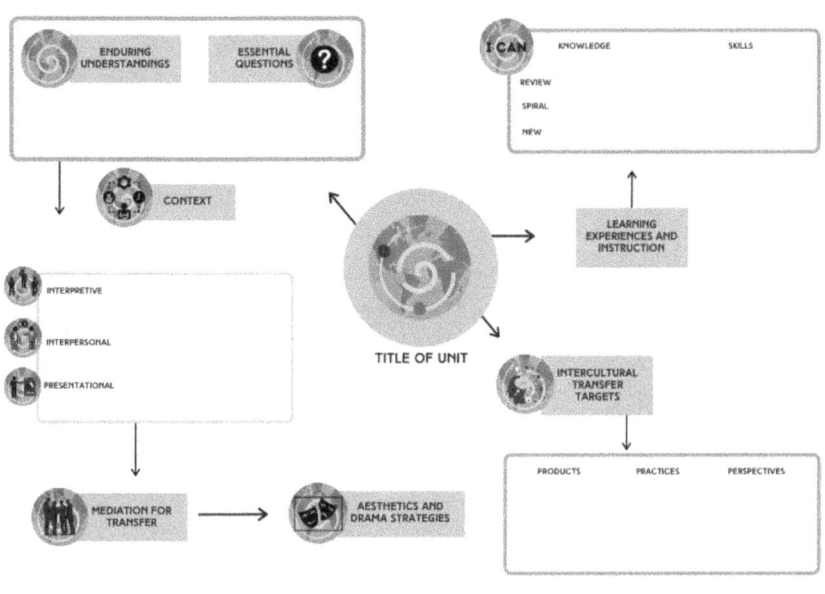

Figure 2.1 ICANADAPT Concept Map

Want to start with the end in mind? Share ideas with a colleague using the annotated ICANADAPT Concept Map (see Figure 7.1)

Developing Enduring Understandings. Exploring Essential Questions: The Channel to Content and Disciplined Thinking

To review from the Introduction, the three stages of Backward Design (McTighe & Wiggins, 2004; Wiggins & McTighe, 2005) are (1) Identify Desired Results, (2) Determine Acceptable Evidence, and (3) Learning Experiences and Instruction.

Teacher candidates at Queens College and in-service teachers and scholars develop the spiral curriculum with intercultural perspectives (Eddy, 2006a, 2007d/e, 2013b, 2016b/c). These perspectives drive Stage One, placing culture at the wheel of articulated programme design. Your desired results are the intercultural transferable goals you set for your programme and your unit.

Enduring Understandings: Routes to Transfer

For this World Language intercultural design, *Enduring Understandings* (McTighe & Wiggins, 2004; Wiggins & McTighe, 2005) are overarching, declarative statements of concepts, perceptions, values, and beliefs that a culture or culture holds close (Eddy, 2006b, 2007d, 2014b, 2017). These may be so fundamental that although they may seem invisible, they are present in almost every personal encounter and are embedded in art, film, sculpture, literature, media, and in all venues and contexts. These are so significant and inherent to understanding that culture that they will reprise and resurface across a curriculum and our lifetime often. Long after pupils have left your school, these will recur again, perhaps in a new context, but learners will respond accordingly with flexibility, confidence and awareness. What do you want the student to come away understanding very well for appropriate interaction and mediation within and between cultures? Stated differently, which cultural perspectives are so essential to thrive in that community or space, that it would be remiss on the part of a programme if it were omitted? From cultural perspectives, let's develop the Enduring Understandings for a chosen concept or theme.

Design for Transfer

Write three Enduring Understandings that enter, reprise and exit throughout the curriculum and over the lifespan as one moves within that culture or cultures. Ask yourself the following questions:
1. What do you want the learner to remember and keep revisiting?

> 2. What are must haves or non-negotiable within cultural perspectives?
>
> 3. Consider your theme and how your culture would respond to that theme. If it were a story the culture tells, what is the moral to the story?
> Students will understand that…
>
> Students will understand that…
>
> Students will understand that…

Students will understand that…

Extended families provide support and celebration across life's milestones and events.

Food is charged with all sorts of personal, familial and cultural symbolism.

These are two possible Enduring Understandings. Throughout workshops, many teachers ask: How are these different from objectives? There is a tendency to conflate the two, but they are very different (see Table 2.5). Enduring Understandings are overarching concepts, not bound by a particular time or context, but transferable to different situations. Objectives are finite, task-oriented statements, limited to skills, functions and facts learned at a particular time. Here is a chart with examples of each, side by side.

Table 2.5 Enduring Understandings and Objective Statements Compared

World Language-MFL Enduring Understandings and Objective statements compared	
Learners understand that…	Learners will be able to…
Social activities are spent with all ages together.	identify social activities and family attending.

Health integrates mind, body, and spirit.	design a menu with community needs in mind.
Colour has special significance for all milestone events.	choose colours for different occasions.
Imagination plays a key role in not only creating but experiencing Chinese opera.	create an infographic for attending Chinese opera.
Proper greetings are determined by age, gender, education, and social status.	say appropriate greetings for elders.
Confrontation is avoided at almost all costs.	disagree or refuse appropriately

Enduring Understandings (EUs) and Essential Questions (EQs) intentionally overlap across other content areas so that World Languages/MFL are integrated into the overall curricular discussion with other disciplines and not sequestered, subordinated or segregated from school or district initiatives. Unfortunately, this is a common practice, because many administrators view MFL/world languages as skills only and not fitting in with other disciplines. Regrettably, we have colleagues that support this treatment, believing aloofness has allowed languages to be left alone to their own devices. In the long run, this estrangement has not served us well in how our discipline is considered and viewed by other teachers, administrators and parents. Indeed, our field is special, but we cannot afford to be aloof and strange to the point we place ourselves out of important conversations that discuss and determine value, time allocation and resources. The model outlined here has been quite empowering for programmes. EUs and EQs serve as touchpoints for deeper inquiry into how cultures respond to and inform the world around them. These are present in different disciplines and are what our learners see and participate in every day. They let our learners see what has mattered to different cultures over time and how they remain relevant now. They allow students to reflect and see how they fit it to the concepts and what they might bring to the table. This framework brings us into curricular discussions with other teachers and administrators as the rightful discipline we are and not subordinated as remedial support or enrichment frill. Furthermore, if a programme chooses to adopt a cadre of EUs and EQs in common, the student leaves that programme with shared, overarching intercultural goals regardless of the language studied in addition to language and culture specific EUs and EQs. How many Enduring Understandings? For any given concept or intercultural transferable goal, plan on four to six. They will enter and exit over your curriculum and not necessarily be addressed every unit, every year. They will all be uncovered by the end of your programme.

Essential Questions: From Where More Questions Come

Essential Questions (McTighe & Wiggins, 2004; Wiggins & McTighe, 2005) are drawn from the Enduring Understandings. EQs provoke more questions, deep inquiry and like EUs, are unfolded and uncovered over time. First, let us understand what an EQ is *not*. Questions such as 'What are the four characteristics of Japanese homes?', 'What are the five key forms in Capoeira?' or 'How do I get around town?' are Focus Questions. These are answerable at the end of a period, focus on recall and facts and for that reason, are finite. Teachers often include focus questions in their agenda on the board or on a webpage. These questions belong at lesson level because their finite nature makes them answerable by the end of the period. Often teachers ask, 'Aren't these essential questions?' Focus questions are not the same as EQs; they function quite differently. Focus questions assist learners in addressing details at lesson level. Just as with objective statements, focus questions reside at Stage Three of our curriculum design. (Refer to previous discussion in Chapter 1 and Appendix A).

Essential Questions are often infinitely big enough to last a lifetime and will recur over the curriculum, across levels, courses, and schools for optimal vertical articulation. You will notice that our EUs and EQs are not tied to a proficiency or performance target level, they are designed for reprise. Neither are the concepts and themes as discussed in Chapter 1. They are constant:Kindergarten through Life, A1 through C2, Novice through Distinguished. What changes are the performance tasks; there lie the complexity and the extent to which the EU and EQ are uncovered with the repertoire the learner can summon now. There are two kinds of EQs: overarching, open-ended and tighter, inquiry guiding questions that are addressed through content in a unit. Like the EUs, they will also recur over the lifespan of the learner in varied intercultural contexts. Essential Questions may enter, reprise and exit; if a particular concept is on hiatus that year, those EQs reappear later. By the end of the curriculum, all are uncovered in varied ways through your performance tasks. EUs and EQs stay constant throughout your curriculum: sturdy and stable as the trunk of a tree: What changes are the AATTs, the performance tasks you design, on the branches that appear each unit year. Through the tasks, they will reveal answers to these questions and uncover the intercultural perspectives with increasing autonomy moving forward in the curriculum.

Essential Questions:

- are not answered in a lesson
- are questions relevant beyond schooling
- are at the heart of the culture
- are recursive and meant to be reprised, revisited, and reevaluated later
- raise more questions
- matter so much that when cultural practices implied in the EQ do not happen, people notice
- activate critical thinking skills

Design for Transfer

Compose Essential Questions for your chosen intercultural concept. To see a selection of EUs and EQs side by side, see Appendix J.

Design for Transfer

Perspectives-Practices-Products Infographics and Intercultural Word Clouds

Intercultural Perspectives become transferable concepts for writing Enduring Understandings and Essential Questions. These Perspectives create the practices and products which in turn inform transfer tasks and the authentic texts we use. It is helpful to have infographics which provide At-a Glance organization and a word cloud to stimulate conversation and questions. Both of these products will be helpful towards implementation with your pupils.

Design three infographics featuring a perspective, practice and product representing the culture(s) you teach.

Create a word cloud of perspectives, practices, products for an Intercultural transferable goal, concept or theme for your articulated curriculum.

What people think

What people do

What people create

Design for Transfer

Intercultural Communicative Competence Inquiry Project
Queens College teacher candidates do this inquiry project twice; in methods and again with different content in curriculum and assessment to see evidence of growth over time. It is one of our key assessments for national accreditation and it is very helpful for our teacher trainees.

- Investigate your unit theme via cultural practices and products but most importantly, the cultural perspectives that informed and shaped the practices and products.
- Discuss cultural comparisons between language communities
- Use a variety of resources to research the material and derive insights from the culture.
- Develop the ICANADAPT graphic organizer that describes the products, practices and perspectives.
- Select NCSSFL-ACTFL Intercultural Competence Can-Do benchmarks (2017) and/or the CEFR Plurilingual/Pluricultural 'I can' statements (2020).

Discuss the Issues

1 Why do we design Enduring Understandings and Essential Questions through the Culture standard? How do they help us uncover content over time?
2 Explain Layers, Lifespan and Level to a colleague. Give an example of each.

3 Enduring Understandings differ from Objective statements and Essential Questions differ from Focus Questions. Discuss.

4 Cultural perspectives are embedded in their products and practices. These come from many disciplines that created authentic texts. Our curriculum is found within every subject.

5 Aesthetic education helps us reveal messages behind a variety of texts and images.

6 Enduring Understandings and Essential Questions help us design for intercultural, transdisciplinary articulation. Discuss.

7 Our curriculum should give learners the tools to continue the inquiry without us. Discuss.

Reflect and Revisit

1 Explain Pluricultural Competence in the CEFR, the Cultures standard in the ACTFL World Readiness standards or your state or national Culture guidelines or standards for our curricular planning.

2 Why should intercultural perspectives and practices drive the curriculum?

3 What are Intercultural Transfer Goals that resurface and recur throughout our lives in every culture?

4 Can the same Intercultural Transfer Goals be used to develop curriculum for any language offered in your school? What will change? What will stay the same?

5 What is a cultural perspective or concept that is understood by even the youngest?

6 How do Enduring Understandings and Essential Questions help us integrate other disciplines in the school curriculum? Why is that important for MFL/World Language Education?

7 How will you uncover these themes over time, over your curriculum? If the theme is the same, what do you think changes, year after year, unit by unit?

Chapter 3

From Coverage without Pity to Designing with Performance for Transfer: Make It New Everyday

Enduring Understandings

- ∞ Early and frequent performance for transfer prepares the learner to make meaningful decisions for novel situations, audiences, needs, conditions and contexts that will change.
- ∞ Transfer tasks require intention to solve them rather than rote skills or recall of cultural facts.
- ∞ The learner needs to be able to handle unanticipated variations flexibly, securely and independently.
- ∞ The more complexity and novelty the task presents, the more it assesses for transfer.
- ∞ Novel, key performance tasks solve problems or create products of value beyond the classroom and support mediation goals.

Essential Questions

- **Q** Why do we create anything?
- **Q** How can we understand the content a culture shares and our participation within it?
- **Q** To what extent are language tasks valued beyond classroom borders?
- **Q** To what extent do our tasks connect to life beyond school?
- **Q** Why does proof of transfer evidence matter?
- **Q** How does novelty prepare us for the unpredictable?
- **Q** What will learners do with language after they have left us?

Key Terms and Concepts

Transfer	Complexity
Context	Autonomy
Summative and Formative Assessment	Novelty
Performance for Transfer	Performance and Proficiency

Research in Practice

The work of the following researchers and practitioners will guide you to cite sources which inform your planning, assessment and instructional decisions in pre-service portfolio assessments or in-service professional learning plans.

Benson, 2011 Eddy, 2006a/b, 2007a/d, 2009a/b, 2010a/c, 2014a, 2016a/b/c/d Holec, 1988 Lamb, 2000, 2001, 2017	Learners should be fully active, take control and be in charge of their own language learning. Learners should solve problems and create new products of value to someone else.
Greene, 2001; Holzer, 2007	Aesthetic Education Capacities of Imaginative Learning.
Heathcote & Bolton, 1995 Maley & Duff, 2005	Drama pedagogy, improvisation and Process Drama strategies support meaning making and socially constructed language for mediation.
Lamb, 2008 Lamb & Reinders, 2005 Little, 1995, 2007, 2009a/b	Teachers shift from information source to catalyst to facilitate learner autonomy.
McTighe, 2014	Learners need to communicate with varied audiences and purposes with appropriate cultural understanding.

McKeough, Lupart & Marini, 1995	Transfer requires students not only to remember but also to make sense of and be able to use what they have learned.
Perkins & Salomon, 1988, 2012	Low (near) Transfer and High (far) Transfer Tasks
Vygotsky, 1962	Learning cannot be separated from social and cultural interaction. Cultural artefacts, tools and symbols to construct meaning are essential. Teacher role is to assist learners to take control.
Wiggins & Mc Tighe, 2005	Learners demonstrate transfer when they can use knowledge and skills in different or new contexts from how the content was originally learned.

I can

- Identify characteristics of performance for transfer
- Turnaround tasks to transfer
- Design the context or scenario for key performance task

Rewind

Which key terms or concepts stand out for you from Chapter 2: *(Re) Imagining curriculum to reveal the cultural story?*

Ask your colleague three questions based on the content from that chapter.

Explain the most compelling idea from the previous chapter in your own words.

Explain how this concept or practice is the same, similar or different to what you know or do.

Which concept or practice do you think will have the greatest impact on your teaching?

Overview

In Chapter 2, we looked at intercultural perspectives for unfolding curriculum and Enduring Understandings and Essential Questions as overarching transferable goals. These provide the routes to transfer, because those concepts help you design tasks that reveal and explain both intercultural communicative goals for the curriculum at each level of learner engagement. Instructors develop EUs and EQs to drive the intercultural theme or concept at programme level. At unit and at lesson level, the learners demonstrate what they can do with performance assessment tasks and culturally authentic materials. These tasks promote both transferable and integrated concepts of language, culture and content, rather than static and formulaic recall of disconnected linguistic, cultural or interdisciplinary content. In this chapter, we define and make the case for transfer and novelty with articulated assessment transfer tasks as an anthology of Key Performances within our curriculum design.

We need to prepare learners for the inevitable unexpected

How do we know we really learned something and truly understood it? Across many content areas taught in schools, often the final assessment resembles the same tasks as taught with identical examples and manipulation of material that pupils experience throughout the unit. The assessment is always for the same audience: the teacher, even if it is presented in front of the class. Corbett (2003) stated, 'the intercultural learner moves amongst cultures, learning to cope with the inevitable changes' (p. 211). The irony is that teacher education often prepares teachers and subsequently the learner for expected routine instead (Eddy, 2017). When our assessments are so predictable in that pupils know not only what is on the tests but also how the material is probed, depicted, solicited or portrayed, what message does that tell them? Is this contradictory to what real language use looks and sounds like? What is the danger of sameness and predictability? Will we have that predictability cushion when out and about, using language in authentic settings, for work or within the community? What happens when they expect sameness and that doesn't work out? The only thing predictable about life in the communication realm is how unpredictable it really is.

Transfer is proven when one can summon their knowledge and skill repertoire independently to solve novel challenges or tasks in varied situations, with no cues from an instructor (Halpern, D., 1998; McKeough, Lupart & Marini, 1995;

McTighe, 2014; Perkins & Salomon, 1988; Wiggins & McTighe, 2005). For our profession, this involves creative tasks beyond facts, procedures, functions and memorized grammar forms. These are performance tasks that solve a problem or create a product, with increasing novelty over time (Eddy, 2007d/g, 2014).

Transfer tasks are the necessary bridge between Performance and Proficiency. *Proficiency* refers to how well someone uses the language in an unplanned and unrehearsed manner at any given time wherever they are, regardless of when, how, or where language is acquired (ACTFL, 2012). Furthermore, to attain a particular proficiency level means that the criteria for that level are sustained consistently, all the time. *Performance* is defined as language learned and practiced within a classroom with familiar contexts (ACTFL, 2012). *Performances for Transfer* provide evidence that one can resolve new problems and create within novel, unfamiliar, unrehearsed or unanticipated situations with someone else's needs in mind, even within classroom instruction. Transfer tasks facilitate proficiency inside the classroom because they mirror the combination of linguistic, social, and cultural demands and expectations outside of it. The AATT exemplars show a series of tasks across different articulation levels of engagement (Eddy, 2014a, 2017, 2019a) tailored to address proficiency target criteria (ACTFL, 2012; COE, 2020; NCSSFL, 2017). These tasks solve a problem or create a deliverable as evidence of transfer. The goal for our curriculum design is to develop Key Performances for transfer set at Articulation Spiral Points, to move the learner to solve problems and create products in new situations with significance beyond school and to consider needs beyond the self.

Every authentic communication transaction is proof of transfer and proof you need transfer

Lack of transfer has happened to all of us, perhaps during an experience with a different subject matter; we all experienced our own transfer vortex. When learning and using another language, you know what it looked and felt like when transfer did not occur. Most of the time learners may not recognize concepts or content to call upon from their repertoire because they never practiced adaptability and novelty. In classrooms, it usually means pupils have to review and relearn information every year and still transfer does not occur. Without transfer, the pupil will not be able to demonstrate the flexibility required when faced with novel tasks or situations that are often ambiguous and require critical thinking and engagement. This is a danger in any discipline, but it is particularly daunting for the language learner that cannot use what they know flexibly and securely for a new situation, audience, or to address someone else's needs. Language that is presented as predictable, contrived and only acceptable when error-free for school does not serve us well outside of that setting, where meaningful language with agility is needed most. Communication does not need to be perfect, but learners need enough poise and flexibility so that mediation and new meaning can occur with the language they have.

Transfer does not occur by chance

Typical scaffolded exercises drill one item or skill repeatedly and often without a meaningful or realistic purpose. Drill/mastery tasks, discrete item cloze activities and memorized dialogues do not prepare the learner for transfer. If language learning is dominated by these types of tasks, transfer will not happen with those alone. You may say, 'I learned my second or subsequent language with fill-ins and drills.' No, learning and true ownership of the language did not happen solely with drills. You took it upon yourself to take risks in real situations where you had to use the language. Those situations were unpredictable and new; you made mistakes, you recombined, mixed it up and were keen to engage in frequent trial and error, perhaps out of necessity. Time and again you created or initiated novel transfer situations and perhaps someone else took part in that. The drills did not accomplish transfer on their own. When learners fill, drill and repeat, they focus on individual items. When world language/MFL curricula resemble an encyclopaedia of grammar and information coverage, item drills of verbs and repetitive sets of the same type often remain a mainstay throughout schemes of work. This costume of rules, lists and patterns with a *lagniappe* of cultural soundbites becomes quite transparent when language learners cannot do anything new with it. No one will ask them to recite these patterns on any street, anywhere. Pupils might absorb these superficially for a test and fill in a blank or answer in multiple choice, but it will not last or it remains so inert and passive, they cannot truly use it. In a coverage-laden curriculum, learners forget, misunderstand a concept or only know it in the rigid, predictable example in which it was taught (Shulman, 1999). They do not have ownership of anything. When prompted exactly as they were taught, students might just fill in the space, prepare longer pieces within expected guidelines and that is its limitation. Rather than repeated drill of the same item with predictable expectations, transfer tasks assess concepts that created the item and the ability to create novel products adaptable to different variables (Eddy, 2014a, 2016b; Wiggins and McTighe, 2005).

Drills give the appearance of understanding but not the reality of transfer

What happens when we are actually out there in the real world? All too often we find out that what we memorized did not serve us well because that assessment and instruction did not teach us how to adapt, adjust, think creatively or flexibly for fickle, unpredictable and changeable demands of actual language use. Drills lull the learner into a false expectation of predictability (Eddy, 2016a). Our pupils often expect and even demand to be tested the way they were taught and if that diverges just one bit, they look at the task like they've never seen it. They look at it and you as if you were both strangers. It can be two months or two weeks from the time they learned it, they look aghast and say, 'You never taught us this.' This problem happens not just in our content area, but in all of them and the crisis of promising the predictable goes all the way up to graduate school, then to the world of work. It leads to inflexibility or collapse when faced with flux, ambiguity and loss of routine. We know now after the painful uncertainty in recent years, it's just not how life is.

Often learners are disappointed at first when they discover language is not the static and predictable exercise as presented but a mercurial and highly creative endeavour. It does our learners a disservice to only offer anticipated drills and task items that suit the same audience. It keeps language too local and fixed for the drill of the moment and then stuck in our past as fragmented recollection. If we want to be fair to our learners and prepare them for honest, future-forward authentic language use, consistent novelty in our tasks is the goal of curriculum and assessment design. When should they have these tasks? Early and often. Remove the scaffolding training wheels sooner rather than later. The tasks we design must instil the message that unpredictability is the only constant in real communication.

The reality of transfer for world languages means any situation where you need to act, solve a problem, create something, respond, engage, alone or socially, when you are 'on the field' and it's real. My first reality of transfer and the lack thereof was my first time in Mexico City. I was down in the underground metro at the onset of rush hour. I thought my experience with New York City subways was sufficient. In an instant, nothing was; my last third-person irregular preterite was gone, it was worth nada, naught, bubkes, zilch, not one ort. I didn't have the strategies to question the reason behind the bedlam, much less to heed the practice of women-only trains during rush hour in that particular metro station. I could not use language flexibly, nor did I wield sufficient intercultural communicative competence to know who, or what to ask or how. OK, a bit of mental as well as physical agility was on my side and I needed every ounce I could muster. I knew in seconds that I made a gross error and kept my wits about me while I quickly planned possible solutions with more information.

Our learners need to be ready to handle abstract and complex ideas, acquire new information, be flexible to change and recognize the need for new strategies (Halpern, 1998). Transfer tasks enable critical thinking skills and encourage flexibility. *Autonomy* helps learners feel confident with the language they own now, use it meaningfully to the extent they can and tackle new uses for it every time they are with us and without us. Autonomy indicates agency right from the beginning whereby pupils plan, implement and evaluate their own learning in the target language as far as they can (Lamb, 2017; Little, 2020). These tasks prime learners to use these skills appropriately in a variety of settings, whatever may arise. Transfer tasks finally put to rest the crisis of the predictable, carefully and intentionally challenging the risk-averse.

Pause to Ponder

What was your transfer moment? It can be related to language learning or something else in your life. Tell a colleague a tale when you were out there and you experienced proof of transfer. Your story can be successful proof of transfer or proof you needed transfer.

Understanding begins with creative transfer

In order to foster flexible, creative and confident language use at any level, it is necessary to challenge the sequential interpretation of Bloom's Taxonomy (Anderson and Krathwohl, 2001; Bloom, 1956) when designing curriculum, assessment and instruction. We have to apply knowledge and create new things in order to understand anything (see Figure 3.1). The idea that the learner has to be mired in 'lower-level' factual and procedural knowledge before they can do 'higher-level' thinking work doesn't agree with what we know from research on how we learn (Agarwal, 2019). A lot of our children, many in lower resourced schools, rarely if ever get to do the HOTS, the higher-order thinking skills and the transfer we are talking about. Instead, they stay stuck in the 'lower-level' procedural

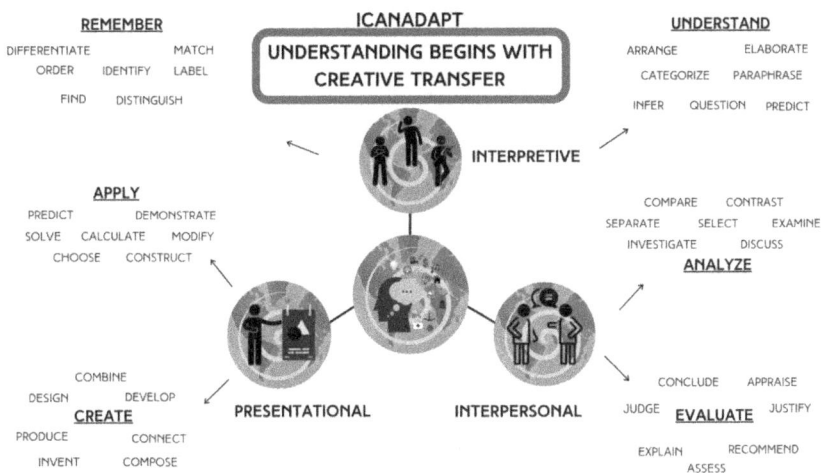

Figure 3.1 Understanding Begins with Creative Transfer

tasks; every question is recall and remember. Worksheets and fill-in-facts prevail, with learners seldom asked to analyse, synthesize or create anything. The floor becomes their ceiling, more like an attic crawl-space, from which many never get out. Creative transfer tasks should not be offered up to just a chosen few. Nor should transfer wait until a higher level of proficiency and only then 'if there's time.'

Novelty is ever present. We combine, retrieve, make decisions, solve problems and create things we may never have exactly seen before. To participate within a language and culture, one cannot rely on rehearsal or think transfer happens by chance. Learners need novel tasks with variation, a complication to solve, opportunities to create and time to analyse those works collaboratively, most of the time, early and often. The two distinctive characteristics of intermediate level (ACTFL, 2012; NCSSFL, 2017) or CEFR A2-B1+ (COE, 2001) are creating original language and asking questions, not just passive answering. Creativity and inquiry are required to get out of Novice. This means they have to experience these right away in novice tasks. The intermediate level is not when those start. For the relatively short time our learners are in the classroom with us, we need to make it new every day from the beginning with creativity and inquiry.

Understanding World Language Performance Assessment: Conception, Consensus, Creation

The Interpretive, Interpersonal and Presentational modes of communication (Glisan, Adair-Hauck, Koda, Sandrock & Swender, 2003) function best as integrated performance assessments (IPA) (Adair-Hauck, Glisan, Koda, Swender

& Sandrock, 2006) rather than separate tasks for receptive, interactive and productive modalities. The IPA recommends authentic texts, with all three mode tasks centered around the same topic. The Interpretive mode uses authentic text that learners listen to, watch or read, with related tasks that infer and make meaning from texts. The Interpersonal mode extends the information in spontaneous and unscripted conversation between two or more people. The Presentational mode is a spoken or written piece developed with time to consult resources and refine the final product. These tasks look quite different from fill-in, discrete point or unrelated multiple-choice item types. In the chapters thus far, we have seen the AATT exemplars engage the modes of communication, extending the concept of IPA for articulation and transfer within the ICANADAPT framework. In the chapters that follow, we will see each mode and components explained with additional AATT exemplars. Although it is not new, many classrooms still do not incorporate the IPA in their assessment inventory, believing that the modes of communication are either too similar to what they do with the four skills or extremely different (Eddy, forthcoming; Stoller, 2009). At the same time, the perception of the IPA and the intention of design are also factors. In a study with teacher trainees, student teacher candidates, in-service teacher mentors and university supervisor, the perception and implementation of the IPA as well as feedback to candidates varied (Eddy & Bustamante, 2020). Additional supports and materials were suggested as well as collaborative opportunities for ongoing professional learning between school districts and university. This gap existed because implementation of the modes was required for new teacher licensure since 2004; however, it was not a requirement for planning, assessment, or instruction in school districts (Eddy, 2009a, 2019a; Eddy & Bustamante, 2020). Even though the three modes indicated a departure from fill-ins and drills, tasks still resemble skills that are low on the pyramid and not requiring intention and thoughtful use of language to solve a problem. Tasks fall short of criteria for performance for transfer when learners do not create new products or solve a problem for an audience, real or fictitious, on their own, without significant teacher supports or scaffolds. Thus, these can be realized only through frequent practice at transfer tasks and teacher development for design of same.

One popular task example for Spanish that is low on the pyramid is the poster where every pupil picks a country and makes a poster with all of the information about the country. There was a time when that information came from an encyclopaedia; now it is all accessed online. In either case, it teaches the learner to cut, copy and paste. A poster or infographic is fine, if it considers purpose, audience, and a repertoire thoughtfully engaged. In *Turnarounds for Transfer* (Eddy,

2008, 2009a, 2010a/b, 2013a, 2014a) groups of teachers and I reforged tired, textbook tasks or any classroom task they thought needed a turnaround. In this case, the task of making the poster about the country and a recall task on tourism sites became a transfer task prototype with a useful product customized to meet people's needs on travel (see Table 3.1). Teachers suggested variations right away, such as an itinerary for mobility accessibility needs. Another suggestion was a time limitation; with only six hours only in one location, decide the 'must-do's' within that limitation. The variable in the former example and the complication in the latter present novel situations that both require critical thinking skills and drawing upon knowledge and skills to solve the problem. The task also trains the learner in mediation strategies, if asked to help someone else unfamiliar with language or procedures.

Turnarounds for Transfer

Original Task: Matching column on tourist locations. Poster on country.
   Turnaround:
   Enduring Understanding:
   Where people choose to travel depends a lot on their interests and needs.
   Essential Question: How do we choose where we want and need to go?
   Context: You are a travel agent specializing in travel to ____. Your clients are all different. Create an itinerary suited for each group, keeping in mind the possible interests and needs of the client.

Table 3.1 Turnarounds for Transfer

Interpretive	Interpersonal	Presentational
Using the different travel brochures and websites from various towns and cities in ___ , categorize on your chart which towns or cities are the best places to visit for the following: Music/Historic Sites/Families/Low Cost/Art/Shopping	Using the chart, share with your partner the towns or cities you would like or not like to visit, based on the information from the categories. Make decisions together on where you would like to go.	Itinerary for: • A family of five with young children. • A person who is a history buff. • Three students with a limited budget. • Grandparents who love small towns, local crafts and music.

Check for Learning

With a colleague, try a *Turnaround for Transfer*. Find a task to turn around. At first it will be the Presentational mode task deliverable. Use the *Understanding begins with Creative Transfer* image to find helpful verbs with creative transfer in mind (see Figure 3.1) and the Articulated Assessment Transfer Task Review Criteria and AATT Design Rubric to guide you (see Appendix K).

Framing the Context

Each target level panel of the AATTs becomes a Stage Two within the ICANADAPT unit template, the summative performance assessment. The *Context* presents a scenario, a situation, need or problem to be solved and a request for a product or deliverable or for a given audience, real or simulated. Learners need to keep the needs of this group, individual, client or organization in mind and create a product in response to the information in the Context and any additional research they do. The Context is for the *summative performance assessment* in Stage Two of the unit. Summative is assessment *of* learning for transfer; the final assessment for the unit when they solve a novel problem and create a new product. Learners must reach back into their repertoire, extract what they need, make thoughtful decisions and choose together on the process and details. In the AATT, the Context is the same across all three levels. Each level creates and contributes a deliverable for the audience in the Context, according to their level of engagement. Learners of the same language but at different levels can do the AATTs simultaneously as a language cohort, so that all learners are working toward the same Context with premise and purpose together. This cohort model engages learners to collaborate, co-construct meaning, practice mediation strategies at their ability and *contribute to the extent they can with the language they have*. This model is intentional and metacognitive, so that the cohort can see language is developmental, all levels can contribute, mediate, and participate actively and socially with the language they own at hand.

The AATT Context and level tasks can be used for linked, vertical articulation between levels, buildings and schools or for multi-level learners in one classroom. Some teachers also choose to do AATTs as a cohort for *formative assessment*, which is assessment *for* learning and *as* learning (Dann, 2014; Earl, 2003) earlier in the unit. This opportunity gives learners more practice at transfer and mediation developmentally and collaboratively. Formative and summative performance assessment done this way make instruction and assessment appear seamless. The AATTs enable active and expert learning, with knowledge constructed to serve a specific disciplined purpose given in the Context. As we have seen, the EUs and EQs (Wiggins & McTighe, 2005) frame key concepts and ideas within disciplines and the cultural perspectives which inform them. When students see these recursive concepts, they enable familiarity and matched solutions in their repertoire. Now the novel situation does not appear as foreign, local or temporary.

Facile transfer teaches us that there are many possibilities, solutions that cross boundaries of disciplinary content, with similarities to be found in diversity. Our transfer tasks provide opportunities for active co-creation of knowledge and collaborative problem-solving. Pupils engage with the creative work of others and then respond to the problem as experts, ready to elaborate, contribute and offer solutions in response to someone else's needs. A community centre would like to welcome newcomers to the neighbourhood. A health magazine needs content for an issue on school food. *HomeTV* is doing a series on new housing developments that match community needs. Learners create an itinerary for a walking tour based on the needs of the participants. Initially, the instructor provides the variations or target audiences for these tasks but soon your learners will offer suggestions for different needs and audiences. These tasks also allow the instructor to see how learners approach a task and choose from their repertoire. This is why it is valuable to spend class time on transfer tasks, what they are and why they are important. Not only do students value tasks done during class time more than those done at home, but it allows the instructor important 'post-production' time to ask questions on learner choices of repertoire and strategy, a judicious use of 10 percent not in the target language (ACTFL, 2010).

Collaboration for Articulation

Your colleague relies on textbook tasks that are expected and rehearsed. Explain transfer to this colleague and why it is important to engage learners in transfer tasks.

Facets of Design

The AATTs often ask learners to collaborate with others as experts in a short improvisational scene to take action on the needs of that audience, group, organization or client. The Mantle of the Expert from Process Drama (Edmiston, 2003; Heathcote & Herbert, 1985; Heathcote & Bolton, 1995) is a pedagogy strategy adapted here within the design of transfer tasks (Eddy, 2019a). Because transfer depends on flexible and novel use of transdisciplinary content, the design space needs to be fashioned for our learners to do so. In order to get past the passive role with content, they need to think, act and be trusted as agents, 'as if' they are experts. Learners become experts 'in role' as planners, curators, advisors, writers, composers and developers related to the discipline in response to need or request outlined in the Context. This role is often stated in the Context. Within the Interpersonal task, it is a short, improvised drama in which they plan, choose, negotiate and come to a consensus on how they will address the needs of others; a group, an organization, an individual, another audience. In this role, they create the deliverable or product for the subsequent Presentational task.

Culturally authentic texts offer us images, symbols, unspoken works of art. Some exemplars feature tasks with each mode creating a deliverable, in that the pupils co-create a piece for an intended audience to do creative inquiry with language. For example, an adaptation of Poster Dialogue (Dawson & Lee, 2018) in the Interpersonal mode asks pupils to use images, symbols and words to reflect collectively and spontaneously to open-ended prompts inspired by a culturally relevant text. After this conversation through writing, learners do a gallery walk to elaborate, clarify, question and respond with other pupils on their posters in small groups. The transfer task is spontaneous and unscripted for the class but it can also be an interactive, improvisational experience at a festival or museum for participants to take part, with each contribution distinctive and unique by the participants.

Sometimes the tasks build to become the spoken and written presentation in response to the purpose or audience in the Context. Once pupils become accustomed to the performance assessments in the AATTs, they will often come up with their own Context, audience or problem to solve. In the exemplars below, the audience in the Contexts are a Sephardic festival (see Table 3.2), a national arts programme (see Table 3.3), an Italian news outlet (see Table 3.5), and a local art museum (see Figure 3.4). Pupils are in the role as experts to create a product or otherwise answer the call to participate or solve a problem for that organization, entity, customer, or patron, whether these are real or fiction. Learners at different levels of engagement can all contribute to these audiences according to their ability, thereby differentiating tasks for an articulated treatment between levels or schools. Their role can also shift to someone else or other people in that same scenario, perhaps a special interest group of attendees, restauranteurs or parents. This change of role will also shift the content and speech register, encouraging flexibility and facility in mediation for different groups of people. The tasks enable experimentation and risk-taking while connecting to the cultural perspectives through the work. These transfer tasks also allow learners to develop an awareness of their own culture, express understanding of the work in their own voice and examine common situations, emotions and issues through new lenses or novel creations. This encourages and challenges the risk-averse to develop empathy, flexibility and a less myopic response to cultural perspectives, values and beliefs, a key objective of intercultural competence (Byram & Fleming, 1998; Byram, Gribkova & Starkey, 2002; Eddy, 2019b).

Teacher as Designer

Music often tells stories of those that might be untold or unknown otherwise. Songs tell us a lot about the culture not only through lyrics, but also by layering different rhythms, suggesting that a blend of influences often shapes the thought, art and emotions of a people (Eddy, 2006b, 2007c). How does music express feelings of despair, hope, longing or resolution? Music has a powerful effect on the emotional centres of the limbic system, the area of our long-term memory. Language delivery through music is 'emotionally memorable'. Current, culturally relevant music often awakens background knowledge on a concept or theme. Learners empathize and relate the themes to their own experience or that of their families and communities. In this exemplar, the concepts of identity through cultural symbolism, imagery and the senses work together in this exemplar for Ladino curriculum through songs by composer and lyricist, Sarah Aroeste. The artist demonstrates creative transfer with two songs; one inspired by medieval poet Samuel Ha-Nagid's *El Leon Ferido/The Wounded Lion* (Goldstein, 1965) and the second with memories, stories, images and reconnection with the place of her ancestors, *Mi Monastir*. Learners understand and connect with concepts in Sephardic culture and language by creating new texts, inviting them to reach into their past for their place in the now. Henry David Thoreau (1857) wrote, 'When I hear music, I fear no danger. I am invulnerable. I see no foe. I am related to the earliest times, and to the latest.'

Voices from the Field

Jews who trace their ancestry back to pre-Inquisition Spain, known as Sephardim, have been bound together for centuries through historical memory, a diasporic identity, and the rich language of Ladino (Judeo-Spanish). Five hundred years later, Sephardic culture still flourishes, despite few native Ladino speakers left today. Both *El Leon Ferido* and *Mi Monastir* are songs about what it means to hold fast to a culture that many people claim is already lost. My inspirations for both songs try to prove that wrong.

El Leon Ferido, which incorporates lines of verse by the Judeo-Spanish poet, Samuel Ha-Nagid, seeks to give hope to those in desperate times. Even in the darkest hour, the lamp still has light before it is extinguished – we must persevere against all odds! This is a universal message, whether taken on a personal level, or on a communal one. Ha-Nagid wrote his poem during a time of great fear in Europe, and I, too, wrote my song as many around me have predicted Ladino's extinction. But like Ha-Nagid's message, I believe Ladino still has brilliant light to share. Likewise, *Mi Monastir*, which I wrote to preserve the memory of a Sephardic community from Macedonia lost in WWII, shows that hope is still possible despite great loss. *Mi Monastir* is based off memories of my grandfather and my surviving cousin, Rachel. I have taken many stories of their generation and tried to convey them in this song filled with honour for them and the city they held so dear. Among many symbolic images I allude to in the Monastir lyrics, the mezuzah is one that stands out. As Rachel's family was taken away on March 11th, 1943, their non-Jewish neighbour took their mezuzah, the signpost on Jewish doors, planning to return it to the family one day. Indeed, years later, the mezuzah was given back to Rachel, an image of which can be found on the song's lyric page. Memories live on through the generations and are what keep cultures alive. By listening to my elders and appreciating the smells, tastes and stories they shared with me from their hometown of Monastir, I have been able to put those memories into song and to preserve them for posterity in their native tongue.

The Ladino language is a complex and beautiful mix of several languages and shows how intertwined so many cultures are. While its core is a 15th century dialect of Spanish, Ladino absorbed bits of Portuguese, Italian, French, Greek, Turkish, Arabic and Hebrew as Jews migrated east from the Iberian Peninsula. Depending on where a Jewish community settled, the dialect of Ladino could vary. *El Leon Ferido* and *Mi Monastir* represent two different variations of Ladino. But both signify the timeless connection that Jews have had for centuries with their Hispanic past.

Sarah Aroeste, Ladino singer/songwriter, author and activist.

Table 3.2 Articulated Assessment Transfer Task
The Wounded Lion Still Knows How to Roar. Sarah Aroeste and Jennifer Eddy

Ladino *El Leon Ferido* and *Mi Monastir*. Music and Lyrics in Ladino by Sarah Aroeste

Enduring Understandings ∗ Personal, historical, societal and cultural symbols create our identity. ∗ Music expresses understanding of the world, human experience and one's self.
Essential Questions ? In the face of adversity, what causes people to triumph and overcome? ? How can images and symbolism tell our story? ? Why is the act of creativity important for the individual and culture? ? What can music from different cultures teach us about ourselves? ? How does music inspire, comfort and support us?
Context A Sephardic festival celebrates music and art over the ages with original stories, poems and songs for all ages.
Articulation Spiral Points @ Create a sensory collage connecting words, symbols and images. @ Compose new poem and lyric stanzas. @ Narrative story for children, @ Plan collaborative interactive exhibits.

Intercultural Transfer Targets	Mediation for Transfer
• I can identify visuals, cultural symbols and imagery represented in the song to people unfamiliar with the culture and language. • I can compare these songs to others with similar themes from my own and other cultures. • I can compare how personal and cultural experiences influence music.	• Bridge and exchange ideas and concepts of emotions, senses, symbols and identity • Describe emotions in the song, the person's feelings and their reasons • Use annotations and visuals to clarify significance of events in song for difference audiences • Summarize information and emotions depicted in song

Novice High	Intermediate High	Advanced Mid
El Leon Ferido	*El Leon Ferido*	*El Leon Ferido*
Mi Monastir	*Mi Monastir*	*Mi Monastir*
Interpretive Task Descriptions		
Listen to the songs and select symbols and images, matching them in order with phrases from *El Monastir* and *El Leon Ferido*. Choose images to represent a town from their family ancestry and culture. These are collected for the Poster Collage.	After listening to the songs, gather photographs that match situation, action or themes and annotate the photographs with descriptions and emotions. Write three questions for the person in *El Leon Ferido* and three questions about *El Monastir*.	As you listen to the two songs, draw a narrative map for each song, with themes, people, events, feelings, senses with the lyrics. Write two questions you have about the emotions in *El Leon Ferido*. What has changed? Write five questions about thevisit to *Mi Monastir*. What would you see, hear, taste?
Can Dos		
I can identify and organize images with phrases and meanings about *Mi Monastir*. I can choose images and symbols representing a town or city where my family lived.	I can infer meaning by writing brief annotations of photographs and posing follow-up questions for the persons in the songs.	I can summarize the song to express emotions, opinions, wishes and changes in a narrative essay. I can pose questions about the people and imagery in the song.

Interpersonal Task Descriptions		
Poster Collage: Learners respond on posters to a series of open-ended prompts with words, symbols and images from the song *Mi Monastir* and *El Leon Ferido*, to make personal connection between the lyrics and their experience. Learners then view the posters in a small group gallery walk and ask and answer questions within the group about the images and phrases on the posters.	A visit to Monastir: Divide song lyrics in three sections and form three groups. Learners depict scenes of a day in Monastir inspired by the lyrics and the images in the song, as people in the town and elaborate content. Greet friends or newcomers to the town, meet relatives, etc. The teacher 'freezes' the scene to pause this 'still image' for questions and responses. Compare scenes and make suggestions. As requested by festival directors, plan a personalized interactive exhibit 'in role' as experts and come to consensus on what participants will see, create, and do to honour their homelands with messages of hope and strength, like in *Mi Monastir*.	Yes…and: Do you know anyone that had to leave everything they knew behind? Have you ever visited where your ancestors lived? What would you see? What would you eat and do? Share these possibilities with your partner. Your partner listens and replies 'yes, and…' offering their interpretation to affirm your wishes and then their own memories or hopes on what they will want to explore when they visit.

Can Dos		
I can ask questions about the images, symbols, emotions, and short phrases paired with the lyrics and ask follow-up questions.	I can interact with others as if I were in the song and in town to elaborate on lyrics, ask questions with others. I can come to a consensus with others 'in role' to develop an interactive experience for the festival and ask clarifying questions.	I can explain to a partner what I would do if I visited a place and elaborate on what I will explore there.
Presentational Task Descriptions		
Festival Poetry and Song Collaborative: Create a seven-line diamante poem describing a town or city of your family and ancestors, like in *Mi Monastir*.	**Kamishibai:** Design and present *Kamishibai* (paper theatre) to tell the story in *Mi Monastir* or about your family and ancestors from your own town, community or neighbourhood, narrating with images, senses and symbols on the illustration boards for an audience of children. **Lyric Lamp:** Offer a new stanza for *El Leon Ferido* to post on a Lyric Lamp, where our collective words show strength and perseverance shines through from pain, abuse, torment and loss.	**In my voice** Write an original short story, song or rap of how you or someone you know showed strength and hope against all odds. ***Mi _____*** Create a video narrative of a family or ancestral hometown or city, how it has changed and what is the same.

Can Dos		
I can write a short poem about a town from my family or culture using single words and phrases with images.	I can summarize a story and create new literature using symbolism from song lyrics. I can compose new song lyrics or a poem in Ladino from personal experiences.	I can compose a song, rap or video narrative reflecting emotions and opinions, life experiences, identity and home.

Bridge to Design

Let's get closer to this design using song lyrics and images. Join colleagues to process and collaborate for additional ideas and reflection on this exemplar before working on your own design.

(See Appendix L in Companion Website Chapter 3.)

Overcome the resistance to (re)vision: By themselves and beyond themselves

Complexity

There needs to be a problem, a reason, request or an impulse of some kind to generate a novel and tailored response. It happens all the time when someone does not have enough language to communicate, is unfamiliar with social behaviours or expectations, or misunderstands a non-negotiable yet tacit cultural perspective; all of these situations request mediation. For example, consider a concrete, popular task: to construct a culturally authentic menu. It is a fine task, but to replicate the menu already exists and reinforces the illusion of sameness. We recall foods, remember images of dishes, or the memory of a dining experience.

Recall and memories by themselves are personal. For transfer to occur those memories or recalled images need to be reimagined, reconstructed and shifted from private to public and (re)visioned. Mediation works in concert with transfer tasks because they model negotiation and reconstruction of new language meaning for other people with their needs in mind. For example, a culturally authentic menu for a non-dairy or low carb restaurant. A restaurant group from X country wants your ideas on a new concept restaurant for your community. The wellness centre is doing a series on popular dishes adapted for different health concerns. A multinational company needs infographics to explain cultural protocol on ordering food, who eats first and what to expect when dining. These tasks assess flexible use of the language and guide learners to clarify concepts and content between people and to navigate social and intercultural situations. Images, memories and recall need transfer. Language makes them accessible to others. Transfer tasks present complexity and variation, value-added features not present in original material and the product is for someone else.

Autonomy

The AATTs are a developmental protocol that prepares learners for novel and unpredictable communication, with reassurance that every level can manage to make sense of some of it and offer new language to someone else. Language learners naturally tend to take control of their learning (Benson, 2011, p. 16; Holec, 1988; Lamb, 2000, 2001, 2017). When learners are agents of their own learning and not always responding to a prescriptive drill, they brandish creativity to consider someone else's needs and use language purposefully. Moving beyond one's own self and needs moves learners to transfer and better language performance. Pupils are always talking or writing about their favourite this, their dream that, and it is fine as an early formative task. Once they have to consider someone else's needs or wants, everything changes. Designing a product or solving a problem with a different audience in mind is purposeful beyond just for self and teacher. It requires them to judge, come to consensus, choose and implement. Practice at transfer helps them refine sensibilities and their imagination, push away from their centre and consider someone else. Design housing developments for different people, families, mobility needs, seniors, college students. Take what they learned for a healthy diet and suggest food options to be sold at a local market. These are all issues that exist, real or imagined (Abugasea Heidt, 2021), that the learner may actually encounter in life and be asked to solve. Once the learner experiences tasks designed this way, they will come up with the contexts, diverse audiences and varied opportunities for mediation. That is how you know they have turned the corner for transfer. When learners design their own transfer tasks, they match activities and tasks to the preferences and needs of someone else. In effect, they are considering solutions for mediation that move communication forward in linguistic, social and cultural situations to facilitate a relationship. They acknowledge experiences that define identity, clarify concepts or deliverables. When teachers allow this to happen, they restore responsibility to the learner, thus enabling learner autonomy. The best gift we can give the learner in any discipline is transfer; it is especially necessary with language.

Novelty

The student has to successfully confront novel challenges before we can say that they really got it. By 'novel' it must be an unfamiliar-looking task that is doable, albeit reaching above the target. Perhaps the authentic materials they have never seen, or the problem is new or they are creating a useful product. It must be new enough that it requires their repertoire, thoughtfully chosen and weeded, with other materials to solve the problem, create the product and offer assistance with the language they can wield now. These are situations new to the pupil as compared to the way in which the original material was learned. Ideally, we are seeking a problem which will test the extent to which the learner has learned to apply the content in a thoughtful and useful way with few to no supports from the teacher. Just because a task is hands-on and educationally worthy doesn't mean that it requires much independent application of prior learning.

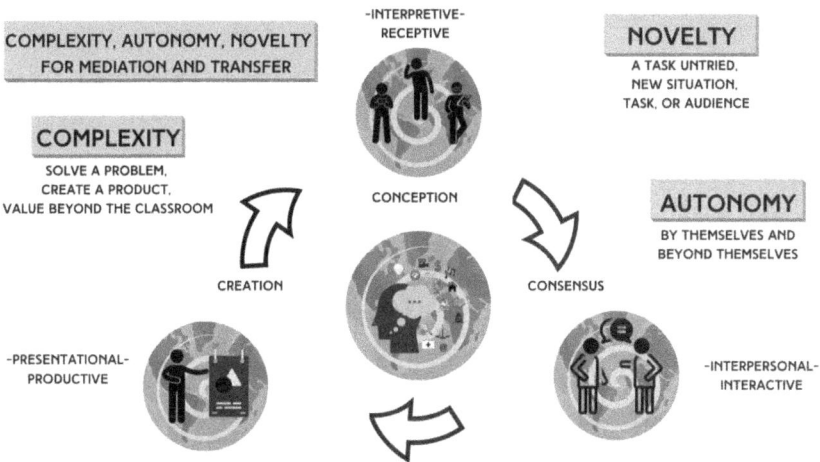

Figure 3.2 Complexity, Autonomy, Novelty for Mediation and Transfer

Rote memorization and recall tasks are assessments, but they cannot assess for transfer. It is all assessment; some are just more powerful than others when it comes to owning and using language. Is the task too familiar? Too scaffolded? Little to no transfer of learning is required and it is better served as a formative task somewhere earlier along the transfer continuum. The more novel the task, with fewer supports, the better it assesses for transfer. (See Figure 3.2.)

Teacher as Designer

In our next exemplar, *Lockdown Yoga*, Ms Singh develops transfer tasks linking Yogic principles and practices during extraordinary times with creating works of art. By presenting it through art, Ms Singh and learners explain and mediate the concepts, terms and practices to make Yoga accessible to people of other cultures. Indeed, learners can choose whichever art form they wish for constructing Yoga meaning and clarifying its concepts through a transfer task.

Voices from the Field

Yoga provides an opportunity to second language learners to value Yogic principles and lifestyles outside their Hindi classrooms, to appreciate and advocate its importance on a global scale beyond self and class. These AATT and ICANADAPT unit exemplars encourage the learners to build well established intercultural competence and at the same time adopt a new healthy lifestyle approach as a lifelong learner and practitioner. This exemplar provides an opportunity to both Heritage Language Learners (HLL) and Foreign Language Learners (FLL) together in mixed classrooms to build intercultural competence in Ayurvedic and Yogic lifestyle under the health & wellness topic. Students learn about ancient Indian practice of Yoga and its importance during COVID-19 lockdown global pandemic as an alternative self-help therapy to improve mental and physical health during lockdown. Students develop and build knowledge and understanding of perspective, practice and products related to Yoga. Various practices like Yoga asana, Yogic diet and chants, and words and phrases relate to Yogic practices and lifestyle and are accessible at all levels of instruction.

The AATT template helps teachers break down our lessons and the general thought process underlying it into individual units that can be easily integrated with target language specific ACTFL proficiency guidelines and performance assessment criteria, and STARTALK principles. AATT design facilitates the necessary merger of research-based second language acquisition principles with language pedagogy strategies. The AATTs provide both student and teacher strong understanding of the topic addressed articulated across a spiral curriculum. Even the novice students can design flash cards/ charts/ posters using various Yoga poses along with its name. They can record in their own voice various words and phrases in the target language that are chanted while practicing Yoga. Through various performance-based activities students collaborate to raise community awareness associated with the therapeutic effects of Yoga incorporating meditation and breathing techniques to improve individual's mental and physical health & wellbeing during COVID-19 lockdown.

'Lockdown Yoga' AATT and ICANADAPT exemplars aim to build Hindi language proficiency and intercultural competence of second language learners while keeping their individual learning needs in mind. This framework incorporates principles of differentiation and backward design which prepare students to take their language proficiency towards performance in real life contexts and scenarios.

Ms Bhavya Singh, Hindi Instructor, New York University

Table 3.3 Articulated Assessment Transfer Task   Lockdown Yoga

Ms Bhavya Singh, New York University	Hindi
Enduring Understandings * Alternative health practices vary across cultures and communities. * Alternative therapy provides cost effective self-care, behavioural and supportive aid options people quarantined at home during Covid-19 lockdowns. * Therapeutic effects of Yoga intervention incorporating meditation and breathing techniques help improve a person's mental and physical wellbeing. * Yoga intervention provides cost effective self-care behavioural treatment and support for overall health benefits. * Maximum benefits depend on age, personal preferences, lifestyle, health and cultural influence.	

Essential Questions
- ? How can we maintain mental clarity, relieve chronic stress, centre attention and build concentration during shelter in place?
- ? To what extent do age, health conditions and personal preferences direct our choices of physical activities that cultivate awareness and a profound state of consciousness?
- ? How do Ancient Indian holistic culture and psychophysiology effects of Yogic diet and exercise help people build connections and communication during Covid-19 lockdown?

Context
The National PTA REFLECTIONS arts programme invites student to submit their completed works of art in one or all of the available arts categories: Dance Choreography, Film production, Literature, Music Composition, Photography and Visual Arts on the topic:
MY LOCKDOWN HEALTH MANTRA IS...

Articulation Spiral Points
- @ Identify Yoga practices and asanas.
- @ Distinguish practices for recommendation across the lifespan.
- @ Explain and report benefits.
- @ Plan and choose content for various audiences.
- @ Compose multimedia works of art on Lockdown Yoga.

Intercultural Transfer Targets	Mediation for Transfer
• I can select and recommend personalized Yoga regime and health routine with community member's needs in mind. • I can demonstrate awareness of subtle differences among cultural behaviour in a diverse community in comparison to the target culture and adjust my behaviour accordingly to situations. • In my own and other cultures, I can identify and compare typical alternative healthcare practices supporting overall health and wellbeing.	• Bridge and exchange ideas and concepts of Yoga to relate to other cultural practices. • Explain and clarify details for different ages and physical conditions. • Use visuals, simple questions and responses to make details accessible. • Summarize and break down information in steps. • Simplify technical language for those unfamiliar with terms and practices.

Novice Mid-High	Intermediate Low-Mid	Intermediate High-Advanced
Interpretive Task Descriptions		
Students (FLLs) and HLLs watch Yoga videos and read the articles to select Yoga asana for their Lockdown Yoga infographic (HLLs)/ Video presentation (FLLs).	Students in triads watch and read pre-assigned videos and articles to identify key details and supporting details of four to six effective yoga asanas and create three questions based on their findings to complete their group Padlet.	Students in breakout rooms read and view authentic resources to understand and analyse the main message and supporting details on the importance of lockdown Yoga and its relevance in maintaining mental and physical health of online learners and summarize the text, main idea and infer facts and opinion along with real life examples to complete shared group resource research template.
Can Dos		
I can identify effective Yoga practices from target culture.	I can categorize effective Yoga asana based on main ideas and key information in TL authentic resources.	I can understand, analyse and organize the main message, supporting details and infer meaning from authentic informational text/audio visual resources on Yoga practice.

Interpersonal Task Descriptions		
Students decide and document effective Yoga practices for lockdown health and wellbeing.	Student groups exchange yoga practices related information based on their findings along with their research-based opinions to support them and ask a variety of questions for information and understanding of the subject.	Students through online synchronous /asynchronous discussion, exchange information and ideas and come to consensus how to: • map out lockdown yoga practice • integrate lockdown Yoga sessions in online curricula as a form of in-home physical fitness routine • convince educational leaders and administrators to lead a discussion via video conferencing between educational institution administrators and student council about the health and well-being situation of students during lockdown. Persuade them to run alternative programmes under student connect resources.
Can Dos		
I can select effective Yoga practices and update and finalize the list after peer discussion and feedback.	I can distinguish Yoga practices based on age, personal preference, health conditions and lifestyle.	I can discuss, explain and negotiate benefits of adopting Yoga practices as alternative health therapy during Covid-19 lockdown to promote overall health and well-being.

Presentational Task Descriptions		
For the National Reflection programme entry, learners in the role of well-being experts present a lockdown Yoga infographic for the *Visual Arts category* infographic presentation.	The National Reflection programme, learners in the role of well-being experts share PSA for the *Film production category* on effective Yoga practices citing examples from their personal connections.	For the Reflection programme in the role of well-being experts, students in the *literature category* write an editorial piece (HLLs) and in the *film production category* record a video entry (FLLs) on the online learners' physical, mental and emotional state and the potential positive influence of Lockdown Yoga.
Can Dos		
I can present effective lockdown Yoga practices as an alternative therapy during Lockdown.	I can give a detailed presentation (PSA/ blog post) on effective Yoga practices as an alternative self-care therapy during home quarantine.	I can report and suggest the positive influence of lockdown yoga on remote learners and discuss intercultural differences of yoga with other traditional alternative therapy from different cultures.

Bridge to Design

How does Ms Singh's work help us think about health and wellbeing across many cultures? Let's get closer to her design process with other colleagues to share additional ideas and reflection before working on your own design.

(See Appendix M in Companion Website Chapter 3.)

None to nigh to near to novel for transfer

Perkins and Salomon (1992) explained that transfer 'occurs when learning in one context or with one set of materials impacts on performance in another context or with other related materials' (p. 2). Practice with forms and structures may yield 'language-like' knowledge but cannot replace input for meaning with interaction and novel application. Transfer task design and implementation use increasingly less teacher guidance and support along a range from no transfer to full novel transfer (see Table 3.4). In addition, the tasks move from familiar to unfamiliar and different from previous experiences and situations. Learners need to recognize similarities in content and concept, predict and choose thoughtfully to solve the new problem given variables, complexities, needs and the audience. In the QC programme, when we consider tasks for summative or formative assessment evidence, we do an assessment evidence inventory and distinguish them as **none, nigh, near or novel** for far transfer using the criteria below.

Table 3.4 Stages of Language Assessment Transfer Examples

None	Nigh and Nearby	Near Transfer	Novel Transfer
Drill Decontextualized content	Familiar Task with Supports	Unfamiliar Task with Supports	Completely New Task No supports
Recall, Drill, substitution of forms. No transfer required or assessed.	Similar content and situations. Details from previous teaching examples or texts. Replication with little variation. Posing questions signals a shift to mediation transfer evidence.	Unfamiliar content and situations. Presented with cues Cues suggested or required approach, process, or content knowledge. Solves problems and creates products.	Unfamiliar and Novel Presented without cues. Learners use a repertoire of knowledge with new texts for novel contexts and situations. Solves problems and creates products.

Fill in with the correct form of the verb. Using the vocabulary box, enter the word in the space.	Using a Venn diagram, compare lunch choices from Latin American and your school menu. Write three questions to the school dietician.	With a partner, plan a dinner party for friends keeping in mind their dietary needs: vegetarian, dairy-free, low sugar, gluten-free, no pork, etc.	*TeenVida* online health magazine wants you to contribute to the next issue on schools. In groups, plan and develop content for this issue.

Check for Learning

With colleagues, do an *Assessment for Transfer* Inventory for a unit or scheme of work using the three criteria above. Examine textbooks, workbooks, tasks you see online, ancillaries or department tasks, activities, exercises and projects. (See Appendix N.)

Teacher as designer

Food is probably the most frequently accessed and commonly taught topic and for good reason; it is an accessible and pleasurable conduit to the culture through all the senses and one fully enjoyed by every community. Far greater relevance to our discipline is the art form of cuisine. It carries with it a wealth of cultural history and provides the perfect transdisciplinary route for a spiral curriculum. Mr Bonanno considers this an opportunity to develop cultural perspectives concerning cuisine with the issue of food piracy and truly artisanal products. With learners 'in role' as expert journalists, these tasks facilitate transfer and thoughtful products across three levels of learner engagement.

Voices from the Field

The concept of *Made in Italy* 'bello e ben fatto' (beautiful and well done) denotes a certain Italian sensitivity towards the art of well-being as well as expert manufacturing skills and fervent creativity. The Italian character of the goods acts as an attraction for consumers in which the role of Renaissance mythology increases the commerciality of the products. However, cultural appropriation distorts their original meanings and cultural contexts erasing the artistic ingenuity and creative process. Learners will develop a set of interlaced skills that foster their understanding of autochthonous values and perspectives through the examination of products and practices to determine what *Made in Italy* means in a global context. As a result, designing with the AATT prepares students to face the challenges of a global and interconnected society by relating to different communities within their own culture and beyond with a deeper understanding that promotes unity in diversity and harmony among all.

Antonino Bonanno

Table 3.5 Articulated Assessment Transfer Task   Made in Italy

Francis Lewis High School, New York	Antonino Bonanno, Spanish and Italian Teacher

Enduring Understandings
* Food conveys a myriad of cultural meanings and values.
* Skilled craftsmanship and artisanal labour reveal a great deal about cultures across the globe.
* Cultural appropriation impacts *Made in Italy* manufacturing which is synonymous with the cultural values of the Italian society.

Coverage without Pity

Essential Questions
? What is *Made in Italy* and its cultural values?
? What is cultural appropriation, and how does it affect cultures across the globe?
? What is the difference between *Made in Italy* and Italian-sounding products?
? To what extent do *Made in Italy* products convey Italian cultural perspectives?

Context
'*La Repubblica*', an Italian news outlet, is investigating the impact of the cultural appropriation of Italian products (food piracy). They are looking for a group of investigative journalists to report on the issue.

Articulation Spiral Points
@ Explain quintessential traits of Italian cuisine.
@ Differentiate between authentic and false Italian foods.
@ Create virtual itinerary of regional Italian cuisine.
@ Present evidence and effects of food piracy with print and video multimedia.

Intercultural Transfer Targets	**Mediation for Transfer**
• I can compare and discuss the values, beliefs, and perspectives that artisanal products convey and how they contribute to creating and shaping national identities and cultural values. • I can determine the impact and effect of cultural appropriation across different cultures. • I can understand what cultural heritage and collective identity are and can discuss the means through which they are passed on.	• Bridge and exchange ideas and concepts of Italian sounding and authentic *Made in Italy* cuisine. • Identify and clarify traits of regional, artisanal products to others. • Collaborate to discuss similarities and differences in views and perspectives on cuisines. • Support intercultural exchanges using known and new cultural references. • Formulate questions and give feedback to make this concept accessible to people from other cultures.

Novice Mid-High	**Intermediate Low-Mid**	**Intermediate High – Advanced Low**
Authentic Italian and Italian-sounding products.	Video reports on Italian-sounding products.	Video reports on Italian-sounding products.

Interpretive Task Descriptions		
Students examine and categorize authentic Italian and Italian-sounding products in a T-Chart. Then, they will scan them with the app to check their answers.	Students watch a video report and complete a Frayer Model giving a definition of Made in Italy and its features to provide examples and non-examples.	Students watch the videos and take notes. Then, students complete a Venn diagram with similarities and differences between Italian-sounding and Made in Italy products.
Can Dos		
I can compare, contrast, identify and categorize authentic Italian-sounding and Made in Italy products.	I can synthesize information from a video and define the main traits of Made in Italy products.	I can acquire information from a video report, then compare, contrast and synthesize factual information about Italian-sounding and Made in Italy products.
Interpersonal Task Descriptions		
Students discuss and agree on defining traits of Made in Italy food.	Students discuss, compare, contrast and select foods and places to include in a food itinerary that resembles the format of the Italian cycling race 'Giro d'Italia'.	Students assign themselves roles to create an editorial board. Then come to consensus about what aspects of Italian-sounding products vs *Made in Italy* to include in their Presentational task.
Can Dos		
I can discuss with a partner and select the defining traits of Made in Italy products.	I can use questions and understand answers to determine an authentic Italian food itinerary.	I can ask and answer questions to assess and rank the defining traits of Italian-sounding and Made in Italy products.

Presentational Task Descriptions		
Students create an infographic for *'La Repubblica'* web portal that resembles a table in which they will report facts about the impact of food piracy on Made in Italy.	Students create a virtual food itinerary for *'La Repubblica'* website using Google Expeditions in which they create visual and textual resources about the places of origin of the foods of their choice.	Students create a multimedia Microsoft Sway for *'La Repubblica'* that includes videos, articles, infographics and charts that they created to present and inform the public about the effects of food piracy.
Can Dos		
I can present data and facts about the impact of food piracy on Made in Italy products.	I can determine the regional origin of Italian traditional foods and create a multimedia informative virtual tour.	I can create an informative and persuasive multimedia hypertext to present factual evidence about Italian-sounding and *Made in Italy* products.

> **Bridge to Design**
>
> Let's go deeper into Mr Bonanno's design process. How can this exemplar inform and inspire our work and that of colleagues? Let's collaborate for additional ideas and reflection on this exemplar before working on your own design.
>
> (See Appendix O in Companion Website Chapter 3.)

Do a task untried rather than just like the last time. Bruner defined creativity as 'an act that produces effective surprise' (1962, p. 3). Each formative task for *near transfer* should move your learners ever more closely to a summative or *far transfer* task through effective surprise. 'To do the same things in the same way' is incompatible with communication. 'To do things a little differently makes the habit healthier, but when pupils engage in tasks they have not done before' (Fisher, 2005, p. 9), that is full creative transfer and the state of the art. Value and respect the inevitable unexpected with novelty.

Novelty yields Bravery. Model for your learners that you are not afraid to try new things so that they understand language requires novelty and expects and rewards partial, fractional control. Both of these tenets foster and promote a self-directed, autonomous learner. Pursuing surprise requires taking risks, but it teaches that not all consequences are predictable. Transfer tasks require a repertoire from which they consider, pick and choose. Dewey (1938) talked about Flexible Purposing or creating a product different from original intent or perhaps unexpected by the teacher. The arts are rife with examples of flexible purposing. Transfer tasks encourage the pursuit of surprise. When you engage in the deliberate design of a transfer task and encourage pupils to follow suit, you support the kind of thinking your learners will do (Eddy, 2016a). It helps them become brave and resourceful; these are characteristics that will serve them well anywhere, abroad or right in their own neighbourhood. Novelty and surprise are better teachers than expected limitation.

Risk taking is inevitable, natural and how we move forward, in language creativity and life. Sir Ken Robinson (2006) said, 'If you're not prepared to be wrong, you'll never come up with anything original.' 'We're now running national education systems where mistakes are the worst thing you can make.' The end result of this, he says, 'is that we are educating people out of their creative capacities'. Indeed, yes and worse: We raise generations of citizens who are risk-averse, and there is some danger in that.

When learners only respond and become accustomed to the predictable and routine, they begin to expect and demand it. Not only does that habit stifle creativity, it oft enables and endorses an inflexible and rigid individual that needs everything all spelled out up front with extreme anticipation, cannot handle even slight change or deviation from plans, has a difficult time on study abroad, is intolerant of ambiguity, becomes nervous when they do not understand every word, falls apart or becomes angry when not in control or is a 'my way or highway' sort. Your learners take cues from you when you exhibit novelty in design. They will be more open to think creatively and deal with small to large challenges in performance tasks. It is important to share stories of risks and examples of creative language mediation that had interesting and innovative results, both yours and those of former pupils. These examples should include successful mediation with partial language, such as clarifying with images, gestures, words or phrases managed with poise, not perfection. It teaches tolerance of ambiguity, flexibility and openness. These consequently are characteristics of intercultural communicative competence, whether that is within a new social group, community, new job or country. Risk-taking thrives on the freedom and efficacy of the unpredictable.

Teacher as Designer

In the article *Children and Art* (Eddy, 2007a), I talk about how artists do performance tasks for transfer all the time. They take one art form and turn it into another (see Figure 3.4). A painting becomes a poem. That becomes a dance, characters and then a play. The play changes time periods or locations. A photograph becomes a song. Transfer tasks are creative ideas, solutions or products made of existing pieces recombined or re-imagined. Any authentic material will do, but the arts immediately provide us with intentional engagement, a relationship involving the learner's response to the art:their experiences, perceptions, and concepts and understandings within the art (Greene, 2001; Holzer, 2007).

Perspectives and ideas essential to a given culture can be uncovered and accessible to the most novice learner through the arts, prompting further inquiry, change in perceptions and then transposing those ideas through your performance assessment task. The arts carry with them keys to critical thinking, widening the cultural lens, encouraging flexibility, tolerance for ambiguity and willingness to change one's mind.

The learner hones these skills by experiencing works of art and creating new interpretations through your transfer tasks. The process starts out as a personal and private impression of the art but it is made public, social and shared through language and becomes new. These tasks notice the subtleties, explore unanticipated opportunities and depend on judgement outside the realm of rules. Transfer asks learners to conceptualize a product, be reflective and transdisciplinary. These qualities will serve them well as, most likely, they will work in more than one occupation in their lifetime (Eddy, 2017).

The best transfer tasks require interaction, a reciprocal relationship between the learner and the authentic materials, any text that you listen to, view, or read or a painting, film, song, play, sculpture or dance. This reciprocity yields new creations shaped by the learner's interests, point of view, emotions, social experience, thereby shortening the creative distance between the original work and the learner.

Voices from the Field

In the painting *A Sunday on La Grande Jatte – 1884* (Georges Seurat, 1884/86. The Art Institute of Chicago) (see Figure 3.3), Seurat blends science and art to create *pointillism*, where your eyes and mind fuse close pinpoints of paint to make new colors then images. It is the only painting in the room at the Art Institute of Chicago. The AATT, *Leisure in 1884 and Today*, learners explore perspectives and practices of leisure and how that has changed over time. The painting depicts everyone of all ages and social classes enjoying their Sunday in their park, together but disconnected. This art inspired Stephen Sondheim and James Lapine to compose a brilliant example of transfer and creativity with their Pulitzer prize-winning play *Sunday in the Park with George* (Sondheim & Lapine, 1984). The play makes this painting come to life, with Seurat interacting with each character on the canvas. He expresses their emotions and personalities through color and light. The dots and dabs of color become the short, staccato notes of the songs (Eddy, 2007a, 2016a). The play reminds us never to stop creating, move forward, make it new.

Figure 3.3 Georges Seurat. A Sunday on La Grande Jatte – 1884. 1884/86. The Art Institute of Chicago. CC0 Public Domain Designation

Figure 3.4 AATT Leisure in 1884 and Today

In the title song, the people in the painting spend their Sunday noticing the changes in their world and the choices they each make, while longing for the connectedness of simpler times.

Dr Jennifer Eddy, Queens College, CUNY

Bridge to Design

How can transfer tasks using works of art bring your learners closer to understanding cultural perspectives and practices? Let's dive deeper into the process and collaborate with colleagues for reflection on this exemplar and then your own design.

(See Appendix P.)

> **Design for Transfer**
>
> Design three *Turnarounds for Transfer* with existing tasks from other textbooks or resources. Try to turn around just the Presentational mode that can be the obvious deliverable.
>
> With learners 'in role' as experts, what do you want them to create and solve?
>
> Who is the audience?
>
> What are their needs?
>
> (For a master list of task types for the modes of communication, see Appendix NN.)

> **Design for transfer**
>
> Design a Context for your Summative Performance Assessment for your AATT.
>
> This will carry over to your ICANADAPT unit template for Stage Two.
>
> Which comes first: The Context or Transfer task? Always remember, you plan to adjust. This process eschews work etched in stone, by design. Some teachers write the Context first, prior to task development. Others find that after they design the full exemplars you see here, the Context inspiration just emerges. Either way, you can always edit and adjust after you design the tasks. Use the Concept Map (see Figure 2.1) to organize and collect your thoughts. (See Appendix OO for the AATT template with fillable fields on the Companion Website, Chapter 7.)
>
>

Discuss the Issues

1 Understanding begins with creative transfer; engage our learners in these tasks, early and often, rather than low-level recall and linear progression.
2 Novelty and unpredictability teach flexibility. Discuss.
3 Learners must engage in tasks by themselves and beyond themselves.
4 Mechanized practice lulls the learner with a false expectation of predictability.
5 Summative assessments should be performed without supports for full transfer evidence.
6 Transfer tasks gently challenge the risk-averse. Discuss.
7 Rote or memorized knowledge and skill drills do not transfer on their own.

Reflect and Revisit

1 How do Intercultural Transferable goals help us develop transfer tasks for an articulated curriculum? Give an example.
2 With the exemplars in the chapters so far, explain at least three characteristics of performance assessment.
3 Why should novel performance for transfer not wait until the end of the unit?
4 Give an example of how you change the audience or need to move a task to transfer.
5 Explain Complexity, Autonomy and Novelty.
6 Give an example of the learner 'in role', and why that strategy helps with mediation and transfer.
7 How does a task that is too familiar or highly scaffolded fall short of transfer?

Chapter 4

Designing for Interpretive Goals: Exploring Meaning for Mediation

Enduring Understandings

- ∞ The Interpretive mode is a receptive yet coactive relationship between the person and the material; it is our silent reaction or tacit response to what we watch, hear, view or read.
- ∞ Tasks and texts provide consistent input that learners react to for meaning, not forms or rules.
- ∞ The Interpretive mode frames context and purpose with cultural meaning and intention.
- ∞ The Interpretive mode explores and processes meaning through identification, inference, organization, summary and questioning.
- ∞ Interpretive mode tasks help us gather new information as we decide, choose and acquire what we need.
- ∞ The Interpretive mode uses texts developed culturally from their language communities and are best unchanged, elaborated rather than simplified. Adapt the task instead.

Essential Questions

- Q What is going on? What do you notice?
- Q To what extent do we need to be told how language works?
- Q What can we do with what we see or hear?
- Q How do we tolerate less than total comprehension?

- Q To what extent is the learner compelled to understand meaning?
- Q How do our experience and understanding influence how we respond and react?
- Q What can we learn about a culture through its texts?
- Q How do arts and media reflect, reveal and shape culture?
- Q How can texts and images from different cultural communities also be about us?
- Q Why do questions matter?
- Q How do these tasks continue to support interpretation without our ongoing instruction?

Key Terms and Concepts

Interpretive Mode	Authentic/Cultural Community Texts
Texts	Conception
Intrapersonal	Ownership and Authorship

Research in Practice

The work of the following researchers and practitioners will guide you to discover and cite sources which inform your curriculum planning, assessment and instructional decisions in pre-service portfolios or in-service professional learning plans.

Byram, 1997 Byram, Gribkova & Starkey, 2002	Learners progress not through static facts but by dynamic exploration and analysis of authentic texts and products representing the ideas and events within the historical memory of a culture or cultures.
Lantoff & Appel, 1994	Meaning is (re)constructed through interaction.

VanPatten, 2003, 2010 VanPatten & Rothman, 2015 Wong & VanPatten, 2003	Learners develop and evolve via consistent contact with input both within and outside the classroom, not through isolated strategies, paradigm rules and grammar drills. Justification for less classroom time on pattern drills.
Kolb, 2014 Vygotzky, 1978, 1986	Learners take active ownership of learning through authentic tasks. The teacher is the facilitator of these tasks which guide problem-solving.
Galloway, 1988 Gilmore, 2004, 2007	Learners are more motivated using authentic materials.
Kramsch, 1993, 2006, 2011	Learners develop intercultural communicative competence through a variety of authentic materials, 'third space' symbolic competence, instead of learning grammar rules from non-authentic materials for teaching.
ACTFL, 2012 CEFR Council of Europe, 2001 CEFR-CV Council of Europe, 2018 NCSSFL, 2017	Learners are 'social agents' who develop competence through action, situation and performance rather than mechanized practice.
Greene, 2001 Housen, 2002 Yenawine, 2013	Aesthetic Education and Visual thinking strategies.
Heathcote & Bolton, 1995 Piazzoli & Kubiak, 2019	Drama Pedagogy with learner 'in role'; using embodying strategies for meaning.
Mishan, 2005	Authentic text criteria: Culture, Currency, Challenge. Texts should not be restricted by proficiency level.
Raphael & Au, 2005	Learners develop questions that are both literal and inferential.
McTighe, 2014 Wiggins & McTighe, 2005	Learners engage in novel tasks aligned with long-term transfer goals across the curriculum; these demonstrate understanding rather than recall and application in the way it was learned.

I can

- Describe and explain the Interpretive tasks for reception and mediation
- Determine authentic texts for your tasks
- Differentiate tasks with exemplars
- Design Interpretive tasks across different levels for articulation
- Develop PASS Can-Dos for this mode aligning to intercultural transfer goals

Rewind

Which key terms or concepts stand out for you from Chapter 3: *From coverage without pity to designing with performance for transfer: Make it new everyday*?

Ask your colleague three questions based on the content from the last chapter.

Explain the most compelling idea from the previous chapter in your own words.

Explain how this concept or practice is the same, similar or different to what you know or do.

Which concept or practice do you think will have the greatest impact on your teaching?

Overview

In Chapter 2, we looked at images and artefacts of different cultures to interpret them and compare how we see them. Intercultural competence unfolds through your tasks so that learners can identify, interpret, compare, explain, and discuss products and practices as would someone from that culture. In Chapter 3, we examined the primacy of transfer, the importance of novelty for learning and proof of transfer for performance assessment as Stage Two of our curriculum design. These key assessments appear at the end of each unit but are designed first, for

Designing for Interpretive Goals

the teacher to know what the final performance looks like and to ascertain goals for learners. In the assessment system, the Interpretive mode gives learners the opportunity to explore texts and images with you, as a class, and on their own. This may be their first encounter with the culture studied or a reprise of earlier experience. Either way, one cannot underestimate the importance of these tasks. This chapter explains how images and texts of all kinds provide cultural context for learners to identify, make inferences, compare and explain. Why should our chosen materials reveal the cultural story? How do our tasks enable the learner to connect, respond and reflect, from the most concrete to abstract concepts? Why is the Interpretive mode so important to design well and for learners to do often?

Interpretive-Receptive mode as Conception

The *Interpretive* mode is one of the standards within the goal area of Communication (National Standards Collaborative Board, 2015): 'Learners understand, interpret and analyse what is heard, read or viewed on a variety of topics.' This definition corresponds to the Receptive mode in the CEFR which describes aural (listening) and visual (reading and viewing) reception (COE, 2001). Both references refer to interpretation of messages and tasks which facilitate meaningful communication in authentic contexts. The Interpretive mode is one-way personal and private communication between the person and the piece, which is anything someone will listen to, watch, or read, but not within conversation with anyone else. It is the first contact we have with anything we need to understand. For that reason, it is communication for conception.

> For the AATTs and ICANADAPT this mode:
> - Details our reaction or response to what we watch, hear, view or read.
> - Explores and processes meaning through identification, inference, organization, summary and questioning.
> - Uses texts developed culturally from language communities and are best unchanged.

For the Interpretive-Interactive mode, learners

- Use culturally authentic, transdisciplinary texts made public and shared
- Own new information from texts in an active, not passive role
- Listen, read, view, or watch and offer personal response or reaction to the text
- Identify, Index, Infer, Inquire, Illustrate, Interpret, Improve

Interpretive mode tasks go beyond low-level comprehension tasks for recall to include inferencing, predicting, organizing concepts, questioning and comparing with what learners already know and with other texts (Shrum & Glisan, 2016). The Interpretive mode is also characterized by the use of *authentic texts*; any oral or written material produced by and for the speakers of a language and their cultural communities and groups (Glisan & Donato, 2017). It is within these authentic texts that the learner can derive cultural interpretation of meanings.

In this curriculum framework, the Interpretive mode signifies *Conception* in two ways. From the onset of a unit, learners take *ownership* of language and begin their understanding of recursive concepts with an intercultural mindset. As teachers, you will design tasks that derive from a line of inquiry from any text, image, audio or video, uncovering the enduring understandings and essential questions (Wiggins & McTighe, 2005) you developed for your recursive themes (Eddy, 2006b, 2007a; 2017). Conception also indicates *authorship;* the texts are creative works in which intercultural perspectives and transdisciplinary concepts begin and reside the moment they were made public and shared. They are physical products, manifestations of our litmus test we used to choose key themes and concepts: Layers, Lifespan and Level. These texts help us make meaning and make sense of life events, relationships and ourselves because someone else created them for our response. Because these concepts are present in a variety of texts, print, works of art, etc., they are accessible to any level of learner. The task you design determines the level of complexity, the text does not.

Interpretive mode for Conception values cultural interpretation, inference, questioning and organization of words, ideas and phrases from material that learners listen to, watch, view, or read. This is a one-way communication between the person and the piece; an opportunity to connect personally and intentionally to meaning rather than study forms or facts. This ability demands tasks beyond traditional comprehension, such as filling in the blanks, completing a drill or answering questions. All too often, well-intentioned language classes rush to have students speaking, sometimes with an expectation of complete accuracy or to produce complete sentences. They might, as long as they read it from a paper or note card, or memorize it, like a script. However, as stated before, life has no script nor is this indicative of true performance. I like to say, 'own before it is shown'. There must be many opportunities to connect with texts and derive meaning from it, before it can be used flexibly and securely. Err on the side of having lots of formative Interpretive mode tasks in each unit to allow more encounters and opportunities for input. These tasks eschew low skill-level facts and forms, because those are fairly easy to obtain.

At conferences or professional learning sessions, I poll participants and ask, 'Which of the three modes do you believe is the most important and the most challenging to design well?' Without exception, they say the Interpersonal mode. The Presentational mode task also has a strong showing, which is still quite relevant as we will see in a later chapter. Participants never choose the Interpretive mode and that has consequences and impact on student learning. In a study of post-secondary learners by Glisan, Uribe and Adair-Hauck (2007) and later with elementary students, Davin, Troyan, Donato and Hellman (2011), found that learners performed least well on Interpretive tasks. Interpretive mode tasks are the most essential to design well because they represent the learner's first contact with culture through texts and what they do with it is very important for anything that comes later. Without Interpretive tasks implemented early and often, the subsequent modes are moot. The challenge is in the design of tasks that enable learners to make meaning interactively with the text before moving on to production. Interpretive tasks go beyond comprehension, true-false and answering questions; these are passive tasks. Interpretive tasks are interactive, whether the learner is alone or in pairs or groups. These tasks enable mediation because they clarify, use visuals and elaborate. In the AATTs, the Interpretive mode focuses and enables learners to own more language and concepts and then again differently across performance target levels.

It was not entirely a surprise that many teachers did not consider this mode of primary importance. Stoller (2009) explained acceptance and implementation of educational innovations rely more on the perception of the innovation more than the reality of the innovation. Eddy and Bustamante (2020) examined this mindset and a gap between trainees and their in-service teacher mentors on the design, implementation and perceptions of the Integrated Performance Assessment (IPA) (Adair-Hauck, Glisan, Koda, Sandrock & Swender, 2006; Glisan, Adair-Hauck, Koda, Sandrock & Swender, 2003). One particular area of interest focused on Interpretive mode tasks. If it is perceived to be too similar or too different from what teachers already know, there is less likelihood of implementation. In the United States, the National Council for Accreditation of Teacher Education (NCATE), now Council for the Accreditation of Educator Preparation (CAEP), requires a dedicated world language teacher preparation methods course (ACTFL, 2002; ACTFL/CAEP, 2013). In that course, any teacher in an accredited programme certified after 2004 was required to plan and assess using the National Standards (National Standards in Foreign Language Education Project, 2006) which meant to do so with the three modes of the Communication standard and designing tasks with authentic materials for the Interpretive mode. If individual states did not adopt the modes, it is not required for in-service teachers to use them with the pupils they teach. In the meantime, new teachers finished certification programmes with these skills but often did not or could not implement them where they taught. States adopted the edTPA (SCALE, 2013), a capstone teacher performance assessment which requires teacher trainees to design, teach and assess in the Interpretive mode and at least one other mode. If teacher certification programmes and licensure exams require design and implementation of Interpretive mode tasks with no corresponding or comparable directive for K-12 instruction, there exist a pedagogical knowledge gap and a perception issue. The latter exist because when state or local education departments do not make the shift, the modes are not only not required but they are also perceived as not important enough to make the change or something only required for certification (Eddy & Bustamante, 2020). With no requirement from states to adopt the modes at least in tandem with other mandates, veteran teachers are at a disadvantage when mentoring new teachers, not to mention the lack of parity with instruction between districts and a genuine misunderstanding of the modes, primarily the Interpretive mode.

When I often see tasks labelled as Interpretive, they are still only practice at recall, discrete point, fill-in tasks, or answering comprehension questions that manipulate forms or grammar structures. There are no items for inference, posing questions, or relating concepts or meaning to images; there is no incentive for reaction. Learners need to interact or respond to texts for what they are conveying and saying. They need to react to its meaning; on *what* it says, not *how* it says it and not with fill-ins or verb substitution drills (VanPatten, 2003, 2004, 2010). The treatment of the Interpretive mode in this way represents a significant shift in curriculum and assessment development. Curriculum and instruction traditionally positioned the learner as a passive recipient of rote knowledge. The expectation was that learners accept this transmission of facts, forms or rules. Duplicating these was indicative of learning and understanding. This was the case in most disciplines or content areas. There was little focus on problem-solving or critical thinking skills to enable learners how to interpret texts and derive their own meaning from input (Gee, 2012).

This shift in focus of interpretation as conception involves both interaction and mediation (COE, 2020). The role of learner as mediator, a social agent (Piccardo, 2013), and the link between two people or groups begins here with tasks in the Interpretive mode. These mode tasks challenge us to rethink our familiar and then reconstruct and organize that meaning right from the onset of learning. Then we can mediate with others between different cultural and linguistic contexts with our intercultural skills, practices and attitudes to the extent we can at that time. Lantoff and Appel (1994) support the idea of tasks that help learners construct meaning through interaction, as opposed to merely answering questions. Vygotsky (1986) recognized the importance of constructing and organizing meaning via 'verbal thought' and called it *Intrapersonal*, an inner dialogue between the person and the piece. This acts as mediation, with the text and from the text as social interaction. This dialogue exists precisely for learners to make meaning from any piece, with many ways to identify, question, analyse, categorize, explain and connect to it. We do this not by changing the text and therefore rendering it intrinsically unappealing. Interpretive skills enable the learner to contact and interact with the original piece in varied ways over time, within tasks that pose it in novel arrangements or formats. This builds knowledge of the concept from the onset, starting with that novice level of engagement: Conception. The tasks you will design in this mode shift your practice from mere transmission to transformation and reconstruction of meaning for the learner. In doing so, you are facilitating strategies to use what they know and own now, for mediation with others.

The table below outlines characteristics of the Interpretive-receptive and presents non-examples, both for use in the AATT and ICANADAPT design model.

Table 4.1 What Interpretive-Receptive Is and Is Not

What Interpretive-Receptive IS	What Interpretive-Receptive is NOT
Personal Inquiry and forming questions	Asking questions with others
What a text means may differ from person to person.	Only one correct answer from comprehension questions
Using authentic texts	Using glossed, edited or adapted texts or vocabulary lists
Identify, infer, index, information and details for active, constructive, meaning-making intended for future use	Listening or reading comprehension out of context for passive, limited and finite use
Summarize main idea or details	Translation
Draw what you hear, label, list, classify, sequence	Fill in the blanks with grammar or vocabulary

Pause to Ponder

So far you have seen nine AATT exemplars. What characteristics do you notice for the Interpretive mode tasks? What does this mode do on its own and in concert with the other mode tasks? Before seeing these exemplars, what other tasks have you seen for the receptive or Interpretive mode? Have you seen tasks that guide learners to 'own before it is shown'? Are the tasks low-level recall and answering questions or do they include inference, categorizing and constructing questions? Consider these while reviewing and designing tasks and share thoughts with a colleague.

Cultural Texts

In Chapter 1, we said we should focus on what our learners can do, so that they can continue to do it without us. In keeping with Vygotskian perspectives and Constructivist Learning Design (Gagnon & Colley, 2001, 2006), our experience with a new language is integrated with cultural resources and socio-cultural contexts within cultural communities. We want learners to make their own meaning, amend and reconstruct their own knowledge and experience in the process, share this with someone else and explain concepts and create new products to the best extent they can, even though they may not understand it all yet. These steps outline effective practice at transfer, which is the expectation beyond the classroom. Thus, our tasks and materials should enable self-directed, autonomous learners (Lamb, 2000, 2008) in preparation for university, career, community and world readiness. Learners need opportunities for engaging these tasks in class. To create this environment, we want learners to interact and derive meaning with materials found in real life, that present with values, concepts, beliefs, perspectives and practices, both implicit and explicit. The materials our learners use will be those that they can (1) encounter within current cultural communities today, or (2) can experience from the cultural histories.

Before designing tasks in this mode, let's consider what you notice, see, hear, or view from a variety of texts. We have said that culture is the organizing principle or framework to our curriculum design. The learners' first contact with a culture will most often be someone they listen to or watch, or a piece to read or view. This opens up the expanded notion of Text. We might think of texts as merely written pieces and the first word that may come to mind is a textbook. The definition is much broader now. *Texts* can be any piece, any artefact that imparts the view of the culture from within that relates to ideas, customs, actions and social behaviours of a particular society. For our purposes, we use the word *text* in its most inclusive sense to refer to all kinds of written, spoken, viewed, or signed material, film, music and all visual arts. They carry with them cultural meaning. *Culturally authentic or cultural community texts* are any spoken, written, signed, created or viewed media designed by cultural communities for the public to consume, use or experience. Galloway (1998) defined authentic texts as 'written by members of a language and culture group for members of the same language and culture group' (p. 133). These materials contrast with those developed specifically for language students, prepared original or edited materials designed to teach language in classrooms (Kramsch, 2006). Students must actively notice and experience the same language in contexts and situations which present in the real world. By truly noticing materials which exist for the cultural community, students at the same time pay attention to how language is used within that culture or cultures.

Remember that an image also is the means by which you can experience and interpret it the way that culture does. When we experience an image, we visualize that vocabulary in its cultural context and consider its cultural perspectives. Texts may take on many forms; symbols on a poster or billboard, a short story, novel, or ode, a video on a national initiative, a blog on teen health, sculpture, food label, a conversation, a song or poem, a magazine article, photographs of people enjoying street food, a podcast, a painting of a picnic in the park or an infographic with symbols and images and many more examples. Culture is inherently present throughout, informing these texts and prompting our response or our reaction to them. The more extended time one has with a text, the more you see, hear and understand.

Visual literacy helps us to identify and interpret the meaning of images, both natural and created, to the extent that people living in that cultural context do. The materials should engage the learner, but that is not enough. Visual thinking strategies (Housen, 2002; Yenawine, 2013) give learners extended, dedicated time to express ideas necessary for language and concept development. Encourage your learners to ask and answer questions such as, 'What is going on? What do you see that makes you say that? What more can you find?' Students comment on what they see, they talk themselves into understanding complex subject matter, even if their comments are at word level.

Mishan (2005) makes the case for authentic texts in the classroom with 'the 3 c's' as rationale for their use: culture, currency and challenge. These serve not only as rationale but criteria for selecting material for the most judicious use across the entire curriculum. This is not to suggest that one will not find a wonderful piece of material that is one and done; solely for one lesson or unit. This will happen. What it does suggest is that one superb text may be used for many different tasks, across all levels of instruction and across content areas. To be sure, novel materials are encouraged so for this case, more is more, not less is more. However, when the teacher finds a piece that answers the call in uncovering cultural perspectives for the curriculum, that economy also guarantees an integration of language and intercultural content.

Complexity and challenge are not consequences of the text but of the task set designed with it. 'Authentic texts chosen not for level but task potential can be used at all proficiency levels' (Mishan, 2005, p.44). In designing Interpretive mode tasks, we should not deprive the learner of interesting material on the basis of their proficiency level. Challenge also brings novelty, which is the means to unpredictability and therefore conducive to transfer. This can occur in small ways, such as guessing the gist, or for deeper inference using audio-visual, context clues or background knowledge to select the correct picture that matches a concept. These challenges are small, yet positive risk-taking measures that are key to ownership and transfer in the Interpretive mode. It is important that our tasks challenge the risk-averse if we want the learner to move forward. There are themes, topics and transdisciplinary content that are familiar concepts and taken up regularly either in school or social settings. Just because a learner is at novice level for language production, it does not mean they cannot or should not experience themes, content, or topics that are conceptually familiar, start building a vocabulary base and manage the concept with what they own at the time. Transdisciplinary concepts also open the door to solving problems and creating a new product which will vary at different intervals unfolded and spiralled in an articulated curriculum. There is only so much one can review and relearn personal details, routines, hobbies, etc. Authentic texts encourage tolerance of ambiguity with partial and imperfect comprehension. We should not demand perfection when even heritage speakers do not expect complete comprehension and production themselves (Guariento & Morley, 2001). Adapt texts to different levels by varying the tasks associated with them.

Claim and Capture

When designing Interpretive tasks, your tasks need to focus on what learners should claim and capture from the piece. This is why it is not enough to play a video or audio, two or three times while they listen. Often that may cause panic because they do not know where their attention should focus. The proverbial 'drinking from a fire hose' is apt here because of a tendency to focus attention equally on the entire lot when we have no focus. The cloze or fill-in type task falls short as well for listening comprehension due to learners' tendency to listen only for missing parts without fully understanding the text. These tasks may show what the learner hears, but not what they understand. The same for answering the questions. In many of our languages, learners can use linguistic cues or tricks to manoeuvre the sentence and answer, but not understand what they wrote or be able to do it unprompted. If one thinks back on a classroom experience learning a language, you may recall that was the case. The task must direct the learner to notice and focus on particular elements for a specific use. In our first language when we see, hear or watch anything for information, we focus on exactly what we need, claim it and are on our way. Once learners see how this skill develops, they will use these strategies whenever faced with new material on their own. Always remember learners will ultimately take information from the Interpretive mode tasks to use for the following Interpersonal mode task. The Presentational task will always be solving a problem or creating the product implied in the Context for the unit. Thus, the Interpretive mode task provides the key pieces for the rest of the tasks.

When we encounter any text we see, hear, view or read, what purpose does it serve and what do we get out of it? They were designed with our response in mind. Do they give information, entertain, or guide us? Do they persuade or convince us? How do they offer suggestions? Is it always with words? Do they do it with images and actions? When you listen to something, an announcement, the news, a song, dinner suggestions or instructions, what do you listen for? When you view something, a poster, infographic, advertisement, sign or mural, what is your 'take-away' from it? How do you use that information; what is your response? What do these materials all have in common? Contrast those materials with those designed for student instruction or set at a particular grade level or year of study. What do these materials look like? How are they structured? Do they have certain characteristics that let you know they are made for the public or classroom instruction?

Check for Learning

With a partner and samples of authentic and classroom materials or activities, categorize three or four texts under each column. Then write three questions about the characteristics you notice. What is the purpose of these texts? Share your questions with your small group or class.

Culturally authentic texts	Pedagogically prepared material designed for classroom instruction

When faced with authentic texts always ask, 'What am I motivated to do next? What do I notice?' This will guide you in designing a task. What meaning does the author of the piece want you to get out of it? What happens now? Why was it written, composed or created? In other words, what is the writer's intention for the piece? Language learners need to mine and unearth meaning, from recognizing words and phrases using images at first for the Novice range, to summarizing paragraph length discourse at Intermediate High through Advanced. The tasks should be compatible with the purpose of the text. In the task description, the teacher helps the learner identify that purpose that matches the communicative intent of the text (Sandrock, 2015).

When learners are only exposed to instructional material heavily edited with cues and supports, controlled structures to complete, they are strategically unprepared for materials, contexts and challenges they will inevitably face beyond school. These strategies need to peel back, connect and reveal what the material gives to us. The tasks we design will help the learner cope independently with a variety of formats, purposes and the full range of plurilingual and pluricultural contexts. Even with texts such as poetry, we design the task to access the text. It is key to not only choose a poem for its topic but also to allow pupils access to the poem by designing for the target level of the task. The source does not change; the task needs to diversify (Diamantidaki, 2019).

Authentic materials provide visual and auditory context clues about the culture that uses them. Can you describe the emotions of characters on TV or in a film based on sounds, tone of voice, music and pitch of the speakers? When you hear authentic speech, it helps you develop proper intonation and features of natural conversation, as opposed to contrived and overly simplified language found in many coursebooks and ancillaries. It is counterproductive to provide materials that suggest routine with diluted subject matter. The learner should be exposed to varied language expressions that communities use every day. Because life in the real language realm has no script, the materials we provide the learner should no less prepare them for that *inevitable unexpected*: Novel materials yield novel actions of improvisation and invention.

Check for Learning

Consider your chosen theme or topic and the language you teach. The table below represents many kinds of texts. What are some examples of texts found in cultural communities today and also some representing their cultural history? Are there any you might add to this list?

What do you want the learner to 'take away' from material? What are your look-fors? Consider our discussion of perspectives and practices. Do we see them in cultural products? How do they reveal themselves?

Table 4.2 Cultural Community Authentic Texts

Audio	Printed	Visual
Commercials	Websites	Sculpture
News	Newspapers and magazines	Street signs
Voicemail	Blogs, tweets, texts	Cartoons and Emojis
Radio	Brochures and Menus	Picture books and Graphic novels
TV	Infographics	Drawing and painting
Film	Fiction/non-fiction literature	Film
Music videos	Advertisements	Posters
PSAs	Promotional materials	Public Information Films
Songs and all music	Lyrics, scripts, and scores	Dance
Interviews	Surveys	Charts, graphs, symbols, images
Talk shows	Food labels	Theatre
Announcements	Maps	Photography

Aesthetic Education and Drama Pedagogy for Interpretive mode tasks

Queens College world language teachers use the Capacities for Capacities of Imaginative Learning (Eddy, 2006b, 2019a; Greene, 2001; Holzer, 2007) developed by Lincoln Center Education aligned with the performance tasks in order to design summative and formative tasks. Texts are always culturally authentic – works of art such as literature, visual and performing arts or informational texts. The Capacities for the Interpretive mode are Noticing Deeply, Embodying, Identifying Patterns and Questioning.

Noticing Deeply acknowledges continuous engagement with the text over time. Learners always come full circle to Interpretive mode tasks over the course of a unit because this is where they gather more information on the chosen texts, images, works of art, whatever they may be. It also indicates the first place where they reach into the text and respond with novelty, new meaning for themselves and begin mediation for others: Interpretation as Conception. Therefore, right from the start, this text is no longer static or foreign; they have established acquaintance and connection to the text piece and begin mediation. In addition, this capacity supports the return to a piece of authentic text over the course of an articulated curriculum with tasks that provide greater challenge. The teacher also can develop tasks using varied media, visuals, music, film and prompts that enable learners to connect personal experiences to key elements embedded in the literary text. Teachers may choose colours, music, images associated with themes in the work for this purpose.

Embodying tasks in this mode asks the learner to not only respond to the text or piece cognitively, but physically experience the work using the senses. In the series of tasks for *One Lucky Day* (Eddy, 2019b) in the next chapter, learners apply *ideokinesis* (Todd, 1937; Linklater, 2006), using visual imagery to inspire body movement to make the shape of concepts with their body, using movements and associated words to make a body poem. Students can then categorize these words. In another task, learners make inferences from text or music, create line drawings to sequence an event, and dance a drawing based on an emotional event. Learners focus on meaning and emotions by creating tableaux (Eddy, 2019b; Piazzoli, 2019; Maley & Duff, 2005). When creating a tableau, the body, gestures, and facial expressions create meaning, relate the story and mediate emotion. This is interpretive and tacit, and it is entirely to demonstrate understanding and embodiment of the emotion and concepts within the piece (Eddy, 2019b).

Embodying is also a design capacity that is accessible, facilitative and inclusive for all learners. Unfortunately, there is practice in many countries to declare a 'disability in foreign languages' and to waive, disapply from a language requirement or advise someone away from taking languages (Sparks, 2009; Wight, 2015). They discredit the notion that neurodiverse learners will fail or withdraw from language courses and that there is no reason someone should be dissuaded from taking one. Embodiment or gesture studies (Stam & McCafferty, 2008; McNeill, 2000) examines how the body mediates learning via gesture. Drama strategies such as improvisation, re-enactments, 'yes…and', pupil as expert 'in role' and other forms of process drama (Baldwin, 2012; Heathcote & Bolton, 1995) had positive effects on language acquisition. Piazzoli & Kubiak (2019) studied neurodiverse learners of Italian using embodying language in action (Piazzoli, 2018) practices. Using a three-phase structure (1) relaxing the body using the image as inspiration, (2) describing in a free association, using contextualized vocabulary, (3) teams prepared a tableau embodying emotion from the image for classmates to identify. Imagery and meaning-making are key here to the Interpretive mode. Mediation for the purpose of meaning is made possible using gestures and whole-body movements as a response to an image, text or work of art. These strategies within tasks are helpful to many neurodiverse teachers and all learners.

Identifying Patterns involves categorizing and organizing images or words using a graphic organizer. This is an important type of Interpretive mode task. Before a learner is even at word level in the language, they can demonstrate comprehension with images, sounds and movements that they group into meaningful categories to chunk information, repeat and revise points (Curtain & Dahlberg, 2016). This capacity also includes drawing an illustration to associate a word with a visual image, remembering word order, putting the words onto a card, cutting up the card into separate phrases, mixing them up and putting them back together again in the correct order.

Questioning is a key feature in designing for the Interpretive mode, often overlooked and still not fully recognized by many world language teachers for the Interpretive mode. Interpretive mode tasks should guide learners to reveal cultural interpretation of meaning. This is different from typical listening or reading comprehension tasks which imply a surface or fact-based treatment of a text. These types of tasks also tend to be satisfied with the standpoint of the learner's culture only rather than engaging a process to fully connect in reciprocity with the culture that created the piece.

One reason for this is the learner remains in a passive role, always answering questions. Most of the time these are fact-based and close to the text. This habit keeps the learner detached from the Interpretive experience both in the classroom and ultimately when faced with language within culture outside of it. Answering questions is also a synthetic response particularly when it is obvious the teacher already knows the answer. Teachers and pupils are accustomed to reading and listening comprehension questions because textbooks traditionally contain a lot of them. This practice exists in many content areas as you recall from your own studies. Typical classroom settings generally do not provide nearly enough opportunities to form and ask questions, and consequently we are not very good at it. This is a problem in every content area, K-20. When learners primarily answer questions to the exclusion of other tasks, they remain passive, dependent recipients, rather than active agents in learning. Our learners do not have nearly enough practice and opportunities to form and ask questions (Eddy, 2016a. 2019b). When we are in any real-world situation out and about in the target language culture, we are the ones that must do the asking! Therefore, all learners need practice on questioning. The Interpretive mode yields more powerful results and demonstrates far better understanding when the learner poses the questions, even simple ones. A key characteristic of the intermediate level of proficiency is the ability to ask and answer questions (ACTFL, 2012). The teacher will be able to follow progression from novice to intermediate by how well and to what extent the learner can form questions. Table 4.3 below applies the *Question Answer Relationship* technique (Raphael & Au, 2005) to Interpretive mode question types. Although the act of this exchange of information with someone else resides in the subsequent Interpersonal mode, constructing questions is a reaction to derive meaning and that is Interpretive. As a reaction to a text, your learners can form questions that are answered directly in the text but also through illustration, the inference from examples. Learners can also improve and elaborate upon texts as they summarize and paraphrase, using solely their own interpretation and collaborative background knowledge (Verhoeven & Perfetti, 2008; Vygotsky, 1978). The value of constructing questions, however simple, cannot be underestimated. Learners need to uncover not only what is directly in the text, but also what is implied and what is not. These offer valuable practice for mediation with others, when we need to point out, clarify, offer examples and our own ideas to make language more accessible.

Table 4.3 Questioning in the Interpretive mode

Literal	Inferential
Identify	**Illustrate**
Fact is in one place in text	Information is covert, hidden, muted or 'between the lines' in the text
Form questions	Form questions that extract and point out tacit and implied example
Index	**Improve**
Facts are in multiple spots in text	Information is not found in the text
Combine to form questions	Form questions to improve or elaborate based on prior knowledge interpretation as bridge to facts 'in absentia'

Designing for Interpretive Goals

Let's consider the following sample text of advice for a popular tourist area:

The area has so many attractions, including three large parks and one of the most beautiful ocean beaches in the state. The rainy season is July-October. You can almost set your watch by when the farmers market gets windy and vendors hurry to pack up and cover their wares. So, grab that al fresco lunch early before they close for an hour or so.

Rental cars are expensive and parking is difficult, so why not walk or take the free buses and trolleys? They run until very late at night to all shops, museums, restaurants, cafes and clubs. These are open every day but Monday.

Rather than ask learners to answer comprehension questions, instead have them form questions from the text. Here are a few that are close to the text and ones that require more inference and move away from the text. Using the table above as a guide, can you construct other questions from this text?

- How many parks are there?
- What are three things you can do?
- What can you do at night?
- When is the best time to visit?

We make meaning by questioning. The Interpretive mode needs to engage students much more actively in the process of constructing meaning if they are ever going to be able to do this on their own. Textbooks typically are rife with an item type found in every content area: the comprehension questions. We do not answer a list of questions after we read any paragraph, poem, song lyrics, article, poster, advertisement, brochure, food label, watch any video or listen to a quick announcement. More likely, our reaction is that the text prompted a few questions in our mind about it. Perhaps we wrote a response to someone. We may have compared the information from the piece to data, news and image or evidence we already knew. Maybe it encouraged or inspired us to plan, make a list or write a tourist review such as the one above. As we listen or read, images may come to mind. This is a reaction, an authentic response to material that our learners need to practice for themselves so that they can then share these points with someone else. These tasks provide the learner with tools to thrive beyond our instruction. Therefore, opportunities for learner-generated questions should occur early and often.

Check for Learning

Exploring and Interpreting meaning for mediation

How do language and culture work together for us to explore and interpret meaning?

Examine a selection of materials for your language and concept. These materials can include images and text: anything to view, listen to, read or watch.

Discuss the following questions with these skills in mind.

1 What information do you take away from the piece?
2 What is one or more specific look-fors, that you discovered from the piece?
3 How does this material make you feel? What emotions do you feel from the material?
4 Does the piece reveal a cultural practice or perspective? How can you clarify it for someone else?
5 Does this piece prompt any cultural comparisons? Can you make a comparison for someone?
6 How might the piece allow you to see yourself, your own cultural practices, your own cultural perspectives?
7 Can this piece connect you to your community through its theme or purpose? To the world?

Teacher as Designer

We have said that complexity lies in the task and not the text. We adapt the task to the target we desire and leave the text original. We start with a text that is wordless by design. Film is a popular culturally authentic text and valuable at all levels of instruction. In this example, the silent film *The Paper Boy* (2015, Aniket Mitra, Writer, Director. Pocketfilms.) takes dialogue out of the equation and places it in the mind of the viewer (see Table 4.4). Any film can become a silent film. With the sound turned off, learners will focus and rely on images, movement, and timing. This story is wonderful for learning any language and this AATT shows us task design for the complexity features and target desired. This story guides the learner to create the self through personal and cultural symbols. The inner dialogue script requested in the context places the learner 'in role' to examine the character's life through different lenses and points of view. Help can come from unexpected sources. Just one person noticing can change an outcome.

Voices from the Field

Our Hindi and Urdu programmes include the theme of child labour. Along with the authentic textual representation in short stories, the silent film *The Paper Boy* is focused on children's lives, poverty and dreams, which are universally relevant topics. The objective is for students to further their critical thinking and develop cultural sensitivity towards these social and psychological issues without sensationalizing and exoticizing them.

The roots, the bottom-up and top-down solutions to poverty are often similar across regions, although the specific symptoms and priorities might be different. The symbolism of the river – of Mother Gangees – bringing him the shoes, i.e. giving hope for the future of the boy might be interpretable similarly in other cultures and the dream-reality dichotomy is also experienced in comparable ways.

The tasks based on *The Paper Boy* and the Child Labour units have been taught usually at the Intermediate and Advanced proficiency levels. However, the silent film can be used at the Novice level when students learn how to describe their routine and surroundings. It serves as a visual context to spiral up the topic by enriching vocabulary and grammar. Students can design a Venn diagram comparing their daily routine with that of the paperboy. The teacher also raises awareness about the specific environment and traditional behaviours (the lanes, the night fire, the singing). The preparatory stage includes teaching phrase level linguistic categories such as noun-adjective gender, number and case agreement (in the big city, on the small lane, on the river banks, alone boy, during dark night, through hard work, with little money, etc.) and present habitual tense for actions the boy performs on a daily basis (he sleeps on a bench, he wakes up early, he delivers newspapers, he earns money, they call him, etc.).

Our programmes include mostly heritage language students who have diverse backgrounds, needs and interests, usually with weaker literacy-skills and stronger aural skills. Planning a unit based on varied authentic resources and designing these performance tasks at different proficiency sub-levels and levels makes the instructor ready for students who learn at a different pace and/or have different extent of exposure to their heritage language/s and culture/s, allowing for differentiation through variation of either process, product or content.

Professor Gabriela Nik Ilieva, Director, South Asian Language Programs. New York University

Table 4.4 Articulated Assessment Transfer Task *The PaperBoy*: Story of identity and hope

Gabriela Nik Ilieva, New York University and Jennifer Eddy, Queens College, CUNY
Enduring Understandings * Identity is both an inside and outside quest and can be about reinvention and change. * Texts and works of art help us construct our understanding of reality. * Dreams combine reality and imagination. * Story, images and dreams are how we remember and recreate our world, thoughts and actions.
Essential Questions ? Do we know who really knows us well? ? What turning points determine our path? ? How does symbolism develop story? ? To what extent does meaning come from the text, from ourselves, or a process between the two that recreates it for us? ? Why is it important for people to construct narratives about their experience? ? What is the relationship of dreams to reality? ? How can images tell my story?
Context A film journal wants an inner dialogue script from the point of view of different people.
Articulation Spiral Points @ Develop storyboard with images and words. @ Examine and elaborate in role to develop meaning. @ Recreate script and story for other genres.

Designing for Interpretive Goals

Intercultural Transfer Targets	Mediation for Transfer
• I can process and create story through my point of view. • I can compare and discuss values and hopes. • I can identify examples of hope and unexpected help in stories from my own and other cultures. • I can exhibit empathy for someone else's circumstances. • I can explain images and symbolism in my own and other cultures to someone unfamiliar with them.	• Bridge and exchange ideas and concepts related to identity, hope, value, personal triumph. • Clarify images, visuals and symbolism in story. • Collaborate in role to resolve situations. • Formulate questions and give feedback on known and new cultural references. • Provide examples to make accessible to people from other cultures.

Novice Mid	Intermediate Mid	Advanced Low
The Paper Boy (2015, Aniket Mitra, Writer, Director. Pocketfilms.)		
Interpretive Task Descriptions		
Student groups receive an envelope with words on flashcards from the story. While watching the film they put the words in order as they see them (shoes, clock, bench, boy, newspaper, alley, river, water, etc.).	Students view segments of the film (without the end) and form questions. They complete a graphic organizer (who, what, where, why, how and what if) and add their ending.	Students view the movie without the ending 'in role'-(a friend, a teacher, an NGO worker) and take notes in a table about the main character's life, needs and wishes while considering solutions.
Can Dos		
I can identify images with words and put them in chronological order.	I can pose questions from facts in the film and categorize info on the organizer.	I can summarize and improve on the plot from the standpoint of another role.

Interpersonal Task Descriptions		
Each pair has three different stills and an envelope with the nouns and adjectives. They describe each still and match the word to the stills. They choose and decide which stills to use for the storyboard.	Jigsaw – students ask their questions and show partners their graphic organizer and ending. Sharing differences, they come to consensus on a common ending which combines one idea from each ending.	Students discuss and agree on five reasons and solutions for this child's situation. Students then jigsaw and report on their ideas 'in role' and come to consensus on the five most efficient strategies.
Can Dos		
I can plan the sequence of a story with a partner.	I can ask a partner questions, compare info and choose an ending for the story.	I can discuss, decide and share solutions and strategies.
Presentational Task Descriptions		
Students design the film story-board and write simple sentence captions.	Students create the director's notes and an audiofile with the beginning and ending sentences for scenes.	Students view the end of the film and discuss what it means (a dream or reality). Students create the narration (script and audio) for a documentary in their role.
Can Dos		
I can develop a storyboard with images and short dialogue.	I can write the script and record the audio for the top and bottom of each scene.	I can develop the narrative and audio for each role for the inner dialogue script.

> **Bridge to Design**
>
> Let's get closer to this exemplar design and the authentic text of silent film. Join colleagues to ask questions about the authors' design processes and collaborate for additional ideas and reflection on this exemplar before working on your own design.
>
> (See Appendix Q in Companion Website Chapter 4.)

Annotations (Fisher, Frey & Hattie, 2016) are a key first step in learner engagement and mediation of texts. Learners can annotate visuals, captions from a video or written material from informational or literary texts. These annotations help learners make connections, ask questions and make inferences. Wolfe and Neuwirth (2001) explain that annotation benefits learners in solo tasks for the Interpretive mode, but also suggest that annotation is social and shared, which strengthens its use for the purpose of collaboration and to practice strategies for plurilingual and pluricultural mediation between other people. These annotations will change over time as the learner develops with the concept and tasks in the curriculum. This is an excellent 'standing-order' task to accompany any Interpretive mode task at home or in class.

Seven Symbols of Transfer and Mediation

- ! is interesting to you
- * is an example or evidence of specific intercultural transfer target
- \# is connected to a social media hashtag
- & is an example of ideal collaboration or connection to another word concept
- ? is an area you question and need to explore further
- + is a new idea, word, phrase or concept as expansion from this learning

Check for Learning

Keep the ICANADAPT Concept Map close by so you can annotate authentic texts with the Seven Symbols of Transfer and Mediation. As you examine authentic texts for use in curriculum and assessment design, use these symbols on the concept map beside your annotations. Share these with colleagues. Use these ideas as you develop your Interpretive tasks for your unit and the AATT. (See Figure 2.1.)

Teacher as Designer

Te Reo Māori is the language of Aotearoa. New Zealand has strong revitalization efforts to build Te Reo capacity through schools, radio, television, events and through www.reomaori.co.nz. There is a goal of one million Māori language speakers by the year 2040, according to Māori language commissioner, Professor Rawinia Higgins. Te Reo is essential for embodying and understanding Māori values, perspectives and worldview. The above website, *Kia Kaha Te reo Māori*, contains many resources for learning Te Reo. They start with a tool to begin small and powerfully, with #MyMihi: how to introduce yourself. Māori values relationships, sense of belonging, connectedness to all things, Whānau wellness and authenticity; what makes you the person you are.

Mr Keri Opai is a community leader and Te Reo Māori and Tikanga Māori educator on culture, principles, values and spirituality. He is author of a glossary of terms in Te Reo Māori for use in the mental health, addiction and disability sectors: 'Te Reo Hāpai – The Language of Enrichment'. This database updates Te Reo Māori already in use, but Mr Opai generated new words that didn't exist previously. These words all come from positive Māori worldviews, stemming from a strengths base, not a deficit base. One of those words is *Takiwātanga*: in my/his/her own time and space. It is the Māori word for autism.

This exemplar uncovers *Takiwātanga* within the Te Reo Māori curriculum through the context of community and Whānau support with Māori perspectives on strength, acceptance, wellbeing and identity (see Table 4.5). Pupils learning Te Reo will understand concepts and new vocabulary to develop creative materials or ideas for outings, recreation and gatherings for positive wellbeing, respect and affirmation of neurodiverse people of all ages.

Designing for Interpretive Goals

Voices from the Field

My kaumātua (elders) always told me: 'He mana tō te kupu' – 'Words have great power'. They meant that the power of language cannot be overstated. Words can crush a person's self-esteem or uplift it to great heights and Te Reo Hāpai not only aims to lessen stigma and discrimination but is also an attempt to reframe thinking about mental health, addiction and disability that has already had far-reaching, positive effects in this country and indeed, around the world. Other indigenous people especially are looking at the glossary and exclaiming, 'If Aotearoa can do it, so can we'.

Keri Opai, healthcentral.nz.

Table 4.5 Articulated Assessment Transfer Task
Takiwātanga: My/His/Her/Our Own Time and Space

Keri Opai and Jennifer Eddy	Te Reo Māori
Enduring Understandings * *Takiwātanga:* in my/his/her/our own time and space. * The importance of Whānau health and wellbeing is key for Māori people. * Ka tipu te whaihanga – Creativity will strengthen. * Ahakoa he aha te rākau he hua kei roto - No matter the species of tree each bears its own unique fruit. * He mana tō te kupu – Words have great power.	
Essential Questions ? What does it mean to live authentically? ? How do people show us that they accept us as we are? ? Why can creativity help us reimagine wellbeing for ourselves, friends and Whānau? ? How does stigma and discrimination affect wellbeing and identity? ? What does acceptance of all neurodiversity look like?	

Context
Tui Ora seeks new ideas for materials in Te Reo Māori on Whānau health and wellness to support *Takiwātanga*, autism and the neurodiverse community.

Articulation Spiral Points
@ Connect words and images with Māori perspectives.
@ Create Video media on *Takiwātanga*.
@ Use of Te Reo Hāpai glossary for updated and inclusive language on Health.
@ *Develop reports on resources, events and supports for* Whānau wellbeing.
@ Compose or create works of art in support of neurodiversity acceptance.

Intercultural Transfer Targets	Mediation for Transfer
• I can identify words and phrases from Te Reo Māori for autism and wellness.
• I can explain *Takiwātanga* from the Māori perspective.
• I can develop Whānau wellbeing resources, events and supports with the community.
• I can work with a partner to exchange and compare Māori values on the subject of *Takiwātanga and* Whānau health and wellness.	• Bridge and exchange ideas and concepts of neurodiversity and supportive vocabulary.
• Explain words and support structure of Whānau to other cultures.
• Present Te Reo Māori perspectives, pose questions and gather others' perspectives.
• Show empathy by asking and answering simple questions for understanding.
• Summarize information on *Takiwātanga* and make accessible for others the main idea of a video by paraphrasing in simpler language.

Novice High	Intermediate Mid	Advanced Low
Te Reo Māori website for use in the mental health, addiction and disability sectors.
Video: Watch Keri Opai, creator of the word *Takiwātanga*.
Video: A Hamilton Māori family raises awareness.	Te Reo Māori website for use in the mental health, addiction and disability sectors.
Video: Watch Keri Opai explain Māori perspectives and language.
Video: Supporting Whānau to navigate *Takiwātanga*	Video: Tūraukawa Bartlett: their own time and space. Video: Autism not a disability, but a different ability – Mom and child at FunFest

Designing for Interpretive Goals

Interpretive Task Descriptions		
Learners watch the videos by both Mr Opai and the family. List and categorize words on the graphic organizer.	Listen to Mr Opai and then the family. Write three questions for each. Check off details from the list as you hear them.	Listen to Mr Opai and then the family at FunFest. Paraphrase and illustrate key points by examples on the video and write five questions and suggestions on positive events for creativity and diverse abilities.
Can Dos		
I can identify and organize key vocabulary related to autism and family engagement.	I can pose questions based on the videos and organize details on Takiwātanga and family support.	I can elaborate by using examples from the video and write clarifying questions and suggestions.
Interpersonal Task Descriptions		
In pairs, plan what words, phrases and visuals to include on the community poster.	Ask extended family about Whānau values, cultural scripts and ideals to support *Takiwātanga*.	Engage with the community and ask and answer questions on positive Māori recommendations to lessen stigma and discrimination.
Can Dos		
I can choose with a partner words, proverbs and images to use for the wellness poster.	I can come to consensus with a partner on what to include in a video to support inclusive and welcoming Whānau support resources.	I can exchange information and decide on suggestions for improved support and events within the community.

Presentational Task Descriptions		
Create infographic posters on Whānau wellbeing and Takiwātanga for the Tui Ora community event.	Compose a short informational video on Whānau wellness supports for Takiwātanga.	Create a poem, song, or work of art for *Takiwātanga*, with positive and uplifting Māori words of strength and support. **'He mana tō te kupu'** Learners write an action plan with on access and supports needed to ensure health, security, inclusivity and acceptance.
Can Dos		
I can use positive words and images for the Tui Ora *Takiwātanga* community event.	I can prepare a video explaining Whānau, *Takiwātanga* and Māori positive point of view.	I can prepare a report for Whānau wellness and health, community resources, events and support for autistic children and adults.

Bridge to Design

Let's explore this exemplar design further and join colleagues to ask questions about Mr Opai's work, *Takiwātanga,* and collaboration for additional ideas and reflection on this exemplar before working on your own design.

(See Appendix R in Companion Website Chapter 4.)

Teacher as Designer

In the exemplar below, Korean teacher Soojin Choi Kim shares her vision for the national song Arirang, a song of the people (see Table 4.6). This beautiful song is known by every Korean and sung for every possible emotion. There are thousands of versions because people compose their own personal Arirang. Arirang is fast and slow, physical and visual. It is a song that unites and expresses individual creativity.

Soojin designs tasks such as the storyboard, graphic organizers, and KWL charts to develop meaning in preparation for composing a new Arirang. Using original song lyrics, the tune and intense emotions, there are so many ways to embody and express your Arirang.

Voices from the Field

The song Arirang is not just a catchy Korean song. It is listed in UNESCO's Representative List of the Intangible Cultural Heritage of Humanity. According to UNESCO, it states, 'Arirang's great virtue is to respect human creativity, freedom of expression and empathy.'

Arirang is the most popular traditional folk song that comforts Koreans and is often considered to symbolize the spirit of all Koreans. Just as Americans crave and eat Chicken Noodle Soup when they are sick, the song Arirang has a similar effect for Koreans when they are sick and need to heal.

Arirang was created to heal the hearts and minds of the Korean people back when their land, language and life were stolen from them. This song kept the Koreans that lost everything grounded. It was a signified cry of help but also a strong voice that encouraged others to never lose hope.

Although Korea is a small country, there are many different regions throughout the country. Interestingly enough, there are different variations of the Arirang song per region. This demonstrates that the physical environment and patterns of life in the different regions influence the people's understanding which led to the creation of many variations. These variations include differences in the melody and speed of the song. Another feature of Arirang is that the lyrics can be substituted with regional characteristics allowing learners to create their own unique Arirang tuned songs.

In this exemplar, learners will compose a modern 'New York' version of poetry that encompasses their everyday lives. Their poems will be inspired by their lifestyle and also have characteristics that highlight their way of expression or feeling.

Ms SooJin Choi Kim

Table 4.6 Articulated Assessment Transfer Task
Arirang: The Song of the People

Soojin Choi Kim	Korean
Enduring Understandings * Music is a universal language that unifies people home or away. * History and culture influence music. * Arirang sings of sorrow and joy, hope and loss, love, resistance and strength. * Life must go on even when faced with challenges.	
Essential Questions ? How does music communicate? ? How do music and history influence each other? ? In what ways have people used music to express their values and describe their experiences? ? Why do some songs go beyond nations and cultures?	
Context The Korean Cultural Centre New York is seeking applicants to compose verses for a modern 'New York' version of Arirang, which will be inspired by aspects of ordinary, everyday life.	
Articulation Spiral Points @ Connect images with emotions. @ Create story. @ Compare versions of Arirang. @ Discuss songs of similar genre across cultures. @ Compose their own Arirang.	
Intercultural Transfer Targets • I can identify concepts and visuals represented in the song. • I can compare versions of Arirang in my own and other cultures. • I can compose Arirang for my own life experience and cultural identity.	**Mediation for Transfer** • Bridge and exchange ideas and concepts of Arirang as a song of all people • Explain and compare similar songs from other cultures • Use visuals to depict range of emotions in versions of Arirang • Summarize information and emotions depicted in song • Elaborate on different versions of Arirang • Relate everyday experiences to clarify meaning of Arirang

Designing for Interpretive Goals

Novice High	Intermediate Mid	Intermediate High
Video of Arirang	Video: Documentary I	Video: Documentary II
Interpretive Task Descriptions		
Students listen/read the 'Arirang' song and draw a storyboard corresponding to the song.	Before watching: students use the KWL chart to write what they know about Arirang in the 'K' column. Then students pose questions on what they would like to know or what they wonder about Arirang in the 'W' column. As students watch the video clip, they find their questions and record new information they learn about Arirang.	Students view the documentary video clip and complete a graphic organizer using the following categories: event, emotion, solution.
Can Dos		
I can create a storyboard based on the given Arirang song.	I can pose questions about Arirang and categorize information on the KWL chart.	I can summarize the story and extract the character's emotions.
Interpersonal Task Descriptions		
Gallery Walk: students walk around the classroom looking at drawings, visual representations, and poster projects that have been hung on the classroom walls or displayed in the classroom. Students can complete a graphic organizer or answer a list of questions as they view each story-board.	Chat Stations: Working in pairs or small groups, students rotate on the teacher's signal from sign to sign to have a conversation based on prompts from students' KWL charts. They talk to one another to decide on the best response to the question posed by the prompt and record it on a graphic organizer.	Students discuss and agree on songs that have a similar cultural and historical background in their culture as Arirang does to Koreans.

Can Dos		
I can pose questions and provide information to represent my story board.	With a classmate, or in a small group, I can come to a consensus on the best response to the question.	I can discuss, decide and share reflections on songs.
Presentational Task Descriptions		
Students create dialogue with simple sentences for their story board based on the given regional Arirang song.	Students create an informative PPT with images and text or short video with a voice recording about various regional Arirang.	Students compose verses for a modern 'New York' Arirang, which will be inspired by aspects of their everyday lives.
Can Dos		
I can develop a storyboard with images and short dialogue.	I can create information slides or videos about Arirang representing different regions and cultures.	I can compose Arirang verses with my own life experiences and record the audio with a chosen regional melody.

Bridge to Design

What else can we learn about Soojin's Choi Kim's design thinking? Let's get closer to this exemplar. Join colleagues to share additional ideas and reflection before working on your own design.

(See Appendix S in Companion Website Chapter 4.)

Designing for Interpretive Goals 151

> **Collaboration for Articulation**
>
> There is a popular adage in the profession: 'Don't change the text, change the task'. Discuss this with your colleague. What does this look like? How could a task help the learner make meaning from the original piece? What about even down to word or image level for the Novice?

Teacher as Designer

When choosing authentic community texts, it is not expected that you 'cover' the material, expect learners to know every word from it, understand the whole piece in its entirety, or speak or write in paragraph length with it, at least not yet. The task you design will have them make sense of it to the extent they can, based on the performance target you set for the unit. You will find that authentic texts can be quite economical, in the sense that the same piece can be examined through varied tasks set at different target levels in an AATT. One great piece can work for any level of instruction; you reprise the material with the content and context later in the year or another year (Eddy, 2019a). They are not expected to master the information in the material at any given time. As we outlined in Chapters 1–3, this curriculum and the materials for it are not framed in a serial or linear way or topic determined by levels. A transfer spiral curriculum revisits the topic, may reprise the material, but does so with a novel task and greater complexity and variation.

The learner develops proficiency in tandem with the pieces they encounter, as their knowledge base grows. This is also why themes, topics, and materials should not be pigeonholed and compartmentalized by the year of study, with some withheld until a higher level (Mishan, 2005). What happens if the learner never takes that course? Worse, what if they chose not to because prior content and tasks were not relevant and applicable beyond classroom exercise? These practices short-change the learner if we hope they will continue on their own and see relevance to using language beyond the school building. As teachers, we want to encourage content that is relevant to participating in society in order to encourage autonomous learning. Just because someone is a novice level speaker does not make them a novice level thinker. These tasks let the learner do what they can do now, with any material for any concept or discipline, even when the encounter just yields word level ownership to start. Ms. Gina Durand offers her exemplar on child labour and engages her pupils in a meaningful and serious topic, showing that no topic or theme is too complex (see Table 4.7).

Many teachers would hold this unit to the end, but our learners can understand these concepts, process and comment, even if it is at word level. Here the pupils construct questions, identify inappropriate jobs for children, categorize the reasons child labour exists. These Interpretive tasks prepare for the subsequent interpersonal and presentational tasks where pupils choose, come to a consensus, and write poems and songs for the campaign.

Voices from the Field

It is essential that students become aware of 'Child Labour' on a global scale. Teachers should not hesitate to teach challenging topics, even with novice levels. The key is to 'modify the task' according to the student's level. The AATT is essential when planning my lessons because I think about the end product and what I would like the students to achieve by the end of each unit. Can-do statements allow me to review with the student as well as provide them with a self-assessment check. Through this AATT and Unit, students will understand that this topic is widespread and can compare children's rights across cultures and their own. Each student can compose a song or a simple diamante poem illustrating the meaning of child labour as evidence of transfer. This exemplar demonstrates that teachers can unfold challenging topics while modifying tasks according to the learner's level. The grammar and vocabulary necessary to do the task is contained within a cultural context rather than presented and retrieved in isolation.

Ms. Gina Durand, Spanish teacher, New York

Table 4.7 Articulated Assessment Transfer Task — Child Labour

Gina Durand	Spanish
Enduring Understandings * Child labour deprives children from their childhood. * Child labour is accepted in some cultures as contributing to the home. * Demographics can influence child labour.	

Designing for Interpretive Goals

Essential Questions
- ? Why do children work?
- ? What is childhood?
- ? To what extent do demographics determine who works?
- ? How does where you live influence why and how you work?

Context
The Pan American Development Foundation is providing a campaign to get informed about child labour. The campaign needs materials to create awareness and promote prevention of child labour that affects millions of children.

Articulation Spiral Points
- @ Identify jobs, hours, conditions.
- @ Outline causes and factors of child labour.
- @ Compare children's rights across countries.
- @ Synthesize prevention and awareness plan.

Intercultural Transfer Targets	Mediation for Transfer
• I can identify jobs done by children. • I can ask questions on how child labour affects children's safety and wellbeing. • I can compare examples of children's rights and protection laws in different countries. • I can gather information from my own and other cultures to develop an awareness and prevention plan.	• Bridge and exchange ideas and concepts on the prevention of child labour. • Refer to visuals to indicate jobs that are inappropriate or dangerous for children. • Use songs and music videos to clarify issues. • Explain and compare with a chart to highlight laws, awareness and action.

Novice High	Intermediate Mid	Advanced Low
Interpretive Task Descriptions		
Students watch music videos and list the jobs that the children mention and what they would rather do with their hands instead of working. Students identify the jobs with pictures provided and write three questions on the video content.	Students read an article and highlight the reasons for child labour and categorize them using the chart. Students compose five questions from the article.	Students read an article on the prevention and enforcement of child labour and paraphrase the article, illustrating the important facts of the content.

	Can Dos	
I can list child labour jobs depicted in the music video.	I can categorize information and write five questions related to the content.	I can paraphrase the article and point out key examples on the importance of preventing child labour.
	Interpersonal Task Descriptions	
Students ask and answer questions about the music video and how the children are affected by child labour and decide what to include on the brochure.	Students discuss the causes of child labour and ask five follow up questions.	Students discuss a plan to effectively combat child labour.
	Can Dos	
I can converse with a partner about how children are affected by child labour and I can label the type of jobs that children do according to the song.	I can come to consensus with a partner on factors that result in child labour in Mexico and compare those with child labour rights in the United States and other countries.	I can discuss/ debate a plan of action to effectively create awareness and promote prevention of child labour.
	Presentational Task Descriptions	
Students compose a simple diamante poem or rap on child labour using words and phrases on jobs, work conditions, ages, etc of children.	In groups, students present a Venn Diagram poster to compare and contrast the rights of children in the United States compared to children in Mexico and other countries.	Students write song for video presentation to include jobs, causes and effects of child labour as a way to create awareness and promote prevention. Students can submit song to the organization *'Iniciativa: La musica contra el trabajo infantil'* which promotes awareness about child labour.
	Can Dos	
I can write a poem or rap about child labour.	I can make a presentation to compare and contrast the rights of children in regards to child labour.	I can create a music video to promote prevention of child labour.

> **Bridge to Design**
>
> Let's go deeper on this exemplar by Ms Durand. Join colleagues to collaborate on how you can adapt the task for a level and develop a topic such as this one over an articulated curriculum. Share additional ideas and reflection before working on your own design.
>
> (See Appendix T in Companion Website Chapter 4.)

Ten design tips for Interpretive mode tasks

1 Consider your perspectives and practices from your Enduring Understandings and Essential Questions for your chosen theme or topic. What are the big ideas and concepts? Do you see these residing in the materials, the products that culture and community bearers provide?

2 Using the chart of authentic materials, choose about nine or ten pieces inclusive of the range of types represented in the chart.

3 Scaffold student independence in the Interpretive mode by designing tasks at all ranges with the same piece.

4 Infographics are wonderful at any level, but particularly for Novices because they are so accessible: many images, short phrases, bullet points, and concise, with a lot of key information 'at a glance'. Always ask yourself, what does this make me do next? Begin with identification, categorization, and posing simple questions. This will build the knowledge base of a more abstract concept early as learners develop image to word recognition, connect with concepts understood in other subjects and expand vocabulary.

5 Intermediate and higher levels have established a mental framework on the topic and can listen, view, watch and read for more detail, higher inference between the lines, and summarize.

6 For multi-levels in one room, use our AATT exemplar to differentiate through tasks but one text. Novice learners might work with an infographic to identify or list, while Intermediate target level learners use it for a task that provide more challenge, such as forming questions or comparing the infographic with a video clip on the same concept.

7 Remember that the task is the liaison, acting as intermediary between the learner and the text. The onus of accessibility is on the task: Make adjustments on the 'ask' of the task and not the piece itself.

8 All learners can make use of the entire set of tools and materials, just for different tasks.

9 Choose materials that will serve as models for learners to recreate anew, perhaps for a different audience, purpose, or even reinvented as a different medium. The materials a teacher provides for the Interpretive mode will become mentor texts, example formats the learner will adapt, edit, innovate, and reimagine for subsequent Presentational mode tasks. If we want learners to be able to compose a digital booklet for a new album, an infographic on good health practices, or a video performance someday, we need to provide these mentor texts accompanied by tasks that mediate a response.

10 The best Interpersonal mode tasks are those which guide learners to discuss what they will include, choose, and decide for the creation of the Presentational mode deliverable. This is why the materials and tasks for the Interpretive mode are so important. Without well-designed Interpretive mode tasks for acquisition and ownership, the other two modes will fall short of communicative expectations.

Table 4.8 Interpretive Mode Task Sampler across Three Levels

Novice0-A1.1	IntermediateA1.2-B1.1	AdvancedB1.2-C1.1
Read nutrition website and identify foods as healthy/unhealthy	Read travel website and write three questions for locals on where they go; what they do	Read article and summarize everyday local fashion with clothing for special occasions
Watch videos on leisure activities and check which are popular for different groups	Watch the video and categorize clothing for different situations	Watch videos on home remedies and compare changes in health practices over time
Listen to descriptions of meals and identify with the image	Listen to the announcement and write three questions for more information	Listen to news clip and summarize local plans to protect the environment

Designing for Interpretive Goals 157

Check for Learning

With your template and materials in front of you (see Tables 4.8 and 4.9), let's consider these questions before design for the Interpretive mode.

- What do you want learners to be able to do as a result of this task?
- What is the 'take-away' from this mode that prepares them for the next task?
- How does this task move us closer to solving the problem presented in the context?

(For a master list of task types for the modes of communication, see Appendix NN.)

Table 4.9 Listening with Visuals Sampler across Three Levels

Listening with Visuals		
Community Health Concerns		
Novice	Intermediate	Advanced
Listen to food choices and select the picture that matches what they hear.	Listen to the public service announcement on diet and place the images in order of the narration.	Listen to interviews on medicinal plants and treatments of indigenous people in Latin America, select images that match and write a summary to elaborate, improve and illustrate by example each plant and treatment.
Listen to the podcast on different foods and health practices and select from four pictures to match what is described.	Listen to the podcast on different medicinal herbs for key details and comparisons, then select from four pictures to match what is described.	Listen to the podcast and select the images that represent health practices past and present.

Design for Transfer

Designing listening tasks: Identifying main ideas and details with images

For these interpretive mode tasks, you want to see that the learner can listen and identify an image that corresponds to the sentence or groups of sentences. Your students will choose a picture, drawing, or image that matches what is being described.

Using your theme, choose four images that depict one simple concept or main idea only or one concrete item. Prepare descriptions of no more than two sentences. The learners may hear the key word represented in the photo twice. Provide additional words that relate and elaborates for context.

In order to engage our learners to use inference and 'listen between the lines' we need to shift from keyword or main idea, to listening for details that infer or imply an image. This is a harder task, but it shows that the learner can grasp details or a concept, even if those words do not exactly match an image. Finally, in our advanced exemplar, learners need to make a distinction between time frames and recognize it as they hear it. That is the first step before they can produce it by saying and writing it themselves.

For your chosen theme, select listening passages and images, film clips or excerpts, photos or objects. Design an Interpretive Listening task for identifying main ideas and details using the images across three levels of learner engagement.

Design for Transfer

Constructing or Posing Questions from cultural community texts

Choose your visuals again or any text or video. Construct questions with the piece yourself. Design an Interpretive mode task for posing questions from cultural texts with the four categories of Question Answer Relationship (Raphael & Au, 2005) questions. Refer to Table 4.9.

Design for Transfer

Using the Capacities for Imaginative Learning aligned with the Interpretive-Receptive mode and design Interpretive mode tasks for your unit and AATT, using the item types below.

- Select an object to match the meaning of a word, phrase or entire work of art.
- Draw emotions relevant to the song or unit theme, then dance what you drew.
- Listen or watch the work and put illustrations in order.
- Gather photographs that match situation, action or themes and give them captions
- Categorize or classify words using a graphic organizer

Adapted from Eddy, J. (2019a). Literature and Drama for Transfer. In F. Diamantidaki, (Ed.), Teaching Literature in Modern Foreign Languages. London: Bloomsbury Academic.

Design for Transfer

With your selected texts and concept, design at least one listening, one viewing and one reading Interpretive mode tasks across **three levels of learner engagement** for your Summative assessment for the AATT. Use the Concept Map (see Figure 2.1) to organize and collect your thoughts. Use the AATT template for your Interpretive mode tasks (see Figure 1.4) and the fillable template on the Companion Website. (See Appendix OO, Chapter 7.)

(For a master list of task types for the modes of communication, see Appendix NN.)

Design assessments first, then say the takeaway

The Performance Assessment Specific Statements (PASS) are can-do statements based upon the work of the *Common European Framework of Reference* and the Can-Do descriptors used in the *European Language Portfolio* (ELP) (Council of Europe, 2001) and with the *NCSSFL-ACTFL can-do statements,* proficiency benchmarks and performance indicators (NCSSFL, 2017) to describe the specific language functions, skills and performances at various stages of language development and learning. The AATTs and ICANADAPT framework supports the goals of Can-Do statements, which facilitate implementation and learner autonomy (Lamb, 2017; Little, 2003; Little, 2009a/b; Little, Goullier & Hughes, 2011; Moeller, Theiler & Wu, 2012) with learners placed at the centre of the process. They receive PASS Can-Dos at the onset of the unit because the teachers design the performance assessments first in this model (Eddy, 2017; McTighe & Wiggins, 2005). These specific can-do statements are different from the overarching unit benchmark statements and general performance target you selected because teachers develop PASS after they design the tasks. This process may seem counter-intuitive; however, it makes sense and saves time. When working with trainees and in-service teachers on task design, it was easy to return to the habit of superfluous coverage when writing PASS can-do statements first. Too many functions, forms and content were listed that did not appear in the tasks but somehow were going to be 'covered' in a lesson. In this model, all can-do statements are accounted for in the formative or summative mode tasks because the task is designed first and the resulting PASS can-do derived from it. This provides excellent accountability and reduces or eliminates the coverage burden habit. Learners receive all the PASS Can-Do statements at the onset of the unit. It gives them a clear idea of what will happen over the course of the unit and eliminates questions such as 'do we need to know this?' Learners can also use them as a self-assessment tool. In the AATT exemplars, although there may be one can-do represented for each mode task, the teacher can derive as many as needed and only those found in the tasks themselves.

Design for Transfer

Design PASS Can-Do statements for your interpretive mode tasks. These are Performance Assessment Specific Statements derived from the task. Remember, in order to avoid previous habits of excess items that do not appear in the assessment, write these can-do's after you designed the assessment. They will be much clearer and focused on only those characteristics or needed elements for that task.

Discuss the Issues

1 The text does not determine the complexity; the task does. Discuss.
2 The task is the liaison, acting as intermediary between the learner and the text.
3 The onus of accessibility is on the task: Make adjustments on the 'ask' of the task and not the text itself.
4 Your colleague plays a video segment three times. Is that an interpretive task?
5 Why is text elaboration better than simplification? How does it help mediation?
6 Small novel challenges are positive risk-taking measures key to ownership and transfer in the Interpretive mode. Give task examples and discuss.
7 Why should the learner pose the questions? What are the consequences of only answering questions?

Reflect and Revisit

1 Why is even word level ownership meaningful when learning intercultural concepts?

2 Why should themes, topics, or materials not be pigeonholed, compartmentalized, or withheld by the year of study? What do our learners already own?

3 Explain Conception as it pertains to the Interpretive-Receptive mode.

4 How do Interpretive tasks help learners for Mediation?

5 How do you align the Capacities of Imaginative Learning with Interpretive performance tasks?

6 With the exemplars in the chapter so far, explain at least three characteristics of Interpretive assessment tasks.

7 How do 'I can' statements help learners understand what they own?

Chapter 5

Designing for the Interpersonal Goal: Consensus on Meaning for Mediation

Enduring Understandings

- ∞ The Interpersonal mode is a productive, improvisational, interactive and cooperative exchange between two or more people.
- ∞ Interpersonal interaction is unscripted, unrefined and unrehearsed and must be purposeful and meaningful for participants.
- ∞ Practice with forms cannot replace interaction nor is it necessary for reacting or responding to input.
- ∞ Interaction for meaning rather than practice on forms encourages the learner to thrive with what they have rather than merely survive.
- ∞ Interpersonal mode tasks engage the learner to interact and negotiate intercultural meaning from input.
- ∞ The Interpersonal mode extends the context for learners to respond to what is said, not how it is said.
- ∞ Interpersonal mode tasks are exchanges that continually use input, helping language grow over time.
- ∞ The Interpersonal mode helps learners plan, choose, decide, get more information, and come to consensus with each other to solve a problem.

Essential Questions

- Q How are we able to communicate when our responses and interactions are not error free?

Q Why does unpredictability matter?

Q To what extent can we operate with partial competence and still make meaning?

Q Does non-nativeness make sense?

Q To what extent is the learner compelled to express meaning through a task?

Q Why does what I can say matter more than how I say it?

Q What does practice at spontaneity and improvisation look like?

Key Terms and Concepts

Interpersonal Mode	Improvisation
Spontaneous	Consensus

Research in Practice

The work of the following researchers and practitioners will guide you to cite sources which inform your planning, assessment and instructional decisions in pre-service portfolio assessments or in-service professional learning plans.

Lantolf & Appel, 1994	Learners need to talk about texts to construct meaning from them, not merely to answer comprehension questions about them.
Heathcote & Bolton, 1995 Kao & O'Neill, 1998 Piazzoli, 2010 Sawyer, 2003 Schewe, 2013	Drama Pedagogy develops improvisational skills in world language education.

Kramsch, 1994, 2008	We use language for social interaction and to interpret meaning through mediation. Language should not be separated from language use.
Lapkin & Swain, 2004	When we speak with each other to solve problems in the language, it facilitates and mediates learning.
Vygotsky, 1986	Learners speak in order to organize, mediate and negotiate for cognitive as well as social purposes.
VanPatten, 2003, 2010; VanPatten & Rothman, 2015; Wong & VanPatten, 2003	Drill practice of forms and rules has little impact on acquisition. Output should be meaning-based, negotiated and interactive.

I can

- Describe and explain Interpersonal tasks for negotiating meaning and mediation
- Differentiate task types from AATT exemplars
- Design key performance tasks in the Interpersonal mode across different levels for articulation
- Develop PASS Can-Dos for this mode aligning to intercultural transfer goals

> **Rewind**
> Which key terms or concepts stand out for you from Chapter 4, *Designing for Interpretive goals: Exploring meaning for mediation*?
> Ask your colleague three questions based on the content from the last chapter.
> Explain the most compelling idea from the previous chapter in your own words.
> Explain how this concept or practice is the same, similar or different to what you know or do.
> Which concept or practice do you think will have the greatest impact on your teaching?

Overview

As you have gathered thus far, our curriculum unfolds intercultural themes through these performance assessments with a focus on meaning, rather than forms. It is not that language structures and vocabulary do not occur within tasks. As discussed, the instructor has a very clear idea what grammar and lexicon are needed after you design the tasks. Acquisition and ownership of language is not the purview of textbooks, the teacher or graded language structures and functions artificially sequenced on curricula, materials, units and scopes of work. What bears repeating here is that to fully realize a curriculum where the learner is an active agent, we must focus on the learner and what they *do* with content. Learners do not own language by intentional practice on forms and repeated sentences merely posturing as language knowledge; they acquire language while they are busy doing something else with it. The Interpretive mode is an exchange between the person and text; the quality and quantity of input and what the learner does with it is the most important factor for what comes next. The learner analyses, explores, questions and makes meaning from texts steeped in content. The Presentational mode gives one the luxury of time and distance, to prepare spoken or refine written communication as we move our thoughts and notions out of spontaneity. This chapter focuses on what we do within that spontaneity. Do we still make and co-create meaning with someone else albeit not perfectly? What practices move us forward in mediation for transfer?

Interpersonal-Interactive mode as consensus

The *Interpersonal* mode is one of the standards within the goal area of Communication (National Standards Collaborative Board, 2015): 'Learners interact and negotiate meaning in spontaneous, spoken, visual or written communication to exchange information and express feelings, preferences and opinions.' In this mode, learners make decisions with each other and exchange information immediately. They can do so in person, on a phone or video call, or text. In the real world we always use many resources to make sense of what we hear, watch or read. We not only do this alone, but we make new meaning for ourselves as we plan, choose, decide and negotiate with others in collaboration. For that reason, it is communication for *consensus*.

Designing for the Interpersonal Goal

> For the AATTs and ICANADAPT, this mode:
>
> - Details a productive, improvisational, interactive, and cooperative exchange between two or more people.
> - Engages the learner to interact and negotiate intercultural meaning from input.
> - Helps learners plan, choose, get more information and come to consensus with each other to solve a problem and eventually yield a novel product.

For the Interpersonal-Interactive mode, learners

- Use repertoire gathered from the Interpretive mode
- Ask and answer questions with other people
- Interact and react to texts, concepts and images with them
- Plan, choose, decide and come to consensus

In order to design tasks in the Interpersonal mode well, one needs to address the one quality in its definition that sets it apart from the others: spontaneous. When something is *spontaneous*, it means the act is unrehearsed. It also means that it can happen without any external stimulus; it just appears out of the blue, on impulse. Although this may occur, I believe the actual act for most of our interpersonal communication experiences with someone else is more aptly defined as *improvisation*. Although both spontaneity and improvisation involve no preparation ahead of time with the terms appearing similar, not all spontaneous acts are improvisation. The distinction is actually quite important. Improvisation is our *reaction* to input from a partner, group or text. Every interaction, whether personal or professional, is an improvisational scene. This involves co-creating conversation and for that to happen, it requires focused listening to another person and mediation is a key part of that. When we are speaking with anyone, we are constantly in the act of improvisation. Even though there may be a subject matter or issue at hand for either one or more parties, you are reacting in real time, with no script. Even if you have notes in front of you for a meeting, your collaborative exchange is still improvised. That is truly the crux of the matter; we *react*. For Interpersonal or Interactive communication, we are reacting, moment by moment, every minute. Communication does not only consist of ideas you share as you react to your own thoughts, but also about your reaction to what you are immediately hearing or watching. Those are truly unanticipated. That is why the input we receive is so important. We are constantly improvising, every moment we respond and react to that input in real time.

Steven Pinker (2003) said, 'Whenever you speak to someone, you are presuming the two of you have a certain degree of familiarity – which your words might alter. So, every sentence has to do two things at once: convey a message and continue to negotiate that relationship' (p. 283). The Interpersonal tasks ask learners to improvise, to create content on their feet. The fact is we never really know what someone is going to say back to us once we engage in conversation. This exchange involves negotiation of meaning, the give and take. In order to do this well, one must have frequent experiences with improvisation. Teacher candidates or trainees often observe classes where learners prepare skits or role plays with memorized lines of dialogue or at least, extensive notes or prompts on cards. Memorized skits or prepared role play in that traditional sense are not Interpersonal mode tasks because learners are not negotiating meaning or improvising. They are also scripted and that is not the reality of Interpersonal communication either. When learners write and perform a skit, they have created a play. When learners create a video, then their script is a screenplay perhaps, but it still does not meet the criteria for this mode. It is fine if pupils write and perform this kind of play, just please to understand its limitations and the purpose for doing it. Writing and performing a play is a good Presentational mode task in an appropriate context, which we will discuss further in the next chapter. The Interpersonal-Interactive mode extends meaning by negotiating and mediating it with someone else. This occurs first from input gathered in the Interpretive mode task. Once again, it is important in assessment and instruction to make opportunities for new meaning every day. This ensures your learners can use what they know flexibly in new and unanticipated situations they will encounter when using the language in the real world.

Table 5.1 outlines characteristics of the Interpersonal-Interactive mode in the AATT and ICANADAPT design model and presents non-examples.

Table 5.1 What Interpersonal-Interactive Is and Is not

What Interpersonal-Interactive IS	What Interpersonal-Interactive is NOT
Improvised exchanges between two or more people	Rehearsed or memorized dialogues, role-plays, skits
Focus on meaning on what is said rather than how	Focus on accuracy with grammar forms

Plan, decide, come to consensus together on task	Taking turns reciting from written materials.
Asking and answering questions with partner developed from the Interpretive mode information	Asking and answering scripted textbook questions out loud
Facilitate, contribute and develop intercultural exchanges for situations, concepts and contexts	Skill practice isolated from intercultural situations, contexts and mediation strategies

Pause to ponder

What characteristics have you noticed for the Interpersonal-Interactive mode tasks? What does this mode do on its own and in concert with the others? Do any of the characteristics in either column above surprise you? Consider these descriptions while reviewing and designing tasks and share thoughts with a colleague.

A closer look at improvisation for the inevitable unexpected

Improvisation is at the heart of Interpersonal mode. Improvisational strategies show us how to adjust, elaborate, and extend the conversation with our response. In order to fully realize curriculum design for intercultural communicative competence, it must include tasks with strategies that listen fully to another person, accept what is offered and then build from it. Improv is genuine language-making because it values the unpredictable. It also recognizes the true nature of teaching should be adjustment rather than fixed scripts, inflexible plans and routines which do not prepare people for inevitable risk taking and how to respond to that unexpected. Many improvisational strategies are influenced by Drama Pedagogy.

The Process Drama (Heathcote & Bolton, 1995; Even, 2008, 2016; Johnstone, 2012; Kao & O'Neill, 1998; O' Neill, 1995; O'Toole, 1992; Rothwell, 2011; Sawyer, 2003; Van Lier, 2010; Wagner, 2002) form contrasts with theatre which traditionally is prepared for an audience. Previously, we used the example of skits as not indicative of the Interpersonal mode. Rehearsed skits and scripted plays constitute theatre. Process Drama is improvised and exists for its participants with no performance for an external audience (Manuel, Hughes, Anderson & Arnold, 2008). Negotiation of meaning takes on particular significance in Process Drama with the ability to create knowledge through the drama (O'Toole, 1992). Improvisation or improv is a discipline that follows forms and practices to enable co-creation between its participants. It is perfect for language learning because it expects differentiation and novelty, new iterations every time which support transfer. Improv is at the heart of collaboration, meaning-making and response because it assumes connection to people within the classroom community and outside of it. In our world language discipline, that connection within a community is oft forgotten where patterns and rules with expected perfection create a lonely learner who is risk-averse.

Drama Pedagogy and Aesthetic Education look at the process of questioning and meaning-making and where learners describe, analyse and elaborate through intentional questions, connecting learners to a larger concept or goal in the text (Dawson and Lee, 2018; Dawson, Cawthon & Baker, 2011; Eisner, 2002). In the previous chapter we discussed the importance of forming questions in the Interpretive mode rather than always answering them. When a learner forms questions from a text, a whole different process is engaged. The learner also becomes active, rather than passive. This requires a shift on the part of the teacher to encourage a classroom culture of risk taking rather than avoidance (Galton, 2008). The teacher needs to be silent and not always ask the questions. The learner must extend and pose the questions in the Interpersonal mode, starting with simple ones at the Novice level. Questioning must begin at Novice to develop flexibility and confidence early and not wait until a higher level that may not come if the learner does not take up or continue language classes. Asking questions and not merely answering them is a characteristic of the Intermediate level of proficiency or CEFR A2-B1 (ACTFL, 2012; COE, 2020); the learner cannot get out of Novice without it. Proper questioning allows them to negotiate, develop mediation strategies and manage incomplete, ambiguous and imperfect bits for their reaction.

When one truly thinks about it, our profession created an artificial construct with memorization for a finite world which never was. It created the environment for mistakes and perfection which is not the nature of authentic language use. One cannot make a mistake with improvisation. One may forget lines in a script and therefore make a mistake with them. In improv that is not the case but there is no script in authentic language anyway. It is all about improv. The imperfections of improvisation contribute to the value of an authentic exchange. There isn't a one right way in improvisation, and just as anything could happen in real language use, so it is with improv. It is ideal for the transition from Interpretive to Interpersonal, because deep listening and response in this way supports our learners to connect and mediate better. This is particularly helpful in light of the fact we have so much technology to connect us yet are increasingly isolated. In addition, at the heart of improvisation is novelty, which serves the learner well for transfer and creating either the spoken or written Presentational mode task.

Language accessible and perspectives visible

Improvisation is a dynamic relationship between teacher and students. Rather than presenting grammar or providing knowledge, the teacher engages with the learners to discover, uncover, share and create content. It is the essence of authentic language use and transfer. Improv as a disciplined practice and art form validates every member in the class, every culture and background.

When we incorporate Process Drama and Aesthetic Education strategies, it enhances the capacity of the learner to construct meaning, solve problems and make decisions within a range of social situations (Cunico, 2005). This process allows the teacher and subsequently the language learner to explore ideas through multiple points of view (Holzer, 2005), adapt to unknowns and be flexible to them. The learner then creates performance tasks to inquire into cultural practices and perspectives and explore its message through other transdisciplinary texts (Eddy, 2006b, 2019b). In releasing the Imagination, Greene (1996) states, "To help kids shape their identity, we've got to awaken them to their own questions and encourage them to shape their identity, we've got to awaken them to their own questions and encourage them to create their own projects. They don't really learn unless they ask" (p. 22).

The improvisational nature of this mode lends itself quite well to using drama for exploring different works of art and texts, including literature. 'This mode can occur between two or more people and involves an exchange to solve an information gap, coming to consensus, planning or decision making.' The negotiation of meaning takes on particular significance in the treatment here of Process Drama and the ability to create their own knowledge through the drama (Baldwin, 2012; O'Toole, 1992). Again, we examine the Capacities of Imaginative Learning (Eddy, 2019b; Greene, 2001; Holzer, 2007) adapted for the Interpersonal mode: Exhibiting Empathy, Living with Ambiguity and Making Connections.

Exhibiting Empathy respects diverse perspectives and understands the experiences of others. 'Yes, and…'Is a Process Drama technique that allows the learner to accept what their partner proposes but immediately retort with Yes…and. Then the partner responds and contributes to the discussion. It helps to build confidence and guide the risk-averse to not be afraid to speak up, a positive attribute whether in the first or another language. 'To accept different ideas and viewpoints in the tasks for One Lucky Day, the technique 'Yes, and...' (Farmer, 2007) asks one student to make a statement and another to listen and offer an idea, Exhibiting Empathy' (Eddy, 2019b, p. 54).

Living with Ambiguity understands that there is more than one interpretation and solutions will not be immediate or clear and can change quickly. The Interpersonal mode adapts Forum Theatre (Boal, 1982, 1992) and Playback Theatre (Feldhendler, 2007; Fox, 2003; Salas, 1996, 2006). These forms practiced in class give people a voice by telling their personal stories or discussing challenging community issues as a tool for social change. The group or individual experiences their story re-enacted and played back through someone else using intentional listening and improvised drama. Learners can also improvise conversation as characters in various stories and texts, suspending their identity to immerse more fully in the experiences of a fictional character (Kingsbury-Brunetto, 2015). For example, a pair or small group are in improvised conversation in the Interpersonal task or in a prepared role play as in the case of a Presentational mode task; the other pupils watch. Learners become 'Spect-Actors' (Boal, 1992). Anyone watching can say 'Stop,' freeze the action, take the place of the protagonist or another character, halt the action and offer another solution. This either continues improvisation and dialogue further but can also initiate improv within a Presentational mode role play. The constant change and flux are good for adapting and Living with Ambiguity. Learners must become flexible and facilitative when the plurilingual and pluricultural contexts we believe that we understand can and will change and the reasons are not apparent or obvious.

Making Connections allows you to notice and align prior knowledge, backgrounds and experiences with others, as well as to other texts. For "let me ask you..." students use the questions they developed in the Interpretive mode to ask a character, author, actor, or director. 'In this way, the learner Makes Connections to the knowledge and experiences of others, giving value to different perspectives and the community expertise that emerges from engagement with the work' (Eddy, 2019b, p. 55). Negotiation of meaning and coming to a consensus tasks allow learners to co-create their own knowledge collaboratively through the drama (O'Toole, 1992). Poster Dialogue (Dawson & Lee, 2018) allows for collective knowledge and reflection with others in response to images, symbols and words and open-ended prompts. After this Interpersonal quick writing task, learners do a gallery walk to elaborate, clarify, question and respond in mediation with other pupils on their posters in small groups.

These strategies train the learner for mediation to facilitate communication in pluricultural space, sensitive situations, social justice themes and to navigate communication when there are different points of view. The goal of the Interpersonal mode is improvisation; interactive exchange and mediation. The learner makes the language accessible and perspective visible with someone else, even if that starts with gesture, single words, images or phrase, awaiting another novel response.

Teacher as Designer

Dr Maxine Greene (2009) explores 'what it means to have an aesthetic experience, focusing on new possibilities and novel creations. She talks about what it means to enter the created world, the fictive world: the literary world. Greene says the work of art cannot reveal itself automatically but must be uncovered with questions. The learner must be engaged in a line of inquiry about the work and pose questions. She concludes that Aesthetic Education focuses on the unanswerable and leaves us with the question, Why?' (Eddy, 2019b, p. 48). The aesthetics of any culture, its beliefs, icons, traditions and history are essential to a culture's identity. Dr Greene affirmed that the Aesthetic Education 'is the intentional undertaking designed to nurture appreciative, reflective, cultural, participatory engagements with the arts by enabling learners to notice what there is to be noticed, and to lend works of art their lives in such a way that they can achieve them as variously meaningful. When this happens, new connections are made in experience: new patterns are formed, new vistas are opened' (2001, p.6). One of the goals of the aesthetic educational process is to engage teachers actively and continuously with a work of art, linking relationships between it and other human experiences, including social, historical and cultural contexts (Greene, 1995).

Voices from the Field

I am thankful to teacher Soojin Choi Kim, author of the *Arirang* exemplar in Chapter 4, who shared the cultural history and voice of the people behind the powerful work of Hyun Jin-geon with me and guided me on the design of these tasks. This short story explores themes of poverty and isolation, painful choices, conflicts, despair, denial and loss of control. One Lucky Day (Hyun,

1924; O'Rourke, 2014) is set against the backdrop of Japanese occupation of Korea. These themes characterized many peoples' lives at that time, living hand to mouth just trying to survive during this colonial period.

In *One Lucky Day*, Kim Cheomji is a rickshaw driver barely existing in an increasingly modern Seoul. With effects of modernity all around them, Kim and his ill wife live in impoverished conditions, barely able to sustain themselves and unable to control their general condition or their world around them.

Raw, unrelenting rain and dismal colours bring the reader into Kim's life and into many other lives in this city. Kim makes the painful decision to leave his very sick wife to go to work, as she pleads that he not leave her alone. The driving rain brings him many fares for his rickshaw and so he can buy the bone broth soup his wife requested. Upon returning home, he finds her dead clutching their child.

Tragic irony with universal, timeless themes of loss, pain, and devastating choices are drawn from this work. Through engagement with different elements in this text, teachers and learners develop sustained, participatory sequences of interactive, creative transfer tasks so that others can process the story through small works of art.

How does Hyun Jin-geon use imagery and language to reveal emotions, context, and irony in *One Lucky Day*?

Dr Jennifer Eddy, Queens College, City University of New York

Reprinted from Eddy, J. (2019b) Literature and Drama for Transfer in Diamantidaki, F. (ed). Teaching Literature in Modern Foreign Languages.

Table 5.2 Articulated Assessment Transfer Task   One Lucky Day

One Lucky Day, **Story by Hyun Jin-geon 현진건, 1924.**   **Jennifer Eddy** How does Hyun Jin-geon use imagery and language to reveal emotions and irony in *One Lucky Day*?
Enduring Understandings ∗ Conditions beyond one's control may lead to painful, difficult dilemmas and choices. ∗ Fortunate circumstances may not always lead to positive outcomes.
Essential Questions ? To what extent can we control life events? ? What determines our decisions? ? How can irony teach us life's lessons?

Context
A museum curator plans an intercultural exhibit on relationships and choices in difficult times of pain, poverty and incomprehensible loss. Participants will interact with various works of art and texts.

Articulation Spiral Points
- Categorize words with images for the story.
- Elaborate in role of character.
- Create interactive museum storyboard exhibit.
- Modify story and change outcome.
- Develop poetry design space for museum.

Intercultural Transfer Targets	**Mediation for Transfer**
• I can connect my emotional response with a literary character from another culture. • I can identify examples of irony in my own and other cultures. • I can exhibit empathy for someone else's circumstances. • I can write a poem or song as response to the culture's story.	• Bridge and exchange ideas and concepts of irony in literary works. • Explain and compare familiar examples of irony in different texts to someone. • Use visuals and movement to convey meaning in the story. • Elaborate meaning by composing a new artform.

Novice High	**Intermediate High**	**Advanced Mid**
Interpretive Task Descriptions		
Living poetry: Learners use themes from the story to write two or three words associated with that theme. Next, use the body to make an object linked to that concept. In small groups, use the movements and the associated words to create a body poem. The class guesses the theme, and categorizes the words with images on a graphic organizer. Ex: Poverty-sad, work, money, tired.	Pose question: Learners create still images or use those from the animated video to write single words and one question to a character.	Drawing dance: Learners recall an event or series of events in their life when they experienced an extreme emotion that changed quickly to an opposite emotion. Draw simple line and shapes to describe event. Use the drawing to move, using space to tell the story. Students write the emotions and story.

Can Dos		
I can identify and categorize words from the story.	I can write questions based on images and scenes.	I can make inferences and elaborate meaning from images and movement.
Interpersonal Task Descriptions		
Yes, and: Using words and themes from the One Lucky Day, the student makes a statement and their partner says Yes, and… and offers an idea. Ex: I have to work. Yes, and you need money. Students share what Kim does that day and why.	Let me ask you: In groups of four or five, each student takes on one character in the story. Each person can ask only one question to the other character in Korean. Ex: "why did you go to work on that day?" Students write words and phrases from a group on a chart.	Forum Theatre: Students receive images and scenes from the story and role play with partners using words and phrases from the story. Any student outside the group can stop the action and take the place of a character to change the outcome.
Can Dos		
I can share decisions with my partner choices and compare mine with my partner and the character.	I can interview a character and respond with empathy.	I can modify a story using words, phrases and emotions.
Presentational Task Descriptions		
Students create a thought tunnel by recording advice accompanied by a visual. The museum participant walks through listening to suggestions or advice, then is prompted to consider a decision.	Storyboard: Design a storyboard with photos or drawings depicting scenes from One Lucky Day. Develop two new scenes not in the story as alternatives. Compose lines for each. Museum participants will use and recombine separate scenes with words and visuals depicting different dilemmas and situations in relationships and life to develop a personal story.	Poetry Participation: Students write a poem based on One Lucky Day keeping the goal of dramatic irony and the unexpected in mind for a multimedia presentation. Alternatively, students can write song lyrics. Using words and phrases from the work and alternative choices provided on separate cards, museum participants are invited to create their own poem as a response.

Can Dos		
I can recommend choices and design an exhibit.	I can compose a new story with alternative endings from multiple perspectives.	I can create a poem and create a poetry design space.

Adapted from Eddy, J. (2019b). Literature and Drama for Transfer. In F. Diamantidaki, (Ed.), Teaching Literature in Modern Foreign Languages. London: Bloomsbury Academic.

> ### Bridge to Design
> Let's go deeper into this design process and collaborate with colleagues for additional ideas and reflection on this exemplar before working on your own design.
>
> (See Appendix U in Companion Website Chapter 5.)

Plan, choose, come to consensus: Poise over perfection

Questioning is the first step to making learned language social and shared. As important as it is to understand what this mode is, it is equally important to understand what it is not. Interpersonal mode tasks are not turn-taking or reading sentences out loud from the textbook or notebook, or reading the answers aloud from questions posed from the textbook or teacher. Learners need to collaborate to create meaning, encourage conceptual thought and facilitate interaction. This is important for learners beyond the classroom in the world of work. Our learners need to organize a plan, elaborate on thoughts and ask their own questions, not just answer them. This is why the questions they ask each other must not yield answers that are already known. This is to say that there is only so much basic personal information one can ask since your learners most likely already know these facts about their classmates. This mode prepares learners to get new information from someone else to act either alone or with another person to move forward on an idea in a creative way. The text and images they receive in the Interpretive mode present enough for learners to ask questions and engage with someone else about something *new and beyond themselves*. The best Interpersonal tasks are those that facilitate the preparation of the Presentational task.

From the novice level, learners can plan, choose and come to consensus. Initially the tasks consist of simple dichotomies, like or dislike, safe or unsafe, yes to include or not, healthy or not, etc. Please remember your Interpretive mode tasks include visuals and images as well as verbal texts. Learners will use these to extend meaning with peers and to plan together, decide, and come to consensus. This is an important strategy for mediation, because we need to be able to do this every day with colleagues at work (COE, 2020). These tasks support compromise, negotiation, consensus, and resolution to solve problems. They also learn to adjust and clarify what they say, based on their observations and reactions. Your learners will have any graphic organizers, tools, and images from their Interpretive mode tasks at hand. Graphic organizers and images provide visual and linguistic support. They not only communicate meaning to us directly from the culture, but also are catalysts for further communication with others. Images stimulate communication about the concept and clarify meaning even if learners cannot talk a lot about the image yet. Van Patten (2003, 2010; VanPatten & Rothman, 2015) says that output in this mode should be meaning-based, negotiated and active. In the Interpersonal mode, learners are active in mediation with the image, even if it is at word or phrase level and they may not have all the words to explain everything yet.

Even at a novice level, one can make language accessible to someone else, who does not expect perfection either. Everyone reading this book most likely is a second language learner. People communicate with partial competence and still make meaning, all the time. The native speaker as an ideal and the norm presents a deficit model and is not useful for use in world language instruction and learning (Cook & Wei, 2016; Davies, 2003; Holliday, 2006; Ortega, 2019). It is important to describe a scale of proficiency (ACTFL, 2012; COE, 2020; NCSSFL, 2017) to indicate to what extent someone can use language across modalities in authentic contexts. We must accept the fact that there is flexibility along this continuum and that competence changes, it shifts and is mercurial. Successful mediation is the norm whereas classifying your language or cultural competence to an unrealistic level of accuracy is not.

One characteristic of higher proficiency is how the speaker fares or copes with a complication. At the lower levels, the speaker can handle simple and smooth situations. It is important, however, to provide learners with small complications they can solve with each other as soon as possible. There needs to be a wrinkle of some kind, a limitation, or small problem built into various Interpersonal mode task prompts. Perhaps they have a budget limit, or they must choose three to four of something from a longer list and therefore must negotiate and compromise. Maybe they can discover suddenly they cannot do something with that time frame or what they want is not available. Any of those scenarios provides just the right amount of challenge for the pair or group to discuss again and solve the problem. This is important at all levels of proficiency and should not wait until Advanced. Learners need to solve small problems along the way with familiar contexts and develop facility with it rather than wait for unfamiliar territory to try their hand.

Check for learning

The Interpersonal mode is the collaborative outcome of the meaning-based tasks from the Interpretive mode. Consider some examples below; see the possibilities for problem-solving, clarification through mediation, and making words and concepts accessible to someone else. Take some notes first before you design tasks for this mode and your AATT and ICANADAPT unit.

Table 5.3 Interpersonal Mode Sampler

Novice	Intermediate	Advanced
Decide with a partner from images which are best to include. Ask questions to compare lists of foods from images	Ask questions and come to consensus to include and suggest with someone else's needs in mind. 'Yes, and…'	Discuss pros and cons of health practices, beliefs and products past and present. Ask questions (How did, if…then?
Choose with a partner as you ask likes and dislikes. 'Yes, and….'	Plan a storyboard together with a sequence of events.	Choose with a partner and explain why. 'Yes, and…'

Exchange similarities and differences with your peers as you create a Venn diagram.	Compare products or practices between two or more cultures using a Likert scale	Debate an issue and come to consensus or not on practices, rules and norms
Accept or reject choices: ideas, words or images to use for later task	Negotiate who does what for a project; collaborate on a shared task	Explain a plan, unfamiliar perspective or suggest a novel approach
Pick and choose from a list	Tweet a response.	Recount an event with peers using notes

Teacher as Designer

Dr Pat Lennon is mentor, professor and university site supervisor to Queens College teacher candidates. With the experience of being supervisor for a school district in MFL, she brings wisdom to our new teachers on administrator's expectations, as well as lifting them up and giving them confidence in often difficult circumstances. This AATT explores social justice across three themes for a spiral curriculum: bullying, human rights and racism.

Bullying can occur throughout the lifespan and includes verbal, emotional, social, physical, passive-aggressive and cyber-bullying. Bullies work alone or in social groups in school or work and professional settings referred to as 'mobbing', subjecting someone to unrelenting, often tacit and private abuse so that the victim has no choice but to leave the group or organization, if they even can. Bullies shame their victims into silence to maintain their innocence, superiority, misuse of power, control or position. This exemplar builds a vocabulary base and explores the problems through the lens of other cultures and their stance and awareness initiatives. The themes of family values and human rights expand to compare these initiatives between countries and cultures. Finally, learners listen to Rigoberta Menchú and collaborate together on activities and presentations at their booth for Human Rights Day.

In these Interpersonal tasks, learners work with others to question, plan and come to a consensus on what to create for the Presentational mode task. They can organize words and concepts and explain it to others, elaborating texts with questions and comments. These tasks guide learners to convey relevant information to others and work collaboratively in simple, shared tasks. These tasks bring learners toward mediation for transfer.

Voices from the Field

The topic of Social Justice must be addressed in our curriculum at all levels to educate our learners about treating others with respect. Although this topic would seem appropriate for upper levels, it is addressed on the novice level as in this AATT.

The topic of bullying and social interactions should be addressed starting with the novice level. As students move to the intermediate level, they will use the vocabulary and grammar already learned to express more advanced concepts about family values and politics.

At the novice level, a popular song in Spanish, "*Soy yo*" (Bomba Estéreo, 2015), shows a young Hispanic girl who is experiencing bullying, but because of her strong self-esteem, she is able to deal with others who are bullying her. For the Intermediate Level, the students read an infographic on family values, which they can discuss and then create their own infographic to share with the class. For the Advanced Level, students watch a video about the human rights activist, Rigoberta Menchú. The students can relate what they learn about Rigoberta Menchú to others who fight for human rights in their own country and throughout the world.

The Novice learner can relate to bullying because it is an issue that many encounter today in school, work, online and in their neighbourhoods. DASA, The Dignity for All Students Act in New York, requires training for teachers, staff and students to help combat the problem.

This is a very important topic for students of all age groups and should be included in all levels of language instruction (novice-advanced). Incorporating lessons on social justice, beginning at the novice level, will help to familiarize students with the topic as it develops higher level thinking skills across levels.

Dr Patricia Lennon, Queens College, CUNY. Retired district supervisor, Sewanhaka Public Schools, NY.

Table 5.4 Articulated Assessment Transfer Task Social Justice: Bullying, Human Rights, Racism

Dr Patricia Lennon, Queens College, CUNY	Spanish
Enduring Understandings * Treating others with respect and understanding positively impacts social justice. * Bullying can occur across the lifespan. * Education can make a positive impact on social justice with action to make better communities. * Words and actions have the power to hurt or heal.	
Essential Questions ? How do our actions support or undermine academic, social and emotional growth? ? Why do people misuse real or imagined power, control or position? ? How does the world see you, and how do you see the world? ? How does lack of respect and understanding affect social justice?	
Context Your community is sponsoring a Human Rights Day. Each club at your school is creating a presentation for the event. You will present for the Spanish Club.	
Articulation Spiral Points @ Edpuzzle or flipgrid video on personal characteristics and qualities. @ Infographic on bullying and social justice. @ Events schedule for Human Rights Day.	

Intercultural Transfer Targets	**Mediation for Transfer**
• I can identify examples of bullying. • I can compare examples of social injustice in my culture with that in other cultures. • I can explain family values in Spanish-speaking countries to someone unfamiliar with these perspectives. • I can collaborate with a partner to discuss human rights issues in Guatemala and other countries.	• Bridge and exchange ideas and concepts on social justice issues with others. • Explain messages on social justice, racism and bullying in a variety of texts. • Recognize the feelings and different points of view of others. • Clarify words and examples related to social justice and bullying in the language for others. • Form questions and feedback to encourage others to clarify and elaborate their opinions.

	- Can give simple, clear instructions to organize an activity. - Collaborate to clarify human rights issues between countries. - Paraphrase main points and details on social justice issues for others.

Authentic Materials		
Bomba Estéreo – Soy Yo (Official Video) – YouTube Bomba Estéreo – Soy Yo Lyrics English and Spanish – Translation & Meaning – I am me – YouTube Anti-Bullying Español – YouTube	Bomba Estéreo – Soy Yo (Official Video) – YouTube Bomba Estéreo – Soy Yo Lyrics English and Spanish – Translation & Meaning – I am me – YouTube Anti-Bullying Español – YouTube	Bomba Estéreo – Soy Yo (Official Video) – YouTube Bomba Estéreo – Soy Yo Lyrics English and Spanish – Translation & Meaning – I am me – YouTube Anti-Bullying Español –I YouTube

Novice High	Intermediate High	Advanced Low
Interpretive Task Descriptions		
Watch the video 'Soy Yo' and answer questions embedded in Edpuzzle. What would you ask her? Write two questions. Read the infographics on workplace bullying and mobbing. Using a graphic organizer, list key words and examples, then write two questions about these texts.	Watch the videos on human rights. Categorize the details and write two questions for each. Compare the concepts presented in the videos. Read the infographic on family values and social justice, identify two concepts and pose two questions.	Watch the video of Rigoberta Menchú and write five questions you would ask her. Paraphrase this interview, using annotations and examples.
Can Dos		
I can identify the main idea of the video and list words that describe the girl's outlook and mindset. I can list and categorize words and phrases about bullying.	I can express and compare two concepts about human rights and social justice and form questions using text materials.	I can form five questions on racism based on the interview. I can elaborate by paraphrasing and using illustrative examples.

Interpersonal Task Descriptions		
Students speak with a partner about the characteristics, mindset and stance of the girl. Share your questions with your partner on her outlook and what she does that is positive. Ask the questions about bullying. In response, say 'yes, and…' adding another characteristic or example of bullying. Compare school and workplace bullying. How are the efforts to combat bullying the same or different in your culture or country?	Come to consensus with a partner on two concepts of social justice and human rights, comparing between two cultures or countries. How has it changed? Plan and decide together what to include in the presentation or video for Human Rights Day.	Come to consensus with your partner about examples of racism and its consequences. Explain with examples to clarify her points. What key points will you include in the activities and materials for Human Rights Day? What will visitors to your booth do?
Can Dos		
I can discuss personal characteristics with descriptive words on outlook and attitude. I can compare bullying in two settings using words and simple phrases.	I can discuss the two concepts that I learned about human rights and social justice with my partner.	I can explain and clarify examples of racism and its consequences to my partner.
Presentational Task Descriptions		
Design a video about your personal characteristics of strength for the Human Rights presentation on bullying. Write a personal four-line lyric for a new stanza of 'Soy Yo.'	Create a video, poster, drawing or a slide presentation about human rights and social justice to share at Human Rights Day.	Create a series of activities and materials for your club's presentation on Human Rights Day.

Can Dos		
I can create video song lyrics using words and phrases of my personal characteristics and strength.	I can express my ideas and opinions about human rights and social justice using multimedia texts.	I can deliver organized presentations using different media on Human Rights concerns.

Bridge to Design

Let's talk about Dr Lennon's exemplar and collaborate with colleagues for additional ideas and reflection on this exemplar before working on your own design.

(See Appendix V in Companion Website Chapter 5.)

Collaboration for Articulation

A colleague at your school wants learners only to answer her questions in class or ask and answer ones from a textbook. You notice they are answering them with simple substitution, but not really understanding what they are saying. What would you say to the colleague? How can you explain Questioning and why it is important as an active learner and mediator in language?

Teacher as Designer

Urdu instructor Romeena Kureishy develops performance assessments for learners across levels to elaborate and clarify practices and products through the values and perspectives of the Eid celebration. How do people celebrate across the globe? Have celebrations changed over time? Are there two sides to how technology has influenced the way we celebrate? How has technology impacted celebrations in different cultures? The Interpersonal tasks in this exemplar highlight cultural practices today and encourage learners to present ideas in a group, pose questions and build upon one another's information for further discussion.

Voices from the Field

Eid is a celebration with family, neighbours and friends. It brings people together. Food is a constant presence. All cultures have similar celebrations and it is very easy to connect with other cultures and their celebrations. Even a novice learner can identify items associated with Eid and compare how they celebrate something with Eid celebrations in Pakistan. They can create presentations such as a poster or an infographic about things associated with Eid.

The concept of celebrations is very important to teach for interculturality as it bundles together Perspectives, Practices and Products in the most authentic way. In the example of Eid, the foods, clothing, henna and the practice of giving 'Eidi' or 'Eid Milna' (Eid hug) or putting 'Mehendi' (Henna) the night before Eid, showcase the products, practices and the perspectives that influence them. Students can then carry the language and culture learned to other content areas easily.

Romeena Kureishy, Urdu instructor.

NYU STARTALK Urdu-Hindi Teacher Program and Kean STARTALK Hindi Urdu Student Program, NJ.

Table 5.5 Articulated Assessment Transfer Task Celebration of Eid

NYU-STARTALK Romeena Kureishy Urdu-Hindi Teacher Program	Urdu
Enduring Understandings * Eid celebrations and certain practices have changed over time.	

Designing for the Interpersonal Goal

Essential Questions
? How has technology influenced the practices associated with Eid?

Context
A cultural website is looking for content on 'The changing trends of Eid'.

Articulation Spiral Points
@ Use visuals to describe items associated with Eid.
@ Create a video to compare Eid celebrations.
@ Describe changes to celebrations across generations via multimedia tools.

Intercultural Transfer Targets	**Mediation for Transfer**
• I can identify ways people celebrate holidays or festivals. • I can promote globalized practices, outlining similarities and differences. • I can compare Eid with other practices and the perspectives which inform them. • I can explain how and why celebrations may change.	• Bridge and exchange ideas and concepts of Eid to others. • Identify visuals and products associated with Eid. • Explain changes and influence of technology on celebrations. • Convey main points about Eid with similarities and differences. • Contribute and support intercultural exchange on values and practices.

Novice High	Intermediate High	Advanced Mid
Interpretive Task Descriptions		
Students watch a PPT on Eid and list all the things associated with celebrating Eid in Pakistan.	Students watch a video on how people celebrate Eid in Pakistan and list all the ways people celebrate Eid.	Students read an article on how the practices of Eid celebrations have changed over the last generation. They identify some main reasons for these changing trends.

Can Dos		
I can identify and list items associated with Eid celebrations in Pakistan.	I can write the ways people celebrate Eid in Pakistan.	I can identify the changing trends in Eid celebrations in Pakistan.
Interpersonal Task Descriptions		
In pairs students ask each other what they celebrate. They find similarities and differences between Eid and what they celebrate.	Students ask each other the best way to celebrate a festival and come up with the top three things to do.	Students interview parents and grandparents to ask how celebrations have changed over time for their own families. Students compare responses with a partner and identify three biggest changes.
Can Dos		
I can compare the celebration of Eid with something I celebrate.	I can exchange information on the best things to do to celebrate Eid/festival.	I can exchange information on celebrations that have changed in my family with a peer.
Presentational Task Descriptions		
Students create an infographic on Eid celebration.	Students create a video presentation of the various ways people celebrate Eid in Pakistan.	Students create an interactive webpage showcasing how technology has changed the way we celebrate Eid.
Can Dos		
I can create an infographic with basic information about things associated with Eid celebrations.	I can create a video showing the various ways people celebrate Eid in Pakistan.	I can research and present how Eid celebrations have changed over time.

Designing for the Interpersonal Goal 189

Bridge to Design

Let's go deeper into Ms Kureishy's design process and collaborate with colleagues for additional ideas and reflection on this exemplar before working on your own design.

(See Appendix W in Companion Website Chapter 5.)

Check for learning

For your ICANADAPT unit and AATT, consider these tasks below that all feature collaboration and working together on an issue.

Table 5.6 Collaboration Sampler

Novice 0-A1.1	Intermediate A1.2-B1.2	Advanced B2.1-C1.1
Choose and come to consensus with a partner between two or more items or practices	Ask questions written from the Interpretive mode task to gather more information from partner	Debate and support opinion on issue
Compare items or practices	Choose and relay information from text with partner, request clarification	Compare and contrast an issue past and present
Select items to include in the Presentational mode deliverable	Join another pair to come to consensus based on varying needs and preferences	Discuss issues with partner from Interpretive mode text

Teacher as Designer

Dr Elcie Douce, World Language Department Chair, develops improvisational Interpersonal tasks that are both spoken and written. Text conversations that happen in the moment develop a shared communicating culture, a space where learners can use simple words to explain things with the limited repertoire they have and develop confidence in doing so.

These performance assessments are complex tasks which compel the learner to relate to images and meanings within song lyrics and reconnect the individual with the society that created the artform. Key to this complex task are mediation strategies to clarify images, ideas and concepts between people who experience this song.

Voices from the Field

The first black nation of Haiti is a francophone country with a rich culture. This song enables students to study French while learning about Haiti's struggles and resilience through the years. This concept is essential to build intercultural competence as it introduces the country to students who may not know about it and its connection to United States history. Other cultures should understand the similarities that exist between Haiti and other countries where songwriters keenly use their inspirations to raise cultural awareness.

Novice teachers can unpack the song using comprehensible Input strategies and scaffolding techniques to help students grasp the message and demonstrate their understanding. Intermediate and Advanced levels teachers can provide opportunities to dive in deeper analysis of the song and enable students to express their viewpoints. I use chat to have text conversations all the time, either via Facebook or WhatsApp. It is very useful for novice learners who are developing their speaking skills. It enables them to build confidence so they can express themselves later on. For remote learning, it offers choices to students with internet issues and it addresses equity issues as well.

Using the Articulated Assessment Transfer Task helps me create real-world tasks that foster students' language skills in all three modes of communication, their cultural awareness and intercultural competence.

Elcie Douce, Ed. D., World Language Department Chair. Nyack Public Schools, New York

Table 5.7 Articulated Assessment Transfer Task — Chanson Pour Haiti

Elcie Douce, Ed.D. World Language Department Chair. Nyack Public Schools, New York
Enduring Understandings * Haiti's struggles and resilience in maintaining its status as the first Black independent Nation. * Cultural history inspires songwriters for all world music.
Essential Questions ? How do Haiti's struggles and resilience bring hope to its people and to the world? ? How does the history of a country shape its culture and affect its songwriters' inspiration?
Context A French magazine wants to publish an article about Haiti and starts a social media line of discussions and blog to gather information.
Articulation Spiral Points @ List descriptive words as cultural history referents. @ Connect images to meaning. @ Compare composer vision with other points of view. @ Persuade and teach others about songs as cultural emblems and anthem of change.

Intercultural Transfer Targets	Mediation for Transfer
• I can identify images connected to cultural perspectives in a song. • I can compare how historical events influence song lyrics in Haiti and my own country. • I can explain cultural messages and the composer's intent expressed in song lyrics.	• Bridge and exchange ideas and concepts represented by imagery within song lyrics. • Interpret images relating to resilience and cultural history. • Connect another person's experience and prior knowledge within song lyrics. • Summarize the significance of the lyrics.

Novice Mid	Intermediate Mid	Advanced Mid
\multicolumn{3}{c}{*Chanson pour Haiti* by Ansy Derose}		
Interpretive Task Descriptions		
Read the song lyrics and create a list of words that describe the author's view of Haiti.	Read the song lyrics and identify the main idea of the song using words from the song to support your viewpoint.	Read the song lyrics and identify the underlying purpose for writing the song and the message the artist wants to convey.
Can Dos		
I can identify and interpret some basic descriptive and familiar words in a song.	I can understand the main idea and key information in song lyrics.	I can identify what motivates the artist to write the song.
Interpersonal Task Descriptions		
Have a video chat conversation with your partner in which you ask and answer questions related to a collage of images that support the vocabulary words and the ideas of the song. Write a Facebook post sharing your opinion of the song in response to other posts.	Have a video chat conversation with your partner in which you compare feelings and personal opinions of the song. Write a post to an online discussion to talk about your feelings and personal opinion regarding the song.	Have a video chat or create a podcast conversation in which you discuss with your partner your interpretation of the song and whether or not you share the singer's idea. Write a Facebook entry to discuss your own interpretation of the song.
Can Dos		
I can ask and answer questions to express ideas related to the images revealed in the song. I can share my opinion about a song in response to other posts.	I can ask and answer questions and compare our reactions to the message conveyed in the song. I can participate in an online discussion where people react to the song.	I can ask and answer questions to discuss my interpretations of a song and express my opinions. I can discuss interpretations of a song on social media.

	Presentational Task Descriptions	
Make a word cloud/a collage describing the author's view of Haiti as described in the song.	Write a simple review of the song and give specific reasons to support your point of view.	Write an article or a blog entry to help others understand the influence of this type of song.
Can Dos		
I can present some simple information about a song.	I can write a simple review of a song and give specific reasons to support my point of view.	I can write an article or a blog entry to convince others of the influence of a song.

Bridge to Design

How does Dr Douce unfold concepts of independence and resilience across the levels and make that comprehensible through song lyrics? Let's go deeper into that process and share additional ideas and reflections that can support your own design.

(See Appendix X in Companion Website Chapter 5.)

Seven design tips for Interpersonal tasks

1 Design Interpersonal tasks with the cultural texts and the Interpretive mode tasks in front of you.
2 In every summative or formative assessment, learners should be asking questions, not just answering them. They should start asking questions right away in the novice level if you want them to progress to Intermediate.

3 Start with two products or practices from cultural texts in the Interpretive mode. Learners choose and decide between two or more items.

4 The best Interpersonal mode tasks are those which guide learners to discuss what they will include, choose, and decide for the creation of the Presentational mode deliverable.

5 The complication or problem to solve should not wait for an advanced target. Generate a situation that learners have to work out together that requires negotiation, consensus and mediation.

6 Improvisation is at the centre of the Interpersonal mode. It values poise over perfection and develops confidence. Try the strategies for Aesthetic Education and Drama Pedagogy.

7 Make sure you see evidence of mediation in the tasks. How would someone use this to make language more accessible or a perspective more visible for someone else?

Design for Transfer

Using the Capacities for Imaginative Learning aligned with the Interpersonal-Interactive Mode
Design Interpersonal mode tasks for your unit and AATT, using the sample item types below.

- Propose solutions with a classmate on issues presented in a work of art.
- Change the time frame of the scene and improvise seconds, minutes, days or years before or after the key event occurs.
- Create an on-air talk show that is spontaneous and unscripted.

Adapted from Eddy, J. (2019b). Literature and Drama for Transfer. In F. Diamantidaki, (Ed.), Teaching Literature in Modern Foreign Languages. London: Bloomsbury Academic.

Designing for the Interpersonal Goal

Design for Transfer

With your selected texts and Interpretive mode tasks, design at least one Interpersonal mode task across **three levels of learner engagement** for your Summative assessment for the AATT. Use the Concept Map (see Figure 2.1) to organize and collect your thoughts. Use the AATT template for your Interpersonal mode tasks (see Figure 1.4) and the fillable template on the Companion Website.

With your template and Interpretive mode tasks and materials in front of you, let's design for the Interpersonal mode.

- What do you want learners to be able to do as a result of this task?
- What is the 'take-away' from this mode that prepares them for the next task?
- How does this task move the learner closer to solving the problem and creating the product presented in the context?

(For a master list of task types for the modes of communication, see Appendix NN.)

Design for Transfer

Design Assessments first, then say the takeaway.
Write the PASS Can Do statements for your Interpersonal mode tasks

Discuss the Issues

1 Some instructors say that language learners should aspire to be like native speakers and error free. Discuss.

2 When I look at an image or work of art, I see perspectives of the culture within. Why do images reveal what matters?

3 Planning improvisation is more realistic than practicing forms. Discuss.

4 What are some benefits for learners when they plan and prepare the Presentational mode deliverable together in the Interpersonal mode task?

5 Why is it important to make meaning and negotiate meaning with the language we have, even if it is not error free?

6 Mediation within this mode is more than just for language; it is for intercultural mediation as well. Discuss and give an example.

7 Drama Pedagogy and Aesthetic Education strategies help learners be free of habit and routine, allowing exploration, experimentation and risk-taking. Why is this helpful for this Interpersonal mode?

Reflect and Revisit

1 What is a characteristic of the Interpersonal/Interaction mode? What is not?

2 Why does improvisation matter? What is the problem with predictable exercises?

3 Memorization of role plays or dialogues is not an Interpersonal task. Why not?

4 How do you use the outcome of the Interpretive or Receptive tasks to design the Interpersonal mode or Interaction tasks?

5 How do these tasks show what the learner can do in this mode along different levels of engagement?

6 How do the Interpersonal tasks uncover cultural perspectives in your EUs and EQs?

7 What evidence of mediation do you see from your tasks?

Chapter 6

Designing for Presentational Goals: Creating Meaning for Mediation

Enduring Understandings

- ∞ Presentational mode is a productive, creative, rehearsed, or refined oral or written piece prepared for an audience.
- ∞ Performance assessment for transfer demonstrates evidence of knowledge and skills applied differently and beyond the context of how it was learned.
- ∞ Performance tasks prepare learners to use a variety of resources, articulate ideas, and become self-directed.
- ∞ Presentational tasks engage learners in real-life, purposeful tasks of value to cultural communities beyond the classroom.
- ∞ Presentational deliverables solve problems and create products for varied audiences and their needs in mind.
- ∞ Aesthetic and drama education support Presentational mode goals.
- ∞ Presentational mode tasks can be done alone or with others and are often planned during the Interpersonal mode tasks.

Essential Questions

- Q To what extent is creativity expected and encouraged?
- Q How are knowledge and skills tested?
- Q Why do people create new things?
- Q Why does transfer matter?
- Q How are novelty, creativity and communication related?

Q What is accomplished by thinking beyond my own needs?
Q What do performance tasks reveal about intercultural competence?

Key terms and Concepts

Presentational Mode	Expressive
Articulation Spiral Points	Transactional
Key Performance Tasks	Poetic

Research in Practice

The work of the following researchers and practitioners will guide you to cite sources which inform your planning, assessment and instructional decisions in pre-service portfolio assessments or in-service professional learning plans.

Britton, et. al. 1975 Hall, 2002	Presentational mode tasks are expressive, transactional, or poetic
Cope and Kalantzis, 2009	Learner is creator of multimodal texts
Eddy, 2006a/b, 2007a/d, 2009a/b, 2015c, 2017, 2019a	Key performance tasks for transfer develop World Language articulated curriculum
Glisan, Adair-Hauck, Koda, Sandrock & Swender, 2003	Performance assessment integrated with three modes of communication
Greene, 2001 Holzer, 2007	Aesthetic Education and the Capacities of Imaginative Learning
Piazzoli, 2010 Kao & O'Neill, 1998 Even; 2008, 2016	Drama Pedagogy techniques for teaching and learning languages
McTighe, 2017 Wiggins & McTighe, 2005, 2011	Learners engage in novel tasks aligned with long-term transfer goals across the curriculum.

I can

- Describe and explain presentational tasks for creating meaning for mediation
- Differentiate task types from AATT exemplars
- Design key performance tasks in the Presentational mode across different levels for articulation
- Develop PASS Can-Dos for this mode aligning to intercultural transfer goals

Rewind

Which key terms or concepts stand out for you from Chapter 5: *Designing for the Interpersonal goal: Consensus on meaning for mediation?*

Ask your colleague three questions based on the content from the last chapter.

Explain the most compelling idea from the previous chapter in your own words.

Explain how this concept or practice is the same, similar or different to what you know or do.

Which concept or practice do you think will have the greatest impact on your teaching?

Overview

By this time, you have seen the AATTs in all the modes of communication, each chapter focusing your design with that particular mode. In the Interpretive and Interpersonal modes, the emphasis is on acquisition, ownership for yourself, then consensus and clarifying meaning with someone else, respectively. With each performance task, the learner needs the opportunity to see how language is a bit more novel each time. Now for the Presentational mode, we create something new for someone else, specialized with an audience in mind, their needs or a purpose or revision that is new. This mode has been described as one-way communication for an audience, because there may be no immediate reaction to what you offer, at least not one perhaps in your presence. However, make no mistake; it is the intention for this audience that makes these works, these creations, truly communicative acts. Whether it is an oral, written or visual text you create, there is a reaction, and someone does notice. Your message was discovered anew, understood from a different perspective. Your deliberate act of transfer extends a new opportunity for someone else to see the concept, idea, or information differently, moving mediation forward. This chapter explores how we can encourage creativity with novel and complex tasks. How does creative transfer make our work relevant and applicable? Why is creativity the tool as well as a goal?

Presentational-Productive mode as creation

The *Presentational* mode is one of the standards within the goal area of Communication (National Standards Collaborative Board, 2015): 'Learners present information and ideas on a variety of topics adapted to various audiences of listeners, readers or viewers to describe, inform, narrate, explain, or persuade.' Some classrooms assign tasks merely for the eyes of the pupil and teacher. Within the framework presented in this book, learners choose from their repertoire of sources what they need to solve a problem or make a new product that is of value to an audience beyond themselves and the classroom. In the real world, we always draw upon a collection of resources and our knowledge to solve a problem or create something new for a given audience. We are given time to revise and refine it. We do this not only alone, but also in collaboration with others. Our creativity clarifies concepts and offers a (re)vision for someone else to consider, the definitive step in mediation. For that reason, it is communication for Creation.

> For the AATTs and ICANADAPT, this mode:
>
> - Details a productive, creative, rehearsed or refined oral or written piece for varied audiences and their needs in mind
> - Prepares learners to use a variety of resources, articulate ideas and become self-directed
> - Engages learners to solve novel problems and create products of value to cultural communities beyond classroom

For the Presentational-Productive mode, learners

- Use repertoire gathered from the Interpretive and Interpersonal modes
- Create oral, written and visual texts of value to others

- Prepare novel product or solve problem alone or in collaboration with peers
- Revise, rehearse, refine, react

The most compelling presentational tasks yield products or deliverables which can be found or created in the world beyond school. This means that these tasks are not just exercises, activities or projects solely for the class or teacher. These are products found across a variety of disciplines present in diverse venues or media. They also can be products expected in the workplace. These assessments involve problem-solving, collaboration and intent to deliver an oral or written product with that audience in mind. These deliverables also convey or clarify a message towards mediation. The AATTs unfold these tasks so that learners participate and create to the extent they can. This process indicates that at any level of engagement, learners can create a product and mediate communication in cultural contexts with confidence, with flexibility. Presentational mode tasks are the tangible outcomes of the processing required from the interpretive and interpersonal tasks. These deliverables are created from data gathered in the Interpretive mode, with stories told, events described, details shared and negotiated in the Interpersonal mode.

To review, the Interpretive mode of reception provides input and opportunities for students to acquire new information. The learner experiences concepts and texts with models that exist in their own and other cultures. The Interpersonal mode asks learners to share information, ideas, choose, plan, come to consensus and make cultural comparisons. These tasks enable the negotiation work needed to create a Presentational mode deliverable. The presentational tasks synthesize and demonstrate content in a new way while remaining purposeful and relevant within cultural contexts and communities.

Presentational tasks provide the learner with evidence of what it means to "do" the discipline, to have abilities tested in various contexts within the target culture. These tasks require the learner to take stock of what they know and are able to do and use that repertoire appropriately in a given situation (see Table 6.1). This means that the learner understands that situations change and flexibility is essential. They may or may not have resources or cues to guide them. In the case of summative assessments in the AATTs for Stage Two of ICANADAPT units, they will not have cues, supports, directions and the like. The fewer supports and directions, the more the task assesses for transfer. To design an articulated curriculum, we do so with *Articulation Spiral Points*, a series of *Key Performances* throughout the curriculum that serve as the catalogue of learner evidence for intercultural concepts within disciplines. Each AATT provides a three-level assessment triptych for that catalogue. As you design, this collection will represent the deliverables for your programme that all learners will do.

Table 6.1 What Presentational-Productive Is and Is Not

What Presentational-Productive IS	What Presentational-Productive is NOT
Prepared, rehearsed, revised written or oral piece with needs of an audience, group or person in mind	Making an oral presentation or product solely for teacher or classroom context
Solves problems and creates novel products	Answers questions from textbook or drills
Assesses for Transfer	Recall and repetition of previous examples with supports
Tasks developed using flexible repertoire of input from Interpretive mode and Interpersonal mode strategies	Tasks in isolation from context and separated from input and interactive exchanges
Oral or written products are designed for intercultural situations, concepts and contexts	Deliverables are isolated from intercultural contexts and mediation strategies

Pause to Ponder

All of the AATT exemplars you have seen include Presentational-productive tasks. What characteristics do you notice for these tasks? What does this mode do on its own and in concert with the others? Before seeing these exemplars, what other tasks have you seen for this mode? In what ways were they different from the ones you see here? How important is the audience when designing these deliverables? Consider these while reviewing and designing tasks and share thoughts with a colleague.

Learning is in the making

The Presentational mode tasks in the AATTs remind us that transfer evidence comes from creating something new, demonstrating flexible and confident use of the language at any proficiency level. In Chapter 3, we discussed that understanding begins with creative transfer (see Figure 3.1) and not to withhold *Create* for a higher target level. At every level of engagement, the learner must be the creator of multimodal texts (Cope and Kalantzis, 2009.) These presentational texts can be written, spoken language, visual, audio, gestural and spatial. The learner will not progress while still mired in low–level tasks. Creativity is the tool as well as the goal that must happen right away, however small the novel works are.

Joan Kelly Hall (2002) describes two kinds of Presentational mode tasks forms: *expressive* or *transactional*. Britton, Burgess, Martin, McLeod & Rosen (1975) included a third form: *poetic*. Expressive products offer our opinions, feelings, experiences, reflections or personal connections in blogs, letters, vlogs, diaries, social media. Transactional products are those which provide information, communicate or share knowledge. We describe objects, narrate events, argue, plan, and persuade people to consider a viewpoint. These also include tasks such as step-by-step instructions, public service announcements, advertisements, infographics or recommendations to an audience on what to do or how to do something. Poetic forms reflect, create and recreate experiences that the audience will enter through the imagination, experiences and emotions. These are songs, plays, poems or stories. These three forms all become transfer tasks in the Presentational mode when the task is novel and requires the learner's repertoire carefully chosen. The Capacities of Imaginative Learning (Eddy, 2019b; Greene, 2001; Holzer, 2007) adapted for the Presentational mode are: Creating Meaning, Taking Action, and Reflecting and Assessing.

Creating Meaning is to create your own interpretations in the light of other people and their contributions. This involves synthesis of texts and expressing it in your own voice. Gestures, body movement, facial expressions, dance, poetry and acting sequences all contain intercultural meaning. This is an opportunity for learners to revise what they have seen, read and heard and make it new in their own words and mindset.

Taking Action is to act on the synthesis of what you have learned in your explorations through a specific product. These include projects in the arts, as well as in other realms. For example: you might write and produce your own play; you might create a dance; you might plant a community garden as a combined service-learning/science project; you might organize a clothing drive for homeless neighbours as a combined service learning/humanities project.

Reflecting/Assessing to look back on a product or problem, identify what challenges remain and revise, elaborate and fine tune the work or text.

Adapted from Holzer, 2007. Aesthetic Education, Inquiry, and the Imagination.

Check for Learning

Using the list of presentational task products below, decide with a colleague if these are transactional, expressive, poetic or a combination of any three. Choose these again, this time with the Presentational Task Tasters below.

Table 6.2 Presentational Task Products

Audio	Printed	Visual
Commercials	Websites, blogs, vlogs, social media	Sculpture, painting, photography
News	Newspapers and magazines	Street signs
Oral presentation	Information list	Cartoons, animation, emojis
Radio	Brochures, labels, menus	Picture books graphic novels
Music (choral and instrumental)	Marketing campaigns	Storyboard, Kamishibai, diorama
TV	Infographics	Games
Film	Fiction/non-fiction literature	Maps
Music videos	Advertisements	Posters
PSAs	Promotional materials	Dance
Songs	Lyrics and scripts	Charts, graphs, symbols, images
Announcements	Surveys, reports, articles	Museum exhibit
Time capsules	Children's stories	Timelines
Murals	Theatre	Questionnaires

Table 6.3 Presentational Task Sampler

Novice 0-A1.1	Intermediate A1.2-B1.1	Advanced B1.2-C1.1
Create a video on healthy activities	Create a video on what to wear for different occasions appropriate to the culture(s)	Write an article on local fashion changes over time

Designing for Presentational Goals

Design an infographic	Develop a culturally appropriate menu for different dietary preferences	Present a report on the pros and cons of school uniforms from the perspective of two cultures
Create a public service announcement	Write a storybook or for young children	Design installations for a new museum exhibit

Collaboration for Articulation

Your colleague provides extensive support on every task and in the end, learners replicate what was in the textbook or material exactly the way it was taught in a previous class. Explain creative transfer to this colleague and why it is important to engage learners in novel presentational mode tasks. Give an example to get started with near to novel tasks.

In Chapter 3 we reviewed the drama technique, Mantle of the Expert (Edmiston, 2003; Heathcote & Herbert, 1985; Heathcote & Bolton, 1995) with the learner 'in role' as the expert. This is an important feature of Key Performance Transfer Tasks in curriculum design. The Presentational mode is usually where the deliverable resides that the expert must create, plan and develop in response to the context problem. The expert must solve the problem differently by creating new material or refashioning it for a different audience and their needs. They are tasks which apply content and skills differently from how they were originally learned or presented.

Check for Learning

When learners become the 'expert', they may not have seen the new task before, but the other modes did provide multiple avenues for complexity, autonomy and novelty. Discuss with a colleague how you have seen the other modes support the Presentational mode to enable the learner as 'expert'. Do you have a task with the learner 'in role?' Share your idea with your colleague.

Changing it all together

After presenting the UCADAPT (Eddy, 2006a, 2007a), curriculum design framework at the conference of National Council on Less Commonly Taught Languages (Eddy, 2010c), the National African Language Resource Center (NALRC) invited me to direct curriculum design leadership institutes with African language, culture, history, and anthropology professors and graduate students at Indiana University, Bloomington (Eddy, 2013b, 2014b, 2015c, 2015d). These scholars came from universities across many countries in Africa as well as from across the United States. Together we explored concepts on varied cultural practices and the perspectives that created them. Our institutes guided these programme leaders on the articulated curriculum design and performance assessment framework which developed further to ICANADAPT that you are learning here. The participants discussed key intercultural themes that should reprise over a curriculum in African languages and cultures. They came to a consensus on *Home, Health, Communal Life, Ritual and festival, Education, Commerce, History, Government and Leisure*. These themes were ones that they felt everyone should experience through performance tasks in order to be able to participate in diverse communities throughout Africa and the diaspora. These became recursive concepts to uncover over the span of the curriculum through the performance assessments and authentic materials providing intercultural response and reactions via the transfer tasks. There were very few materials designed for classroom instruction; those that existed were mostly grammar or vocabulary books. These scholars collected videos on dance, traditional farming, religious practices, food labels, posters and photographs, government pamphlets and PSAs, greeting cards, folktale story books, real estate advertisements and radio/TV broadcasts. These were the catalyst for the Interpretive tasks and the inspiration to create new products and solve problems and needs relevant to their communities. By collaborating together on articulated Key Performance tasks, these African scholars became curriculum designers, with exemplars on housing negotiation, conflict resolution, greetings, trading and advertising, time and space, dance therapy and many others. We continue this important work together and it has become a model for many cultures and communities, especially endangered and indigenous languages where materials and curricula are scarce.

Check for Learning

Do you teach or learn a language less commonly taught where there is a dearth of classroom-based materials? Do you use authentic materials? What are the benefits? If you learned a language that traditionally has had a lot of materials designed for instruction, what are the advantages and disadvantages? What was your experience? Share your comparisons with a partner.

Teacher as Designer

Dr Kazeem Kẹ́hìndé Sanuth is one of the scholars from our first group in the leadership institutes at the National African Language Resource Center (NALRC). His exemplar on Yorùbá celebration within the context of weddings examines the diversity of celebration within Nigeria and beyond, unfolded across levels for articulation (see Table 6.4). His tasks also assist learners with points for mediation, such as elaborating specifics between Nigerian wedding customs and clarifying traditions and planning steps for someone unfamiliar with the customs.

Voices from the Field

The concept of celebration in the Yorùbá context is essential in an articulated curriculum for intercultural competence, mainly because it is a prevalent authentic affordance for learners in the Yorùbá social context. Wedding events are everywhere all time of the year and it offers common resources that can be used for pedagogical purposes such as (1) wedding rites items, (2) food and drinks, (3) cloth types, and (4) colors on display, among other items. Also, sociocultural practices are abundant such as greeting, songs, dance, social demeanors at social gatherings, etc. All of these provide context for pedagogical tasks.

The practices and products involved in a Yorùbá wedding present a vast variety of content that can provide access to the language and culture and stimulate learners' interactions across multiple levels of competence. Even with a limited linguistic capacity, a novice learner can connect to and identify some items and cultural practices which can be easily identified, named and even used to express their preferences.

I like the fact that designing this way centers on language use for real-life functions, such as collecting, processing and sharing information through reading, discussing, and writing. Focus on pedagogical task description prompts instructors to find creative ways to design using the authentic material. With the ultimate outcome mirrored on practical life events and activities, it makes language teaching relevant to not only the target context but also as a medium for teaching useful 21st-century skills. Also, the idea of the vertically articulated assessment is an effective way to both produce and view the effectiveness of scaling a single topic across multiple levels.

Kazeem Kẹ́hìndé Sanuth, PhD, Associate Director, National African Language Resource Center (NALRC) Hamilton Lugar School of Global and International Studies. Indiana University-Bloomington.

Table 6.4 Articulated Assessment Transfer Task
Wedding Celebration of the Yorùbá People

Kazeem Kẹ́hìndé Sanuth, PhD	Yorùbá
Enduring Understandings * Although a wedding ceremony is celebrated across all communities, the way and manner it is celebrated varies across cultures. * How every community celebrates weddings is determined by their outlook on life, belief system, social and environmental affordances.	
Essential Questions ? What makes a Yorùbá wedding celebration? ? How do community, social constructs and beliefs influence how people prepare for celebrations? ? What cultural products or practices distinguish a wedding celebration from one culture to another?	

Designing for Presentational Goals 209

Context
A social service/event planning startup in South-West Nigeria, for its multimedia blog on event planning, is seeking content that will appeal to the Yorùbá audience in Nigeria and the diaspora, with a focus on wedding celebrations.

Articulation Spiral Points
@ Design multimedia material on Yorùbá wedding rituals and activities.
@ Compare traditions between Yorùbá and other celebrations in Nigeria and diaspora.
@ Report on changing traditions and essential rituals.

Intercultural Transfer Targets	Mediation for Transfer
• I can identify traditional rites for marriage and weddings. • I can explain the diversity within Nigerian wedding celebration and practices and relate those to perspectives. • I can compare practices and preferences between different wedding rites in Nigeria and the diaspora.	• Bridge and exchange ideas and concepts related to Yorùbá wedding rites. • Identify wedding items connected with rituals. • Ask people to elaborate specific points between Nigerian wedding customs. • Clarify traditions and planning steps. • Collaborate on shared tasks and exchange values and practices.

Novice High	Intermediate Mid	Intermediate High
Interpretive Task Descriptions		
Musical video on Yorùbá wedding Students watch the music video that presents Yorùbá wedding and identify and list the recognizable wedding rite items (Ẹrù ìyàwó) used in the Yorùbá culture (such as iṣu, oyin, aṣọ, ẹja, ohun-mímu, òrùka.) that are shown in the video.	A collection of Event Schedule outlines used for a variety of Yorùbá weddings. Students examine the collection of Yorùbá wedding Event Schedules and use the information in the printouts to categorize the way Yorùbá people celebrate wedding/the various activities and practices for celebrating a wedding in the Yorùbá culture.	Nigerian bridal websites and wedding blogs. Students will study and research several authentic Nigerian bridal websites and blogs and compare Yorùbá wedding celebrations with other Nigerian wedding celebrations.

Can Dos		
I can identify common items for a wedding in the Yorùbá culture.	I can categorize Yorùbá steps in planning a wedding celebration in the Yorùbá culture.	I can compare and contrast the Yorùbá wedding celebration with other Nigerian wedding celebrations.
Interpersonal Task Descriptions		
In pairs, learners come to a consensus on which wedding activities/rituals are the same or different between the Yorùbá culture and their culture.	Learners will debate with a partner choosing what aspect of the Yorùbá wedding practices they like and the aspect they do not like and ask questions on preferences.	Learners will discuss with a partner, agreeing on the aspects of the Yorùbá marriage celebration that have changed over time and provide explanation.
Can Dos		
I can compare wedding celebrations between the Yorùbá culture and my culture.	I can decide and provide information to a partner about my preferences on Yorùbá wedding practices and ask follow-up questions.	I can come to agreement on Yorùbá traditions of marriage celebration that have changed and discuss the reason.
Presentational Task Descriptions		
Create a poster to present a comparison of wedding rites items (Ẹrù ìyàwó) between the Yorùbá culture to their own culture.	Create a multimedia presentation on the traditional rites/steps of activities during a Yorùbá wedding ceremony.	Write a short article for a wedding blog to describe the essential requirements and stages in planning a Yorùbá wedding.
Can Dos		
I can present a comparison of wedding rite items (Ẹrù ìyàwó) between Yorùbá culture to my own culture using visuals and organizers.	I can make a presentation with information on traditional rites/steps of planning activities for a Yorùbá wedding ceremony.	I can deliver detailed requirements and stages in a written report on planning a Yorùbá wedding.

Bridge to design

Let's get closer to this exemplar design and go deeper on the concept of celebration throughout cultures. Join colleagues to ask questions about Dr Sanuth's design processes and collaborate for additional ideas and reflection on this exemplar before working on your own design.

(See Appendix Y in Companion Website Chapter 6.)

Check for Learning

Keep the ICANADAPT Concept Map close by so you can research, brainstorm and annotate with the Seven Symbols of Transfer and Mediation below. Use these ideas as you develop the key summative assessments in the Presentational mode tasks for your unit and the AATT. (See Figure 2.1.)

Seven Symbols of Transfer and Mediation
- ! is interesting to you
- * is an example or evidence of specific intercultural transfer target
- \# is connected to a social media hashtag
- & is an example of ideal collaboration or connection to another word concept
- ? is an area you question and need to explore further
- \+ is a new idea, word, phrase, or concept as expansion from this learning

Teacher as Designer

For the initiative, 'Creating a Safe Space', The American Association of Teachers of German (AATG) resources inspired the following two AATT exemplars: *Familienstrukturen in der deutschsprachigen Welt* (Diverse Families in the German-speaking world) (See Table 6.5) and *DIE Imbissstadt* (THE Food City)

(See Table 6.6) by Dr Paul Garcia and Michael McCloskey. Both exemplars demonstrate diversity, within families and also of cuisine in Germany. The requisite topics of food and family life appear in all World Language/MFL curricula. These exemplars provide a fresh, uncommon examination of concepts and practices that are ever present in daily life yet infrequently explored in our curricula. Both exemplars clarify and extend diversity beyond the 'one and done' appearance we may see in materials, if at all, to one which reprises for greater depth over an articulated, pluricultural German curriculum for our times.

Voices from the Field

Our world endures – both within and beyond the tragedy of COVID-19. Approximately 150 million of our planet's 7.9 billion population have been infected. Over three million have died.

To be sure, there are many, many lessons to be gleaned from these sobering statistics. The pandemic is just that; it is pervasive. COVID-19 recognizes no national boundaries. No language, no cultural differences prevent its omnipresence. We have certainly learned both the positive and negative extent of globalization. Historically, humanity depends on its interconnected relationships – in real time and space. We were isolated from physical proximity to one another, and that loss of "place" made us even more dependent on machinery than in the last 150 years. Earlier periods, such as the "Age of Aquarius," of "Angst," and even the "Atomic Age" have been overtaken by the pandemic and our consequent reliance on the "Computer Age" to regain the loss of place.

It is not just a consequence of disease that we seek connections for information and health news. We know that additional influences beyond the pandemic will continue to reshape our globalized life experiences. Each existential force has its roots intertwined in technologies that collapse time and place as they develop our 21st century, and do so, irrespective of location, language, and culture.

Among these apparently permanent – and Hegelian – vectors that reconfigure the present into the future, let us consider their impact on our unconditional need to learn about "the other." For us in the field of languages and cultures, we must understand these extant forces:

1. A youth-informed culture of freedom.
2. Media-delivered contemporaneity.
3. Migration patterns – from poverty to hope and opportunity – that are not only geographical, but emotional and cognitive affective as well.

The pandemic year 2020 – and years before and after – challenge language educators to separate our profession from "traditional" modes of teaching languages to engage tomorrow's students by attending to the reality of a blended time and space that spill over national boundaries. Two ideal examples of this internationalized pedagogy serve as templates for teachers of German. Family structures in the German-speaking world are one; food consumption in Germany, Austria, Switzerland, and Luxembourg are the other.

Unquestionably, traditional family structures continue – and will remain, but as part of a larger and more complex canvas. At the same time, non-traditional family units thrive. They are state-supported and individually approved. Not everyone must be part of a heteronormative, nuclear family. Teachers (and not just teachers of German) have students whose parents may be perhaps foster parents of the same gender. They may be part of a voluntarily single parent home, for instance. To assign students a course of language/culture study in which every representative of the culture in question belongs to a traditional family structure is wrong. Teaching a lesson as though "family" equals "blonde, blue-eyed, white mother/father" homelife is demonstrably untrue – and risible, were it not a sad attempt at stereotyping. Students of the German-speaking world – and pupils of all other languages, have as their present (and future) the reality of multiple family units. Language usage and terms have changed. Pertinent vocabulary has expanded, not only because of the pandemic and the usage of specific terms. (German has created some 1200-plus words dealing with COVID-19.) Students must become acquainted with "meine Einelternfamilie" (my one-parent family) or "ein gleichgeschlechtliches Ehepaar" (same-sex married couple). They must be conscious that as the world's interconnectedness has made it possible to enjoy an "authentic foreign meal" in many cities of the world; that "authentic foreign food" may well have started life as the "Döner Kebab" did – not in Turkey, but in Berlin, around 1972.

We seek to help our students explain that the stereotype of a monochromatic Germany is not valid – nor were they 3 and 4 generations ago. In understanding multiculturalism as commonplace, be it in family life or in cuisine, we validate the various contributions of our global society to its constituent parts to create a world where different cultural traditions intertwine and flourish. Be it the women selling Thai delicacies in Berlin's "Thai Park" (Preußenpark) or "Elternabend" (Parent Evening) in Vienna with a child's mother and same-gender partner in attendance to check on their son's academic progress (rather than one parent staying at home to cloak the same-gender parenting nature of their household), today's language students cannot be permitted to develop their knowledge of another tongue and its culture(s) as an exercise in stereotypical thinking. The family members depicted in traditional textbook formats do not represent the totality of today's families, period. Admittedly, contemporary German-speaking parents – whatever the adult configuration – do what earlier parents have done. New challenges, however, exist in the non-traditional household, to be sure. How, for example, does a same-sex couple arrange their child's birthday party plans to ensure that the (many?) invitees' parents recognize that their children's hosts are not them, 'Mutti und Vati'. Similarly, going for a lunchtime meal does not mean a pork cutlet with red cabbage as the daily staple of every Berliner. The *Leitmotiv* throughout our vectors of change (freedom, media, migration) is the diversity and inclusivity that the globalized societies, replete with examples of migration towards hope and a better future, represent. To teach languages in and for the future, we must accept that the past (and many past practices) no longer is the appropriate perspective from which we may teach.

Dr Paul Garcia, Professor of German, University of Kansas (Ret.)

Table 6.5 Articulated Assessment Transfer Task   Familienstrukturen in der deutschsprachigen Welt   Diverse Families in the German-speaking World

From "Creating a Safe Space," An AATG Initiative	Paul Garcia & Mike McCloskey
Enduring Understandings * German-speaking families are increasingly diverse in their make-up. * Same-sex parenting, single parenting homes, and other forms of raising children are not taboo. * The stereotypical nuclear family found in traditional textbooks does not represent the totality of today's family units.	

Designing for Presentational Goals 215

Essential Questions
? How does contemporary German-language culture define families?
? How do laws, national, regional social programmes support families?

Context
Contemporary German-speaking parents do what families have always done: they raise children, they take part in school events, they make plans. Some aspects of modern life differ from those issues faced by stereotypical families, however. Certain challenges exist in a non-traditional household. How are these met in a diverse Europe? Prepare information on 'Die neuen Familien'.

Articulation Spiral Points
@ Describe diverse families in Germany.
@ Resolve potential conflict.
@ Develop a family profile.
@ Plan a party.
@ Share experiences to sites in Germany which highlight its diversity.

Intercultural Transfer Targets	**Mediation for Transfer**
• I can identify examples of family diversity in Germany. • I can compare details of diverse families in my own and other cultures. • I can explain and resolve questions on diverse families.	• Bridge and exchange ideas and concepts of diverse family groups. • Recognize when others disagree or when difficulties occur in interaction. • Explain information about values and attitudes on diverse families in Germany and other cultures. • Use visuals to clarify family diversity. • Summarize information and statements made and ask others to share points of view.

Novice High	**Intermediate Mid**	**Advanced Low**
Authentic Material Audiofile	Short documentary 'What is a family'	Students review two German-language websites about party suggestions, taking notes as to their preferences about foods, decorations, a theme, foods to prepare.

Interpretive Task Descriptions		
You are staying with a host family in Germany and your younger host brother wants you to draw with him as you discuss your families. Listen as he discusses his family and draw/notate as many details that you hear as possible.	Students listen to different occupants of the apartment building describe their definition of family and provide details about each of the families with as much information as possible in the graphic organizer. Compose three questions about the families.	To prepare for a discussion about party plans made by a non-traditional family, students review two sites and list five to seven party ideas: Students list five considerations (*Überlegungen*) that a same-sex couple might discuss in hosting the child's party.
Can Dos		
I can identify terms relating to different family groupings and relations
I can understand descriptions about the diverse families of German-speaking areas.	I can form questions about the different family types as depicted in the documentary and on the posters.
I can organize words and details referencing different types of family units.	I can read and understand information about ways that German-speaking families use the internet to plan a birthday party for a child.
I can use new vocabulary terms that relate to party planning in writing a paragraph of 150–200 words on the topic.
I can exchange information with others on party plans.

Interpersonal Task Descriptions		
Your host brother asks clarifying questions about your family. Ask and answer questions with supporting details.	Using the posters or other authentic realia, student partners ask questions to gather additional information about the people in photos or posters (or both) and their own families. Students design 'Steckbriefe' on selected individuals/families and do a "speed-dating intro" to their 'Steckbrief'.	In pairs, students choose a photo from the *Familienstrukturen* posters. They ask and answer questions about the depicted family – clothing, ages, birthdays, professions, relatives, national origin, etc. In groups of 3, they discuss the plot, '*Geburtstagszauber im Frühling*' then write questions to ask another triad, and answer questions from a 3rd group.
Can Dos		
I can describe, ask and answer questions about families, both traditional and diverse, with supporting details. I can share two "new" facts about families in my own and other cultures.	I can ask questions about different families and family member details. I can answer questions about individuals on a given *Steckbrief*.	I can ask a student partner questions about the family depicted in the photo, using appropriate time frames. I can read a story about a springtime birthday in a magical garden, compose questions about the story and answer others' questions about the plot.

Presentational Task Descriptions		
Family is often not only what we are born into but what we choose as well. Write about your "chosen family" or "*Wahlfamilie*". Include details and information about your own chosen family or figures in popular culture.	In groups, students should write a ten-minute family drama script between members of a family and define a family conflict or decision to be made, making the desires/opinions of all clear, and come to a resolution by the conclusion of the script. Matters at the centre of this script can be either serious or minor in nature.	Using "*Wir machen einen Ausflug*" *and "Wir gehen ins Museum."*, student pairs rehearse and retell their weekend "birthday excursion" with a parent or friend(s) to a museum/ historical site in Berlin "*Mein fantastischer Geburtstagsausflug*" Students each present a PowerPoint lecture on the excursion destination itself. Possible Berlin sites: *Jüdisches Museum, Schwules Museum, Gründerzeit Museum, Gedächtniskirche, Museuminsel.*
Can Dos		
I can describe non-traditional families. I can provide additional non-demographic information descriptive of the relationship individuals have to each other.	I can write, rehearse and present a dramatic family scene. I can use language with appropriate register levels for "parent/student" who meet for discussion or resolve a family matter or conflict.	I can present my 'Berlin birthday trip' story. I can present a lecture about the site of interest and its importance to Berlin.

> ### Bridge to Design
> Let's examine this exemplar and discuss similar themes on family and identity in the cultures you teach. Collaborate with colleagues for additional ideas and reflection on this exemplar before working on your own design.
>
> (See Appendix Z in Companion Website Chapter 6.)

Table 6.6 Articulated Assessment Transfer Task   DIE Imbissstadt   THE Food City

From 'Creating a Safe Space', an AATG Initiative by Paul Garcia & Mike McCloskey
Enduring Understandings * Diversity in Germany today is experiencing that quintessential Berlin dining custom: street foods and food trucks. * Contributions of immigrant communities include foods, arts, and a cosmopolitan "world city." * Many influences on German cuisine past and present stem from immigrant experiences.
Essential Questions ? Can cuisine shape one's identity as a community? As German-speakers? ? What/how is Berlin?
Context Berlin's 'new heritage', its diversity and the availability of foods from around the world are just a brief bus or subway ride away. We present a contemporary perspective on diversity in the German-speaking world through one Berlin custom: street foods. Prepare a culinary tour of **DIE Imbissstadt,** highlighting Berlin's multicultural reality with arts and music to accompany Berlin's food scene: 'Eating on the Go in **THE Food City**'.
Articulation Spiral Points @ Present examples on a cultural topic using visuals and charts. @ Recognize areas in Berlin that are home to its immigrant citizens. @ Present diversity of cuisines between communities here and abroad. @ Compose customized materials for others on Berlin.

Intercultural Transfer Targets	Mediation for Transfer
• Identify information on ethnic street foods. • I can compare Berlin's ethnic cuisines with those from my community. • I can explain food preferences from diverse cultural perspectives. • I can suggest dishes and places of interest to others.	• Bridge and exchange ideas and concepts of diverse culinary contributions to Berlin. • Recognize ingredients and clarify tastes and flavours. • Facilitate collaborative interaction with others on navigating the choices in THE Food City. • Explain customs and cuisines that are new to others. • Use visuals and charts to clarify various choices of cuisine and locations of food trucks and stalls. • Summarize content information of personal interest.

Novice High	Intermediate Mid	Advanced Low
Watch Berlin's *ThaiPark* video and visit the *ThaiPark* website and others about maps, music, population growth and contemporary aspects of Berlin's culinary life.	Visit *ThaiPark* Berlin Website. One well-respected and popular area is *ThaiPark* on Preußenplatz, where locals and tourists alike compare flavours from Southeast Asia with their own food cultures.	Maps and materials on Berlin's street foods customs and related patterns of immigration growth combine with information on 'must see' sites of interest for advanced learners in all communicative modes. English as a Weltsprache and Anglicisms in German usage offer additional fertile topics for discussion.

Designing for Presentational Goals

Interpretive Task Descriptions		
Watch the video on *ThaiPark*, answer the questions below and write five more about *ThaiPark* and your favourite cuisine. 1. Wo kann man *ThaiPark* finden? 2. Kann man thailändisches Essen im *ThaiPark* finden? 3. Wann findet Thaipark statt? 4. Sind die Stände improvisiert oder sind sie jeden Tag da? 5. Wer hat Thaipark begonnen?	After studying in Berlin, your friend needs suggestions about food locales to try in the city. Using the website, organize information in a chart about *ThaiPark*. Include important information to have for a visit, the types of foods available, opening times, as well as other points of interest that would get your friend excited to go.	Using *Migrationshintergrund*, students use markers on blank maps to locate *Bezirke*, famous landmarks. They listen to/read demographics, locate street food sites/trucks in Berlin's central areas, such as '*Vatos Tacos*', Mexican foods in Markthalle 9. Students find landmarks, districts, foods by name, and locate food trucks.
Can Dos		
I can identify foods and cultures from diverse backgrounds. I can ask and answer questions about the *ThaiPark*.	I can organize authentic text related to food, different cultures and other important information on locations and events. I can identify and restate the most important information needed to pass on to others based on the necessities of the situation.	I can summarize information on Berlin's districts, ethnic groups, foods and famous landmarks. I can follow information on maps regarding districts, transportation hubs, tourist attractions, ethnic food locations (*ThaiPark, Türkenmarkt*)

Interpersonal Task Descriptions		
Ask your questions about ThaiPark with your partner. Decide foods you would like to try there. Pick a favourite recipe or dish representative of your culture or other cultures. With your partner, identify the ingredients, the origin of the dish, why you like it, the special connection you have to it or other pertinent contributions to this discussion.	For many of us, food is the most tangible representation of culture. Pick a favourite recipe or dish representative of your culture or other cultures. Compare and contrast the ingredients and flavours and explain the origin of the dish. Come to consensus on the diversity of foods available.	Students in triads pose questions about Berlin's demographics, districts, foods and important landmarks. Student pairs exchange information on songs about Berlin, ask another pair five to seven questions about the singers' (Dietrich, Alpa Gun) Berlin/ethnic connections With maps, students explain to partners how to use the U-Bahn from Hbf to reach specific food sites.
Can Dos		
I can recognize ingredients from various dishes. I can relate these foods to the greater world around me. I can answer questions about the food.	I can compare my experience with food beyond community with a partner. I can describe food from different cultures. I can ask and answer questions about my experience with different foods.	I can ask and answer questions about daily life in multicultural Berlin. I can express past and present life in Germany through songs. I can use a Berlin map to ask questions and use public transportation.
Presentational Task Descriptions		
Now that you have heard about *ThaiPark*, you decide to help others check it out.	Prepare a written letter to a friend on the following topic:	Pairs create "Facts & Stats" talks on Berlin: street food/truck sites near a famous landmark, getting from one site to another, returning "home" to Alexanderplatz.

Designing for Presentational Goals

Write a scenario with a stand owner in *ThaiPark*. Discuss different foods you would like to try, ask questions about ingredients, and even ask for suggestions. The stand owner can ask questions, make suggestions and clarify ingredients in foods. Use the *ThaiPark* website for common dishes found in the park.	Using the internet as a resource to research locations, write a letter to a German friend about the diversity of foods in your community. Compare and contrast the cuisines available in your own area to those available in the German speaking world (including Berlin) and comment on your desire to try a variety of diverse foods in German speaking regions.	Write a Berlin restaurant review known for its ethnic cuisine. Present a five-minute talk on a visit to one of the following: Deutsche Kinamathek; das Museum für Film und Fernsehen; Pergamom Museum; Gründerzeit Museum; other sites. Create a collaborative tour of THE Food City.
Can Dos		
I can prepare a scene to guide visitors new to *ThaiPark* to promote the cuisine. I can describe food choices in *ThaiPark*. I can navigate intercultural exchanges in German.	I can compare and contrast food cultures from my own community to those in the target culture using German. I can express cuisine preferences from different cultures.	I can design and deliver a five-minute presentation on Berlin as a multicultural city. I can prepare a collaborative talk about Berlin – its population, districts, famous Berliners, historical sites, its food scene I can write a review about an ethnic meal at a Berlin restaurant I can create a tour of Berlin on a self-researched topic.

> **Bridge to Design**
>
> Let's get closer to this exemplar design. Join colleagues to ask questions about the authors' design processes and collaborate on more ideas before working on your own design.
>
> (See Appendix AA in Companion Website Chapter 6.)

At the onset of the unit, learners receive the Context for the summative performance assessment. This tells them what the unit is about, the 'movie trailer' for the unit, if you will. It does not reveal too much or how they will create the deliverable, only the audience and the need. As you design these tasks, you may find that they took on a life of their own and veered away from the Context. This happens; it's part of creativity and a good sign. It is recommended to hold onto those tasks because you may have the foundation for an entirely different AATT or at the least, you now have formative assessments for Stage Three that occur prior to your summative assessments. After teachers develop in practice with design, some groups have designed Presentational mode tasks first and worked backward towards the Interpretive mode. After they see the entire sequence, the Context manifests from the tasks. This process is fine; you and your colleagues will decide which order works as you design together. The most important part is design for the audience's needs with deliverable and participation according to the performance target of your learners.

Check for Learning

As you are designing your Presentational tasks, this is a good time to check the Context in the AATT. Does this product or problem align with what is in the Context? Don't worry if you need to adapt this.

Teacher as Designer

Dr Ida D'Ugo builds awareness of gender-based violence (GBV) into a spiral, articulated curriculum, unpacking key concepts right from the Novice level (see Table 6.7). This example depicts how a complex theme can and should be started at early levels. When designed backward from performance targets with complexity in the task rather than text or theme, it becomes feasible for teachers of this AATT to unfold the concept and develop the concept and vocabulary base early. The tasks support plurilingual and pluricultural mediation by tasks that clarify images and examples of GBV to others and elaborate on themes relevant to community campaigns on this important issue.

Voices from the Field

Gender-based violence (GBV) is one of many important social justice issues that transcend cultures. With the proper scaffolding and support that address different learning styles, a novice learner, or a learner at any level, can break down the concept of GBV into manageable units that are easier to process. Using these units and student choice with respect to the format of the deliverable, learners can prepare a product that is commensurate with their level of proficiency. Learning experiences that are relevant to real-world situations, rather than limited to an instructional setting, promote student engagement and interest. Once students are engaged and are given a voice, they will become motivated to do more with the content, including advocating for a cause.

Dr Ida M. D'Ugo, EdD, Empowering Creative Minds LLC.

Table 6.7 Articulated Assessment Transfer Task — Gender-Based Violence

Dr Ida M. D'Ugo, EdD	Empowering Creative Minds LLC.
Enduring Understandings	
* Gender-based violence represents one of the most systematic and widespread human rights violations.	
Essential Questions	
? Aren't all human beings entitled to the same human and civil rights?	
? Who makes decisions related to the allocation of these rights?	

Context

The Global Leadership campaign encourages communities around the world to create and submit events, videos, photos or public service announcements to advocate for the elimination of gender-based violence.

Articulation Spiral Points

@ Identify examples of human rights.

@ Recognize teen behaviours of GBV with survey and steps to protect teens.

@ Paraphrase details of human rights and GBV in community discussion panels.

@ Create a PSA on protection and prevention strategies.

Intercultural Transfer Targets	Mediation for Transfer
• I can identify steps to protect human rights in my community. • I can make comparisons between my own and other cultures to support local campaigns. • I can explain strategies to others on preventing GBV in my community.	• Bridge and exchange ideas and concepts of human rights and GBV to others. • Identify images associated with GBV. • Support communication on the issue through clarifying questions to make concepts accessible. • Elaborate and provide appropriate examples.

Novice High	Intermediate High	Advanced Low
Interpretive Task Descriptions		
Students first view an image and react to it. Then they will read an authentic infographic, scan for cognates and complete a *cloze activity* to identify examples of basic human rights. Students brainstorm individually on examples of gender-based violence (GBV) *among adolescents* using a graphic organizer brainstorming web or Circle Thinking Map.	Students view an image, react, then using an infographic provide a *short response example* for each human right explained. Students then brainstorm individually on examples of gender-based violence (GBV) using a graphic organizer brainstorming web or Circle Thinking Map.	Students view an image, react in *long response or narrative* in the first-person point of view. They then read selected articles of the 'Universal Declaration of Human Rights' and provide an example for each human right explained. Students highlight and paraphrase the main points of the articles.

Designing for Presentational Goals

Next students view one to five short videos to recognize some behaviours associated with GBV *among teens* and answer questions embedded in the videos using EdPuzzle. Students use the responses from the comprehension questions to determine which human right listed on the infographic was violated and how. This information will be noted on a graphic organizer or Tree Map Thinking Map.	Next students view a video/playlist for a campaign against GBV and develop comprehension questions to recognize some behaviours associated with GBV. Students paraphrase the main points associated with the campaign (*#AmigoDateCuenta*) against GBV.	Next students brainstorm individually on examples of gender-based violence (GBV) using a graphic organizer brainstorming web or Circle Thinking Map. Afterwards students will view videos on GBV and answer questions to recognize some behaviours associated with GBV and how human rights were violated.
Can Dos		
I can identify human rights based upon an infographic. I can identify how a human right was violated based upon a video (or videos).	I can analyse the definition of human rights based upon the infographic of the United Nations' Universal Declaration of Human Rights. I can view a video/playlist on a campaign against gender-based violence and understand how to protect a human right.	I can read articles of the "Universal Declaration of Human Rights" and paraphrase the main points. I can view videos on gender-based violence and analyse how a human right was violated and determine how to protect this right.

Interpersonal Task Descriptions		
Students will then work with a partner/group to select two or three basic human rights. They prepare questions on WHAT steps should be taken to protect these rights among adolescents. Working with a partner/group, students will ask four or more classmates the questions on WHAT steps should be taken to prevent GBV among adolescents. Students will also answer their peers' questions. (Google Forms, Microsoft Forms or Kahoot can be used to prepare and administer a survey to the class instead.) After reviewing the results of the interviews or surveys, students will complete the graphic organizer key details or Tree Map Thinking Map with steps to prevent GBV among adolescents.	Students will then work with a partner/group to select two or three basic human rights. They prepare questions on HOW students and the local community can protect these rights and prevent GBV. Working with a partner/group, students will raise questions on HOW students and the local community can protect these rights and prevent GBV during a virtual/in-person discussion panel or breakout sessions with community organizations (e.g. women's shelters, law firms, or District Attorney's office) involved in helping victims of GBV. Students will note responses of the community organizations.	Students will then work with a partner/group to select two or three basic human rights. They prepare questions on HOW students and the local community can protect these rights and prevent GBV. Working with a partner/group, students will raise questions on HOW students and the local community can protect these rights and prevent GBV. Students will offer advice and opinions during a virtual/in-person discussion panel or breakout sessions with community organizations (e.g. women's shelters, law firms, student counsellors, or District Attorney's office) involved in helping victims of GBV. Students will note responses of the community organizations.

Designing for Presentational Goals

Can Dos		
I can ask and answer questions on steps to prevent gender-based violence among adolescents.	I can exchange information on human rights and preventing gender-based violence with a community member and/or my peers.	I can explain my opinions and provide advice on how to support Human Rights Day with community organizations and/or my peers.
Presentational Task Descriptions		
Students will work alone or with a partner to create a VoiceThread, short video, or design a T-shirt on how to prevent GBV among adolescents. Students will also reflect on how these steps can be implemented in their own community. Students write a hashtag and draw a symbol (e.g. emoji) representing their response.	Students will work alone or with a partner to create a Public Service Announcement (PSA – 30 seconds to 1 minute) or digital campaign poster on how to prevent GBV for the campaign. Students then write a Tweet to promote their PSA or campaign poster. Students will also reflect on how these steps can be implemented with local organizations.	Students will work alone or with a partner to create a Public Service Announcement (PSA – 1 to 1 ½ minutes) on what they will do to prevent GBV for the campaign. Students then write an Instagram message to promote their PSA. Students will also reflect on how these prevention strategies can be implemented with local community organizations.
Can Dos		
I can present information in my VoiceThread, video, or T-shirt to prevent gender-based violence among adolescents. I can identify practices in my own and other cultures to help me understand different perspectives.	I can create a PSA or campaign poster stating ways to protect human rights and prevent gender-based violence. I can make comparisons between my own and other cultures to help me understand different perspectives.	I can create a PSA stating opinions and advice to protect human rights and prevent gender-based violence. I can make comparisons between my own and other cultures to help me understand different perspectives.

Bridge to Design

Dr D'Ugo's exemplar reminds us that any concept can be treated at any level; it's the tasks that determine the complexity, not the text, topic or theme. Let's collaborate on this exemplar and apply these insights as you work on your own design.

(See Appendix BB in Companion Website Chapter 6.)

Check for Learning

With learners 'in role' as experts, what do you want them to create and solve? Which key performances and products will appear as Articulated Spiral Points?
Who is the audience?
What are their needs?

Teacher as designer

In Nahuatl, two separate words or ideas often come together carefully in *difrasismo*, a meticulous pairing of words to express a new, single metaphor and concept. *In Xochitl, In Cuicatl;* Flower and Song, is poetry.

Irwin Sánchez is a poet, chef and Nahuatl instructor for the Endangered Language Alliance (ELA) in New York City. The ELA, founded and co-directed by Queens College Assistant Professor of Linguistics Daniel Kaufman, supports linguistic diversity and endangered languages in New York City and beyond. In his exemplar, Mr Sánchez wants learners to understand the Nahua perspective of balance as a theme in his poetry, through food, healing and medicine. These tasks across three target levels help learners identify themes in emotions, nature, spirituality and balance, to describe their own healing experiences and explain to others unfamiliar with the products and practices. Nahuatl scholar Miguel Leon-Portilla said the Nahua poets found '*azo tle nelli in tlalticpac*' – the only truths on earth – are in the language of poetry (Gingerich, 1987, p. 86). Personification is

Designing for Presentational Goals   231

a key element in Nahua poetry. Mr Sánchez gives learners the opportunity to write and give life and animation to abstract ideas and inanimate objects. The concepts of healing and the sacred spiral and reprise throughout an articulated curriculum for Nahuatl.

How do we live in balance and be our most authentic self?

How can we flower and sing?

Voices from the Field

The learner should understand that food is sacred in Nahua culture. It is a gift from the gods and the ancestors and should thus always be respected and never wasted. Foods also have various properties that can directly affect our mental and emotional state. Just like some foods are poisonous, many foods are medicinal. The poem *Chili uan Xocolatl* explains how two very different foods affect the body and mind and how both are necessary to maintain a healthy emotional balance. The poems attempt to capture essential elements of a culture. It is one thing to learn about a culture by reading history and gazing at artifacts but it is entirely different to hear the voices of people speaking directly to you. The language itself works in concert with the content to deliver a deeper view of the culture. For instance, it is one thing to read that "respecting elders" is an important value in some culture or another, but it is another thing to embody that respect by daily use of language. In the case of Nahuatl, respect is shown with the suffix *-tzin,* which is attached not only to names of respected people but also to the names of objects that are generally considered inanimate in western culture. We show how we must embody our respect through language even when we are speaking in a third person, or non-person, for that matter.

I want the learner to think about emotional balance and how people try to achieve it in the learner's society. Are there healing foods or healing activities in your culture? I also want the learner to think about how respect is shown in their language. What differentiates respectful language from casual language or even disrespectful language in their culture?

Personification begins with a name. When we give an animal a name, it becomes a member of our family. Nobody, after all, has a nameless pet. So begin the process of personification by thinking up a meaningful and

> fitting name for something and let the attributes and personality flow from the name. Naming is a very important and sacred activity in many of the indigenous cultures of this continent. In Nahuatl, *tōcāyoh* refers to a relationship between two people with the same name. This word was so commonly used that it was adopted into Mexican Spanish. I understand this word as being related to *tōca,* which means 'to plant', as both seeds and names are planted without knowing what will develop. A plant grows from a seed and a personality grows from a name. When you plant a name in an object or animal, you are planting a personality that will emerge in your interactions with it. I want the learner to try and "plant" a name of their choosing, either in Nahuatl or their native language, and see how personification takes its course naturally.
>
> Irwin Sánchez

Table 6.8 Articulated Assessment Transfer Task   in Xochitl, in Cuicatl

Irwin Sánchez	Nahuatl
Enduring Understandings	
* Happiness is achieved with balance in mind, body and spirit.	
* Mole is a symbol of balance and divine gifts.	
* Words of our ancestors cure us, strengthen us and lift us up.	
Essential Questions	
? How do our ancestors keep teaching and caring for us?	
? What is sacred? What is divine?	
? Why does creativity help us maintain balance?	
? What lifts us up?	
Context	
Learners of Nahuatl prepare for the community event, 'In xochitl in cuicatl, Flor y Canto' – Flower and Song.	
Articulation Spiral Points	
@ Compose visual poetry of food and feelings	
@ Develop examples of personification	
@ Create poem and prose on healing	

Designing for Presentational Goals

Intercultural Transfer Targets	Mediation for Transfer
• I can identify words and images to convey emotions in Nahua culture • I can explain healing practices in Nahua and another culture • I can compare personification examples in my own and Nahua poetry • I can name foods associated with emotions in different cultures	• Bridge and exchange ideas and concepts on Nahua healing and balance • Identify words and images connecting feelings with healing, food, emotions and balance • Clarify healing practices and its importance • Collaborate on shared flower and song

Novice	Intermediate	Advanced
Interpretive Task Descriptions		
Chili Uan Xocolatl (Chile and Chocolate) Irwin Sánchez, Author. Learners receive an envelope with words and images from the poem. While listening and reading the poem, they group the words and images together.	*Pahtli* (Medicine) Irwin Sánchez, Author. While listening and reading the poem, group the words and images of curing and healing together and write three questions.	*Tlen Nexehua* (That Which Lifts Me) Irwin Sánchez, Author. While listening and reading the poem, they group the words and images together. Write five questions about the healing experience and explain a healing experience you had.
Can Dos		
I can identify images with words.	I can form questions with images and phrases from the poem.	I can form questions and illustrate a healing experience in a paragraph.

Interpersonal Task Descriptions		
For the author, chili represents suffering and chocolate represents pleasure. What does chocolate and chili represent to you? What foods represent suffering and pleasure to you? With a partner, ask and answer questions on foods that represent both suffering and pleasure.	Learners ask each other questions on concepts related to curing in Nahua culture vs. concepts relating to curing in another culture. What are the elements of curing in Nahua culture? How can words heal?	The sweat bath is a traditional healing method in many Native American cultures. What other healing methods are familiar to you? Ask your partner your questions and compare your healing experiences or techniques and explain the connection between mental and emotional health to physical health.
Can Dos		
I can ask and answer basic questions about food items and how I relate them to feelings with simple words and phrases.	I can ask questions and come to a consensus with a partner on curing and healing and give examples from different cultures.	I can ask and answer questions to compare healing practices and experiences on mental, emotional and physical health.
Presentational Task Descriptions		
Students collect the basic elements of a poem about foods and the emotions and feelings they represent. Create a visual or concrete poem or mobile with the words and images of food and feelings.	Juanita is a personification of a *temazcal*, or sweat bath. Create a personification of something that's important to you. What is its name? What are its characteristics?	Compose a *Xochicuicatl* or *tlahtolli* expressing how they feel after a healing experience. Try to answer the question: *Tlen mitzehua?* What lifts you up?
Can Dos		
I can relate food and various emotions using simple words, phrases and images.	I can develop and expand a personification of something that heals me or is important to me with simple sentences and imagery.	I can write a poem or prose paragraph about healing as an emotional, physical and spiritual experience.

Designing for Presentational Goals

> **Bridge to Design**
>
> Let's go deeper with this design and explore poetry in the cultures you teach. Join colleagues to ask questions about the process and tasks Mr Sánchez uses and collaborate for additional ideas and reflection on this exemplar before working on your own design.
>
> (See Appendix CC in Companion Website Chapter 6.)

Ten design tips for Presentational tasks

1. Strive for products, needs, problems or action issues that exist in a particular career, organization, group, individual or community setting.
2. Focus on value beyond school or classroom.
3. Give learners class time to revise, rehearse, edit and consult new resources that they obtain or you provide.
4. Provide new authentic materials and resources to use.
5. With each presentational task, strive to make meaning new every day.
6. For the summative assessment, this task should be without supports and directions.
7. Learners may come up with their own complexity or variation, audience, demographic on their own as an extension or elaboration to your task. This is how you know they have turned the corner to transfer when they provide their own complication to solve.

> **Design for Transfer**
>
> Using the Capacities for Imaginative Learning aligned with the Presentational-Productive mode.
> Design Presentational mode tasks for your unit and AATT, using the sample item types below.

- Write a response to a character in the literary work.
- Create a multimedia presentation.
- Compose a different ending for the song, poem, story, novel, film, dance or play.
- Create a third-person journal entry.
- Draw a cartoon strip on the ideas generated from the work.
- Curate a museum exhibition based on themes from the work.
- Construct a game of the products, practices and perspectives of the culture.
- Create a storyboard with words and graphics to tell a story in a work of art.
- Write a four-line song plot for a literary work as liner notes.
- Set the storyline in different time frames.
- Write a spoof, parody or skit based on original work of art.
- Be a song, literary, dance, theatre or art critic.

Adapted from Eddy, J. (2019b). Literature and Drama for Transfer. In F. Diamantidaki, (Ed.), Teaching Literature in Modern Foreign Languages. London: Bloomsbury Academic.

Design for Transfer

For your AATT, design the summative presentational tasks for the highest performance target first (see Figure 1.4).

Design summative presentational tasks for at least two other levels, working backward from the target goal.

(For a master list of task types for the modes of communication, see Appendix NN.)

Designing for Presentational Goals

Design for Transfer

Develop the PASS Can-Dos for each Presentational mode task. Make sure that as you read backward from this Presentational back to the Interpretive the Can-do aligns with what is required of the task. If there is anything that is not assessed in that task, remove it and keep it aside. These may be knowledge and skills for formative assessments that you will design in Stage Three of your ICANADAPT template (see Figure 1.3).

Design for Transfer

Derive Intercultural Transfer Targets for your set. As you noticed from each AATT exemplar, the ITTs reflect the takeaway from the task and address products, practices and the perspectives which created them. They also describe clarification, collaboration and explanation to someone else unfamiliar with the culture(s). The ITTs indicate mediation in order to make culture accessible to others who may be new to the culture and need a bridge to understand these elements.

Design for Transfer

Now that you have completed key performance assessment in the three modes across all three levels, each set of tasks becomes the summative performance transfer task for Stage Two of ICANADAPT (see Figure 1.3). Enter these now to build Stage Two of your articulated units.

Discuss the Issues

1 The process of creating novel texts for an audience engages us in strategies for mediation and transfer. Discuss.
2 What kinds of thinking does the presentational task push learners to do?
3 Performance based assessment helps teachers evaluate and plan future instruction. Discuss.
4 How do learners use the outcomes of the interpretive and the interpersonal tasks to fulfil the presentational task?
5 Now that we have seen many AATT exemplars, how are these performance assessments different from memorization or fill in the blank tasks? How do they differ from other performance tasks?
6 How can we use can-do statements to help ourselves and the learner to implement these tasks?
7 Why do transfer tasks provide the best evidence of understanding concepts for intercultural competence?

Reflect and Revisit

1 What are characteristics of high-quality Presentational mode tasks?
2 Does the new task have value beyond teacher, classroom and school?
3 Does the deliverable align with the context for the summative performance assessment?
4 If these tasks are formative assessments, how do they move the learner from near to far transfer?
5 How do these tasks show what the learner can do in this mode along different levels of engagement?
6 How do the Presentational tasks uncover cultural perspectives in your EUs and EQs?
7 What are the 'look for's' as evidence of student learning in this mode?

Chapter 7

Putting It Together for Articulation and Transfer

Enduring Understandings

- ∞ Articulated, spiral curriculum design favours all level participation.
- ∞ Spiral, bespoke curriculum is flexible yet is responsive to required standards.
- ∞ Formative assessments must show content discipline performance with minimal prompting.
- ∞ Formative tasks remain aligned with larger intercultural transferable concepts and goals.
- ∞ Assessments imply the knowledge and skills needed to do them and are chosen after tasks are designed.

Essential Questions

- Q What does collaboration for articulation look like?
- Q Is absorbing or consuming facts and forms a priority?
- Q What happens when knowledge and skills are fragmented and out of context?
- Q What does an expert do?

Key terms and concepts

Formative Assessment	Summative Assessment
Review, Spiral, New	Intercultural Transfer Targets

Research in Practice

The work of the following researchers and practitioners will guide you to cite sources which inform your planning, assessment and instructional decisions in pre-service portfolio assessments or in-service professional learning plans.

Bruner, 1961, 1973	Curriculum designed with disciplinary content on a spiral curriculum and inductive thinking to reveal concepts
Byrnes, 2008	Articulation through content and culture
Eddy, 2007f, 2010a, 2017, 2019a	World Language curriculum vertically articulated with concepts, themes and performance tasks for transfer
Erickson, 2007	Concept-based curriculum and instruction
Ornstein & Hunkins, 2004 Sahlberg, 2007	Curriculum must be live, responsive, always in revision, not a fixed product. Focus on flexibility, meaning, creativity and social experience
Wiggins & McTighe, 2005, 2011	Curriculum designed backward from conceptual goals and key performances

I can

- Identify formative tasks from exemplars
- Design tasks that are near transfer to support the summative key performance assessment
- Collaborate with colleagues to design for articulated, spiral curriculum

> **Rewind**
>
> Which terms or concepts stand out for you from *Chapter 6: Designing for Presentational goals: Creating meaning for mediation?*
>
> Ask your colleague three questions based on the content from the last chapter.
>
> Explain the most compelling idea from the previous chapter in your own words.
>
> Explain how this concept or practice is the same, similar or different to what you know or do.
>
> Which concept or practice do you think will have the greatest impact on your teaching?

Overview

The last chapter on the Presentational mode explained culminating tasks which for the AATTs represent the final, summative Key Performance task for a unit or scheme of work for Stage Two on your template. Now that you have Key Performances at three levels of engagement that represent at least three *Articulation Spiral Points* in your curriculum, it is time to shift to formative assessments for Stage Three. Long-standing practice in most language departments is planning individual lessons from lists of grammar and vocabulary first. The fact that it is considered last always surprises the seasoned and novice instructor alike, so here we are. In this chapter, we review components for Stage Three of ICANADAPT with some unit sample exemplars from teacher work seen throughout the book. In addition, we explore relevant steps to initiate or augment articulated design for faculty and instructors at any level of instruction to consider. A unit implementation plan guide and key steps are included in this chapter to facilitate a smooth 'step in' transition to this design. Department chairs and faculty who have typically not designed together before will see the flexibility inherent in their curriculum and clarity within their programme for articulation goals.

It's all about performance assessment for transfer and practice at mediation

The AATTs were designed as summative assessments *of* learning, the final performance assessment of the unit or scheme of work. They serve as the Key Performances on your spiral curriculum. Key Performances require thoughtful, flexible use of content, knowledge and skills for transfer. Many teachers also use these tasks as formative assessments *for* learning along the course of the unit. Then they are particularly useful for multi-level learners in the same classroom and ideal for differentiated assessment. Formative tasks for transfer still show evidence of the thinking and support behind the response, not just the response itself. Just as with the summative assessment, the formative assessments in Stage Three of your ICANADAPT template (see Figure 1.3) should show increasing novelty for a new situation or work on a product. The learner needs to be able to perform them with minimal prompting by the teacher to do the content or discipline. These near-transfer tasks show the ability to adjust, draw inferences, generalize, compare and contrast, argue, critique and evaluate the work of others as well as one's own: assessment *as* learning (Dann, 2014; Earl, 2003). It is in this place that assessment and instruction appear seamless. Lesson-level tasks call for learners to apply their skills with flexibility, variation and increasing novelty until they receive the summative assessment which is new and has no supports (see Table 7.1).

For this reason, formative assessments must be designed after the summative Key Performance Tasks in the AATT. When you know what the final assessment looks like, it is judicious as well as genuine to develop the ones that must lead up to it.

For ICANADAPT, this Stage:

- Details formative assessments for learning
- Assists the teacher in selecting only relevant grammar and vocabulary needed to do the tasks
- Organizes spiralled content and aligns its purpose with Cultures standard and intercultural goals in Stage One

During the lessons, learners

- Develop their repertoire with near transfer tasks
- Use content as review, spiral and new
- Self-assess with PASS and Intercultural Transfer Targets

Teachers in world languages and most other content areas habitually plan lessons first. Unfortunately, they often attempt to cover large portions of content, plan a lot of activities that may not address a performance or conceptual goal and consider assessment last. When designing summative or formative assessment tasks, remember the 'must-haves' or non-negotiables of true performance. Consider what happens anytime we communicate:interactions are non-scripted; information has gaps. Materials are not filtered, arranged cleanly or adapted. We must sift through anything we hear or see to get precisely what we need to solve a problem, create something of any use and move on. These are characteristics of tasks that simulate what it is like to do a subject in real life. It is not a repetitive drill or mastery of facts.

How often have we drilled something repeatedly, but the learner still cannot understand the concept behind the example? Sometimes we teach without allowing the desired performance to inform the instruction. Do our materials focus too much on discrete facts and four skills in isolation? Consider that experts in their fields manage their knowledge repertoire not by amassing lists of facts about their chosen discipline but by arranging and structuring their knowledge and skills around a few 'must-have', non-negotiable concepts (National Research Council, 2000). The transferable concepts are embedded in the culture or cultures that live, work and inform every subject and discipline. This is why this curriculum framework asks you to focus on those few must-haves, to let the performances that prove learner flexibility be novel and frequent.

Table 7.1 Summative and Formative Assessment

Stage Two	Stage Three
Assessment **of** learning	Assessment **for** learning and **as** learning
Summative Assessment end of unit	**Formative Assessments** during instruction
Key performance for transfer requiring flexible use of knowledge and skill repertoire	Near transfer tasks with supports and scaffolds to adjust, infer, generalize, compare, and evaluate the work of others as well as one's own
Prepared for an audience, group, or individual beyond the classroom, real or fictitious	Can be internal only or with other's needs and value beyond the classroom

Pause to Ponder

Now that you have designed key summative performances for the AATT, what do these tasks imply for knowledge and skills required to do them? At each of the three levels, what will the learner need to do the task?

Check for Learning

Examine your performance tasks thus far.

Ask the question: What does this help me to do? Why are we learning this? Art and music students can always answer this question. Many textbook assessments fail the criteria. Is it valuable as solely a classroom exercise? Is the task one that asks for exhaustive lists of grammar forms out of context? What is this for?

What does it mean to 'do' in relation to intercultural transferable concepts and goals?

Our tasks for formative assessment still support transfer with the goal of making new meaning every day. Drill-tests are exercises out of context, a discrete, isolated element that is unrealistically setup and prompted. This item does not transfer without practice in adapting it to new situations. Drills give the appearance of understanding but not the reality of transfer (Eddy, 2009b). True performance even in formative assessment will have all its messiness and interest value. These tasks still require a repertoire, used wisely and thoughtfully. The less prompts or guidance the learner receives, the more it assesses for transfer (see Table 7.2). As we have seen from designing summative assessments for AATTs, the learner judges what to do and when. Transfer tasks, however small and guided initially, provide the steps towards the Key Performance tasks and your Articulation Spiral Points throughout your curriculum. The AATTs represent not the occasional treat but "mains", an anthology of Key Performances indicating how the learner *does the discipline*. The formative assessments completed in class and at home support them.

Putting It Together for Articulation and Transfer

Table 7.2 None to Nigh to Near to Novel Transfer Annotated

None	Nigh and Nearby	Near Transfer	Novel Transfer
Drill Decontextualized content	Familiar Task with Supports	Unfamiliar Task with Supports	Completely New Task No supports
Fill-in-the-blank Multiple choice Matching Vocabulary quizzes Spelling quizzes Dictation	Read menus and design your own menu	Students read several authentic menus and identify which dishes from the list are appropriate for different people based on their likes/dislikes	A new concept restaurant needs menu ideas for authentic cuisine that is dairy free, no pork, gluten free, etc.
Verb conjugation Listing verb endings Chanting verb endings Choral repetition Multiple questions of the same item	Students read real estate ads and design their dream home.	Students read several apartments ads and listen to the needs of four groups. Decide with a partner the features and apartments best for: kids under 12, accessible, public transport, college students, etc.	*HomeTV* is doing a series on new communities in ___. Plan new housing development in a chosen neighbourhood, keeping the community's needs in mind.

Check for Learning

As you review your catalogue of Key Performance Tasks for your AATT and Stage Two, consider the table above. Are your tasks Nigh, Near or Novel for transfer? As you look at your ICANADAPT exemplars for Stage Three, what kind of formative assessment do you see? How do these compare with tasks from textbooks or other materials?

(For a master list of task types for the modes of communication, see Appendix NN.)

Assessment as instruction

Below is an AATT followed by a sample of a Stage Three unit by Ms LingLing Xie (see full unit sample Appendix DD). The formative tasks and content chosen here will support the Novice High summative assessment in the AATT. The goal areas of Connections, Communities and Comparisons support the Cultures standard (National Standards Collaborative Board, 2015) in ICANADAPT. Ms Xie aligns those PASS Can-Dos back to the intercultural goals of the EUs and EQs. In addition, the *Intercultural Transfer Targets* (Eddy, 2017) enhance the Can-Do statements (NCSSFL, 2014/2017), to focus on perspectives, practices and comparisons within transdisciplinary connections and community engagement, for utility beyond the classroom. These statements show how this task explains and clarifies the cultural response within another discipline and makes it accessible to someone else unfamiliar, unacquainted or otherwise inexperienced with the culture(s), to make it accessible to them. This feature reinforces transfer through mediation, that the learner can do this via strategies at the point in which they can perform right now and not think they must have perfection in the language in order to do so.

The panel for *Review, Spiral and New* (Eddy, 2017), lists only the grammar, vocabulary and content needed to do the task. This process makes sure there is no extra material that is not addressed in the assessment. *Review* indicates content taught earlier that same year. *Spiral* designates the vocabulary or grammar point that is spiraled from a previous year. *New* specifies that this unit is the first time that learners will encounter that content. This feature works smoothly with any curricula or scheme of work that specifies vocabulary at particular stages or points, since the pupil can revisit and reprise words as they engage in performance tasks requiring new terms, deeper abstraction and further transfer.

Teacher as Designer

Ms LingLing Xie examines values of education and school life for a Chinese curriculum. Each task transitions the learner through the concept of education in Chinese culture, with each level contributing to the new student exchange programme. With this collection of tasks, learners develop intercultural communicative competence strategies for mediation as they learn to clarify visuals and school procedures to others and compare US and Chinese school systems and expectations, with the use of the *Intercultural Transfer Targets*. Note the use of time frames as it applies to Chinese in the Intermediate High tasks. This performance target addresses those criteria (ACTFL, 2012) for Advanced Low, even though learners cannot perform consistently in all modalities at that level.

Voices from the Field

The important role of education in Chinese values and daily life make this concept essential in an articulated curriculum for intercultural competence for teaching my language and culture. Students will understand that education is treated as the key channel to personal success and studying hard can lead to a bright future. Chinese students spend long hours in school and learn the same curriculum in the same classroom. In order to give the children a good future, Chinese families make every effort to prepare their children for college. Even a novice learner can unpack these concepts by exploring authentic Chinese school schedules and then prepare a daily schedule with a particular audience in mind. Designing this way helps me implement intercultural competence into my daily class teaching. In addition, it helped design the presentational task for students to demonstrate and apply their understanding of Chinese culture.

LingLing Xie   Herricks Public Schools, New York

Table 7.3 Articulated Assessment Transfer Task   School and Education

Chinese	LingLing Xie, Herricks High School, NY
Enduring Understandings	
* Education is the key channel to personal success in China.	
* Intense study for a good grade in the college exam can lead to a bright future.	
* Chinese families make every effort to send their children to a good college or to study abroad.	
* Chinese school curriculum and school life reflects the culture of collectivism.	

Essential Questions
? How do we define success and plan for it?
? What matters in our schools?
? What do priorities in educational systems tell us about our own culture?
? To what extent does family play a role in education?

Context
A high school in China is developing an international exchange student programme with a US high school. They need your help for presenting Chinese family school and education between two countries. The programme wants to combine the advantages of both Chinese and American education and meet the needs of both Chinese and American students. You are presenting to the Chinese audience the best school schedule, a day on a high school campus, and comparison of the educational system and benefits of studying abroad.

Articulation Spiral Points
@ Identify school requirements in daily schedule.
@ Explain school culture, expectations and educational environments in Vlog.
@ Compare details and give opinions on school systems in Vlog.
@ Create report for families on the ideal school system.

Intercultural Transfer Targets	Mediation for Transfer
• I can compare school schedules between cultures for someone unfamiliar with them. • I can identify aspects of school culture and how they reflect the values of the culture in general. • I can explain Eastern and Western school systems and make these two concepts accessible. • I can describe similarities and differences of learning environments in China and other countries.	• Bridge and exchange ideas and concepts of schooling and education between cultures. • Clarify typical visuals, signs, materials in schools. • Explain features of school procedures to others. • Share expectations of school here and abroad.

Novice High	Intermediate Low-Mid	Intermediate High
Chinese high school schedule	Vlog about Shanghai high school student & Vlog about Beijing high school international student	Chinese college examination vs. study abroad
Interpretive Task Descriptions		
Read an authentic school schedule and answer the questions.	Watch a vlog about a day in Chinese high school, arrange the sequence of the activities and pose questions about the video.	Read an article about the road to college, taking Chinese college examination or studying abroad. They will answer questions and form five questions on their own.
Can Dos		
I can respond to simple questions about a school schedule.	I can infer, ask and respond to live or recorded introductions, details and descriptions by students from a partner school.	I can elaborate on the main idea of the article about the goal of high school with follow-up questions in various time frames.
Interpersonal Task Descriptions		
Share their comments with their partners about different school subjects on the schedule.	Discuss with the partners about similarities and differences between Chinese and American school schedules and learning environments.	With a partner, talk about the different products, perspectives and practices between Chinese and American school culture.

Can Dos		
I can differentiate which classes are harder or easier than others and why.	I can express opinions about the length of the school day and the learning environment between different cultures.	I can justify and exchange opinions about education in different cultures.
Presentational Task Descriptions		
Create the optimal school daily schedule which fits the needs of Chinese and American students.	Create a vlog to present about what is the best school and learning environment.	For a blog on viewpoints on Eastern and Western education, present the ideal school system.
Can Dos		
In my own and other cultures, I can identify some elements of a school schedule, and how they reflect the culture.	I can create a video to describe my ideal school day and learning environment.	I can compare school and curricula to determine what is valued now and then in my own and other cultures.

Bridge to Design

How does Ms Xie's work help us think about the role of education across many cultures? Let's get closer to her design process with other colleagues to share additional ideas and reflection before working on your own design.

(See Appendix EE in Companion Website Chapter 7.)

Table 7.4 Stage Three Unit Sample Education

Stage 3: Learning Experiences and Instruction: Connections-Comparisons-Communities				
Formative Assessments during lessons	**Mode** **IN** **IP** **PR**	**Performance Assessment Specific Statements I can…**	**Vocabulary and Grammar Review (R) same year Spiral (S) previous year New (N) for this unit.**	**Intercultural Transfer Targets**
Students will read a schedule about a Chinese school and answer the questions. With a partner, students will interact and come to a consensus on the type of subject schedule that fits their needs. Students will develop a survey for their peers about school subjects and their needs for the China high school. Students watch an interview video and fill out the chart about the typical Chinese student daily schedule. Paired with a partner, the students ask questions and create Venn diagrams to illustrate similarities and differences between their daily schedules at their school and in China. Students will present the Venn Diagram and talk about the similarities and differences between Chinese and American school schedules.	IN IP PR IN IP PR	I can understand the class schedules of a day at a Chinese school. I can interact and exchange information to select the type of subjects that best fits my needs. I can develop a simple survey about school subjects and schedules. I can listen and interpret the information in the video. I can compare the daily school schedule at my school and in China. I can present and compare the daily schedule between Chinese and American schools.	中文(S) "Chinese"老师 (R) "teacher" 学生(R) "student" 课 (S)"class" 英文 (N) "English" 数学(N) "Math" 音乐(N) "Music" 喜欢 (S)"like" 点(N) "O'clock" 分(N) "Minute" 刻(N) "Quarter" 早上(R) "Morning" 中午(R) "Noon"	I can identify some elements of a school schedule, or levels of schooling in my own and other cultures. I can indicate differences in school schedules to someone else unfamiliar with the Chinese system. I can clarify routines which characterize Chinese cultures and schooling to someone else. In my own and other cultures, I can compare school routines and curricula to determine how they reflect the culture.

Teacher as Designer

Ms Hanna-Wicht's AATT exemplar explores three Arabic communities: nomadic, rural and urban. Note the connectedness in concept and presentation of the three homes and the scaffolding used in the unit sample (See Appendix FF in Companion Website Chapter 7.)

Voices from the Field

When I took your course back in 2016 to design my own Arabic-language articulated curriculum, my inspiration for this AATT and Unit was the diversity of a landscape that spans twenty-two Arabic-speaking states. From the Atlantic Ocean in the West, to the Gulf in the East, and from the Mediterranean in the North, to the Indian Sea in the South, the region spans 5,070,420 sq miles and is home to some 500 million people.

The tasks are designed to introduce learners to three dwellings مساكن ثلاثة in the Arabic-speaking countries العربية باللغة المتحدثة الدول. Participants will discover a nomadic Bedouin tent رحل ودب خيمة; a rural farm in a village مغربية قرية في ريفية مزرعة; and an urban home منزل مدني. Authentic resources will provide the context by which students will explore the layout and contents of dwellings.

My choice of nomadic, rural and urban communities is intentional in that each of those populations presents homes, lives, and practices that are interconnected and build on one another. The life of a Bedouin in Jordan is, by its nomadic nature, quite minimalist. Therefore, the vocabulary is meaningfully restricted. As learners move from Novice to Intermediate Low, they visit a Moroccan rural farm, where a more complex landscape of a village setting is introduced. Lastly, at the Intermediate-Mid level, learners discover the ultra-modern urban Dubai in the United Arab Emirates.

Each level builds on the previous in authentic contexts that represent people's homes and lives. By clearly articulating the end goal of the unit and connecting it to future and previous units, instructors provide learners with an awareness of how language will be acquired and of the path to increased language proficiency. Furthermore, learners can establish a range of interdisciplinary connections and experience true intercultural citizenship. All these places, I trust, will spark an interest to further discover this rich region and its languages.

Susan Hanna-Wicht, Arabic Instructor

Table 7.5 Articulated Assessment Transfer Task — Our Lives, Our Homes

Arabic	Susan Hanna-Wicht
Enduring Understandings * Our homes are unique yet meet universal human needs. * Our dwellings are shaped by our environment and personal, family, social and cultural values. * Our home sustains essential human needs for shelter, food and interaction.	
Essential Questions ? Do our homes shape our lives? ? What makes our homes both unique and similar? ? How does the environment influence our home? ? How do social practices determine our home layout? ? To what extent are cultural practices, homes and lives interconnected?	
Context In preparation for trips to Jordan, Morocco, and Dubai, learners prepare texts and materials to compare homes, describe lifestyles and communities and explain cultural practices.	
Articulation Spiral Points @ Develop models or drawings of Nomadic tent @ Acquire items in the village centre @ Plan a typical week in Dubai	
Intercultural Transfer Targets • I can identify characteristics of homes in three distinct regions • I can make comparisons between nomadic, rural and urban lifestyles to people from other cultures • I can describe common items to someone unfamiliar with homes in these regions • I can express myself in different communities appropriately and help others new to the cultures	**Mediation for Transfer** • Bridge and exchange ideas and concepts of homes and lifestyles • Clarify concepts of diversity and interconnectedness • Describe features of nomadic, rural and urban lives to others unfamiliar with these communities • Instruct others on how to acquire items according to location and need

Novice High	Intermediate Mid	Intermediate High
Authentic Materials		
Learners discover the layout of a Bedouin tent, trace Bedouin tents to early human settlements and appreciate the indigenous, nomadic way of life and how it may be endangered. Watch a tribal dwelling in Jordan video YouTube on the Jordanian Bedouin population.	Learners travel to a village in the Atlas mountains in Morocco and discover a farm with animals and crops. They will compare this with the Bedouin lifestyle. Watch excerpts from video بالج الطالس الكبيرى. بالمغرب: وادي الزلات Moroccan Atlas farmsteads.	Learners are moving to Dubai for six months to study Arabic. Watch this video and be welcomed to an urban home in Dubai دبي
Interpretive Task Descriptions		
Organize items or practices that are a) unique to nomadic way of life and b) universal. Draw comparisons between nomadic community life and your own. See unit for Items. Answer these questions: كيف يعيش الناس في الصحراء؟ لماذا اذا نجد بيوت مصنوعة من الوبر؟ ما وسائل التنقل في الصحراء؟	Take notes on the village in the Atlas mountain farmstead using the graphic organizer. Answer these questions: كيف يعيش الناس في قرية جبلية؟ لماذا نجد بيوت مصنوعة من الطين؟ ما وسائل التنقل إلى القرية؟	Summarize three interesting points from the video, answer these questions: كيف يعيش الناس في مدينة مثل دبي؟ لماذا نجد بيوت مصنوعة من الطابوق؟ ما وسائل التنقل في المدينة؟ and write three more questions. Vocabulary includes: ،أهل، عائلة، أطفال، حديقة، مدخل، مطبخ، غرفة نوم، صالون، غرفة جلوس، ،ستارة، زريعات، دارب، ورق جردان، أحذية، أصفر، ستوديو

Putting It Together for Articulation and Transfer

Can Dos		
I can label and distinguish familiar words, phrases and sentences related to everyday living in a Nomadic home. I can recognize the main idea and phrases. I can compare Nomadic life with lifestyles of other communities.	I can infer the main idea in a short excerpt from the video on communities living in the Atlas mountains.	I can summarize the main idea and supporting details on the video describing an apartment in Dubai. I can answer and form follow up questions on urban homes.
Interpersonal Task Descriptions		
Watch this video and share likes and dislikes about living in the desert, eating certain foods, drinking certain beverages, wearing certain clothing items. أنا أحب \ ال أحب أن أسكن في الصحراء أن أنا ما في خيمة أن أشرب أن القهوة \ بي الحلب آكل الخبز \ اللحمة \ ألبس الجبنة أن اللباس التقليدي	Learners ask and answer questions with a partner and come to consensus on differences between Atlas mountain farm community and the Bedouin lifestyle.	Watch this video on urban apartments and ask your partner three questions about city life and preferences.
Can Dos		
I can express culturally appropriate greetings and present my family. سهلاً السلام عليكم، مرحباً، أهلاً تفضل	I can ask and answer simple questions about the farming community. I can compare two lifestyles and homes.	I can exchange information about homes in a large city like Dubai.

Presentational Task Descriptions		
Plan to visit Jordan and discover the nomadic Bedouin way of life. Draw or create a model of a nomadic tent and include labelled (in Arabic) items for the dwellings. In pairs, students present to each other their tents, its contents. They may exchange items (barter), using polite expressions to ask and provide something.	Make a 3D model of a farm and include animals of their choice. Present items they need for their farm, for travel to the village centre and to acquire what they need. Note similarities or differences between the rural farm, Bedouin and other communities.	Prepare a video describing (1) what a typical week in Dubai will involve or city of my choice (including weekends, places to see, trips, etc.), and (2) what kind of home they need.
Can Dos		
I can identify items pertaining to nomadic life in the desert. I can exchange and barter for items appropriately.	I can use a model to describe life in the Atlas Mountains in Morocco and compare with other communities.	I can describe a week's activities in the city and expectations for homes and lodging.

Bridge to Design

How does Ms Hanna-Wicht's AATT exemplar unfold the concept of home and lifestyle in these three distinct yet deeply connected communities? Let's go deeper into these formative tasks and how her unit excerpt provides the supports. Share additional ideas and reflection with colleagues before working on your own design.

(See Appendix GG in Companion Website Chapter 7.)

Putting It Together for Articulation and Transfer   257

Check for Learning

The annotated ICANADAPT Concept Map (see Figure 7.1) shows the unit conceptual design for Viva La Vida, the first AATT exemplar in this book. The area for knowledge and skills has an area for notes on instructional strategies, now that the performance tasks are designed.

Compare your ICANADAPT Concept Map with the annotated map. Have your concept map next to you when you design with the unit template.

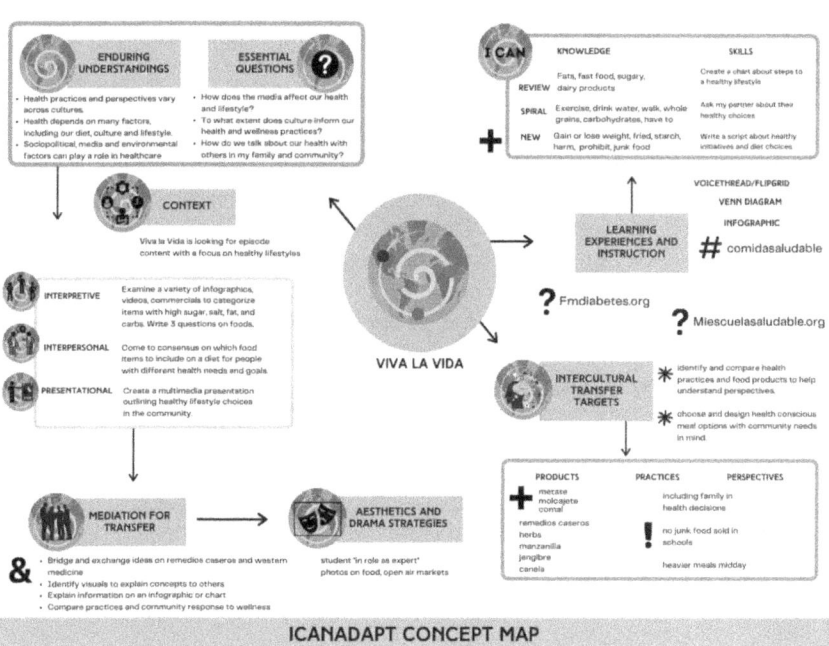

Figure 7.1 ICANADAPT Concept Map Health

Teacher as Designer

Ms Ekaterina Kalmanson presents one of her lessons here on Axe Porridge (see Table 7.6), from the AATT in Chapter 2. This lesson plan from Stage Three breaks down further the specific instructional strategies and supports prior to the AATT Summative Key Performance Tasks. This lesson was planned last, after the summative and formative assessments were designed. How do you think this process helped the teacher? How are learners more accountable for what they know and are able to do?

(For this ICANADAPT unit, see Appendix HH. For additional lessons, see Appendix II in Companion Website Chapter 7.)

Table 7.6 Lesson Plan

Teacher: Ekaterina Kalmanson	Proficiency Target: Novice High	Unit Theme: National Identity
Central Focus: The central focus of this lesson is to introduce students to *smekalka* and to engage them in simple conversation about themselves and to share their experiences and reflections about *smekalka* using the three modes of communication and language forms to convey meaning.		
Enduring Understanding (s): The ability to think outside the box is highly valued in Russian culture. There are differences and similarities between people of different cultures in their values, beliefs, and ways of thinking.		
Essential Question (s): How do we emerge from a difficult situation with no support or resources? How can we think outside the box? Is ability to think outside the box intercultural?		
Standards Addressed: (National Standards Collaborative Board, 2015)		
Cultures: Students can reflect on an idea that *smekalka* is not only an ability to think outside the box to get what we want using the means handy and an ingenious mind, but also the ability to cope with a difficult situation or crisis and act effectively. Students can identify what *smekalka* is and its intercultural nature.		

Putting It Together for Articulation and Transfer

Communication Standard Informal/Formal Assessments	Comparisons- Connections- Communities
Interpretive: Students will infer meaning from the memes about *smekalka*.	**Comparisons:** Students make comparisons of their personal experiences of thinking outside the box with the meme's content and the moral of the story.
Interpersonal: Students ask each other's opinions about memes.	**Connections:** Students use their knowledge of people's ability to think outside the box to infer meaning from the Axe Porridge story and Russian memes.
Presentational: Students will create and present new memes about *smekalka* proving that this is an intercultural trait.	**Communities:** Students use their knowledge and skills developed in this unit to express their reflections about the interculturality of the ability to think outside the box.

I can distinguish what *smekalka* is.	**I can** ask questions about *smekalka*	**I can** present examples of my ability to think out of the box.

Step by step delivery of lesson
Warm Up: To enter the room students need to whisper to the teacher six axe porridge ingredients.
Focus Question (s): What is *smekalka*? Who has *smekalka*, the Old Lady or the Soldier? Do only Russian people have *smekalka*?
Motivation: Teacher announces that today detectives will investigate smekalka. Students need to indicate who has smekalka, The Old Lady or the Soldier?
Interpretive Mode Tasks: The teacher presents memes about *smekalka*. When there is text in a meme, the teacher reads it out loud and scaffolds comprehension using synonyms, TPR and visuals. Students inspect Russian memes about *smekalka* and rank them from the most favorite to the least favorite, using Poll Everywhere.

Additional Mode Tasks/Activities: The teacher models communicative situations by declaring her preferences and using ordinal numbers. Some students share their preferences using ordinal numbers. Students vote for each meme finding the most popular and the least popular memes. The teacher displays the ranking results. The teacher models questions, asking one of the students if she/he has *smekalka* and can prove it with a picture. Then the teacher asks two students to exchange questions and answers. Then all the students go around the class and ask their classmates if they have *smekalka* or personally know people who have it. Can they prove it with pictures? Students need to count positive answers and report it to the class.	
Homework: Create and present your own meme about smekalka. Post it on the Google Classroom *Smekalka* Discussion Board.	
Summary and Closure: Do only Russians have *smekalka*? (no)	

Learning Objectives/ Forms/Functions	Learning experiences and Instructional Strategies:
Students will infer meaning from the story and memes, ask questions, discuss *smekalka*, create their own memes about *smekalka*, express likes and dislikes, apply appropriate cultural responses for situations, exchange information while creating axe porridge infographics and present them to the group using appropriate sentence structure, ordinal numbers and expressions to exchange information.	Differentiation: I provide strong comprehensible input using a lot of visuals, props and TPR. Furthermore, I will use flexible grouping. Presentation and modelling: The teacher presents new material using visuals and TPR, also the teacher models questions and answers. Guided and independent practice: Teacher gradually releases responsibilities, models questions and answers, scaffolds understanding using a lot of props and visuals. Addressing misconceptions: Explain how common misconceptions are addressed for example, include common misconceptions (in language, culture or form) and how you will address those errors or misconceptions. A common misconception is that Russian people cannot think outside the box to get what they want using the means handy, an ingenious mind, and are not able to cope with a difficult situation or crisis and act effectively.

Materials:
Authentic texts Axe Porridge cartoon and Memes
Materials/supplies needed: Smart Board
Instructional resources: Axe porridge cartoon, *smekalka* memes, the anonymous letter
Technology platforms/apps Google Drawings/meme generator

Research in Practice Alignment

Researcher/ Practitioner	Concept, theory or practice	Specific example in my planning, assessment, or instruction
Eddy, J. From Coverage Without Pity to Performance: World Language Curriculum and Assessment Exposed in the Light of Backward Design. NYSAFLT Journal	Eddy believes that performance assessment design engages the learner in transfer tasks with less reliance on supports and repeated drills. They teach the learner to expect variation.	The AATTs are designed to prepare students to use Russian language outside the classroom and to engage cultural transfer by introducing students to the *smekalka* concept. Using memes at this early level, they can mediate and explain this cultural concept with examples to someone unfamiliar with the word. In this unit students grow an ability to be tolerant of new circumstances and to be able to apply critical thinking to solve problems with almost no cues.
Sandrock, P. (2014). Keys to Assessment. Alexandria, VA: ACTFL.	Sandrock believes that performance assessments focus the instructional activities toward a clear communicative purpose. If students skim material in the interpretive task in order to pull out the main idea and key details, then the teacher also models this process while leading students through an example.	In this lesson, I incorporated the idea of *smekalka* throughout all three communicative modes to prepare students for the summative assessment where they need to be able to not only understand that *smekalka* is an ability to think outside the box and the ability to get what you want using the means handy and an ingenious mind, but to differentiate between *smekalka* and artifice and to clarify *smekalka* as a great intercultural trait.

VanPatten, B. (2017). While We're on the Topic: BVP on Language, Acquisition, and Classroom Practice. Alexandria, VA: ACTFL.	Van Patten believes that if we teach communicatively but test the same old stuff, we are doomed to failure.	In this lesson students discover the idea of *smekalka* and I assess their understanding by assessing students' ability to apply new knowledge in real life and to create a meme about *smekalka*.

Encores from our designers

Any theme, any concept, any level in the spiral: Examine Unit samples for the AATTs *Child Labour, Lockdown Yoga* and *Gender-Based Violence* for additional insight and ideas on making these themes, language and cultural contexts accessible for learners at all levels.
(see Appendices JJ, KK, LL in Companion Website Chapter 7.)

Design for Transfer

Using your Stage Three ICANADAPT template (see Figure 1.3), decide the grammar, vocabulary and other content needed to do the formative assessment in one of the three modes. Only select what learners need to use to do the assessment and indicate if the element is *Review, Spiral or New*.

Design for Transfer

Using your Stage Three ICANADAPT template (see Figure 1.3 and fillable template Appendix OO), derive the Intercultural Transfer Targets from the formative assessments on the left. Remember that these clarify the cultural response within the given disciplinary content and make it accessible to someone else unfamiliar, unacquainted, or inexperienced with the culture (s), in order to make it accessible to them.

> (To see another sample of the ITTs, see Appendix B. ITT Articulation Chart)
> (For fillable AATT, ICANADAPT, and Lesson Plan templates, see Appendix OO in Companion Website Chapter 7.)
>
>

Towards a flexible, bespoke curriculum

The AATT and ICANADAPT curriculum framework is flexible, yet is responsive to required standards, particularly those which maintain planning habits with Stage Three topics, vocabulary lists and grammar. Even with national or state curricula where there are fixed topics by level, grammar and vocabulary, begin with Intercultural transferable goals first and design the summative performance assessments for transfer right away. Learners will thrive with Key Performances presented in your curriculum catalogue rather than fragmented and decontextualized knowledge and skills.

The following implementation tools, *Tips to Articulated Design* and subsequent *Design for Transfer* tasks are intended to start conversations within your departments and reflect on principles in this book. If you are a new or seasoned teacher, this is a great time to discuss these with your school colleagues or in a professional learning community. If a department wishes to start curriculum revision, these tips guide the curriculum team as they use this book.

In *Designing World Language Curriculum for Intercultural Communicative Competence,* the teacher designers have made the case for curriculum design driven by intercultural and transdisciplinary competence as the hook for sustained inquiry across levels, buildings and schools. Hopefully their exemplars have inspired you to design your own AATTs and ICANADAPT exemplars for your curricula, schemes of work, units and programmes.

Design World Language/MFL curriculum for transfer and make meaning new every day.

Prepare language learners for the inevitable unexpected.

Implementation for articulation

The Unit Guide (Eddy, 2010a, 2017) (see Appendix MM) is an implementation tool designed to be distributed to pupils at the onset of a unit or scheme of work. This tool presents a clear overview of the unit within the big picture conceptual scope as well as details for its appearance during this unit. It functions as a 'movie trailer' to your unit as it does not give too much away to the learner. All of the EUs and EQs for that Intercultural Transferable Goal or concept/theme are included, even though they may not all be addressed during that unit. The teacher checks off only those that are present. This is so the learner recognizes the continuity throughout the programme and sees these enter, exit, reprise and recur as they should during the programme. Just as a *basso continuo* provides structure during a Baroque musical piece, so do the EUs and EQs for the curriculum design and implementation. On this sheet is the Context for the AATT, the PASS Can-Dos, and the *Intercultural Transfer Targets*. These tools let learners know that everything they will learn is relevant, applicable and aligns back to the Context. It prevents questions such as 'Do we need to know this?' and 'Is this going to be on the test?' Learners have a very clear idea what the unit is about, recognize past ideas to reach back, to reflect and have Can Do's to prepare for what will happen.

Design for Transfer

Using the Unit Guide as a model, develop your own unit guide and share with a colleague. Walk your colleague through the unit using the tool. Does it present a complete picture?

Use in tandem with your Concept Map.

Seven tips to articulated design with AATTs and ICANADAPT

1 As a department, choose the intercultural transfer goals, those concepts and themes that matter for your cultures and are present throughout transdisciplinary works. These will recur and reprise K-12, 7-12, 9-12, KS2-KS4, KS5; Pre A1-C.

2 Design Enduring Understandings and Essential Questions at programme level for those themes. Every EU and EQ does not have to be treated each year.

3 Decide which years these concepts will occur, some may reappear and exit over time, as long as at the end, all are done. Not all units need be of equal length.

4 Design Summative performance assessments for each concept for each unit year with the AATTs. Gather the culturally authentic material for the tasks.

5 Design Formative assessments which move towards full transfer for each unit year.

6 Then and only then, plan activities, instruction, and knowledge and skills required for those assessments. Grammar, vocabulary and the points illustrated in this design are not mutually exclusive, but work together more powerfully and with intention toward transfer and flexible use and performance capital beyond the classroom.

7 If your department is large, you may wish to have a smaller design team. Other department members can develop the repository of authentic materials. Make sure the design team has teachers from different levels. All levels and languages work with each other. Middle School and High School or KS2-KS3-KS4-KS5 are not separated in this work. If there is an early language or elementary programme, a representative should also be on this design team. If K-16 articulation through university is desired, form the team from both secondary and post-secondary levels. ICANADAPT is ideal for any college or university wishing to revise their major and coursework with intercultural themes that reprise through cultural history and disciplined themes.

Design for Transfer

Take another look at the formative assessments for your unit and scheme of work. How well do they move the learner towards far transfer and the summative performance task at the end?

Take any activity or task your students currently do. Does it use the material in a novel way from how it was originally taught? Is this a situation they might actually encounter in some way in the target culture? Is there a new result they can create, however small?

With that in mind, move your task along that transfer path now.

(For a master list of task types for the modes of communication, see Appendix NN.)

(For ICANADAPT template with fillable fields, AATT, lesson plan and Scheme of Work companion templates with fillable fields, see Appendix OO on the Companion Website Chapter 7.)

Collaboration for articulation

At the start of this book, we considered **Seven guiding principles for world language curriculum design:**

1 Intercultural perspectives and transdisciplinary content unfold articulated curriculum and scaffold key tasks of meaningful performance.

2 Learners acquire and own language not by linear and predictable memorization of functions, structures, and forms but through creative, unpredictable interaction in tasks using transdisciplinary content in texts.

3 Key Performance Tasks are designed for transfer to novel contexts, situations or audiences.

4 Complexity differentiates tasks, not topics, themes, or texts.

5 Learners are active social agents co-constructing meaning through mediation and complex tasks across languages and cultures.

6 Tasks solve problems and create products relevant to college, community, work and world.

7 Learners take risks to apply their repertoire flexibly but not with native-like accuracy.

- Choose two of these and discuss with a colleague, giving examples or non-examples with curricula you already know. How do you see these principles within those curricular plans, schemes of work or materials? Use the Tool for Articulation with the seven guiding principles for world language curriculum design. (See Appendix PP.)

- As stated, with any curriculum design re-vision, it is important to start small, with two or three concepts and key assessments first, rather than do the entire curriculum in a year. Discuss with colleagues which concepts you will choose first to spiral and reprise.

Design for Transfer

We all come to curriculum design in a different *place* and at a different *pace*. Where do you see yourself, programme, department, or colleagues? To what extent do these principles align with your practice?

Not yet	Getting Started	Still at it-Needs Work	Almost there

Design for transfer

Intercultural perspectives and transdisciplinary content unfold articulated curriculum and scaffold key tasks of meaningful performance.

Choose two intercultural transferable concepts or goals, perspectives, or themes and decide where these two will enter, exit and reprise throughout your curriculum. Do these concepts also appear in Social Studies, Health, or Arts? If so, perhaps they can appear during the same year, but it is not required.

Place the tasks from your AATTs in those years along the curriculum on an articulated timeline. For these two concepts, you now have a short catalogue of the Key Performance Tasks, the Articulation Spiral Points.

Task: Create a multimedia presentation of these for your curriculum and assessment course, your PLC, or department.

Design for Transfer

Learners acquire and own language not by linear and predictable memorization of functions, structures and forms but through *creative, unpredictable interaction in tasks using transdisciplinary content in texts.*

Task: Go deeper into this principle and make the case to a colleague or department lead that language within content texts is key, with evidence that the language repertoire we truly own happens while we are busy doing something else with it.

Design for Transfer

Complexity differentiates tasks, not topics, themes or texts.

Task: Examine a curriculum framework for your state, local district, or country and find any evidence and examples of this principle or evidence to the contrary. Compare with a curriculum from another county, parish, state or country. Do you see tasks designed for complexity or are topics and themes allocated by level? Are materials chosen by their complexity or are tasks designed with those materials to meet a target requirement? Do this research and present it to colleagues.

Design for Transfer

Consider Principles 3 and 5. Have you seen this in practice at your school or department?

Task: If so, give examples of tasks. If not, share a task that you can Turnaround to Transfer as a Key Performance in your curriculum.

Design for Transfer

Consider Principles 6 and 7. Why is it important for learners to use the language they own and to the extent they can to help someone else? How do the Key Performance Tasks in the AATTs and the formative tasks prepare learners for making language and culture accessible?

Task: Explain how your AATTs clarify perspectives, expectations and behaviours. Give examples of how the tasks in your AATT point out words, symbols, and images, rendering various texts comprehensible or bring new knowledge to someone unfamiliar or unexperienced with the text.

Discuss the Issues

1 'EUs and EQs are the same throughout the programme; what changes are the tasks which gather assessment evidence of those EUs and EQs every year.' Discuss.

2 Explain to a colleague why lesson planning and instructional strategies are in Stage 3 and not developed or completed first?

3 How will Stage three be a good check-up to make sure all appear in the assessments you created?

4 Formative assessments should move students ever closer to Transfer. Discuss.

5 A colleague or department chair wants to redesign all the curricula in one year. What do you say?

6 Explain to a new colleague about Enduring Understandings and Essential Questions and why they are key to an articulated curriculum for intercultural communicative competence.

7 You are about to start choosing intercultural transferable concepts and goals that recur and reprise. A colleague wants to make a list of all the grammar and vocabulary first. What do you explain to them?

Reflect and Revisit

1 Why is it important to have colleagues of all instructional levels design the curriculum together?

2 Why does choosing intercultural transferable concepts and goals for your cultures and languages come first in this curriculum design framework?

3 What is the difference between summative and formative assessment? Why are the summative assessments – the Key Performance Tasks – designed before the formative tasks?

4 Why is it best practice to develop PASS Can-Do statements only after you have designed all the performance assessments?

5 How do you know what language grammar and vocabulary learners need to use?

6 How do I plan learning experiences and instruction that match intercultural communicative competence goals?

7 Your department teaches five languages. How might the same EUs and EQs be the same for all?

Key Performance Task catalogue from this book

This book advocates a Key Performance Task anthology or catalogue for learners as they move throughout a World Language/MFL curriculum and shows teachers how to develop this within this framework of curriculum and assessment design.

Ideal for use during the methods/curriculum and assessment course for teacher candidates or teacher trainees, below is the list of the Key Performance Tasks found within this book in the section *Design for Transfer*. These would also be of interest for in-service teachers to align with departmental or professional learning community goals.

Chapter 1

- Consider a concept or perspective that you envision can be unfolded throughout your curriculum
- Consider a possible task that could solve a problem or create products of value to the community

Chapter 2

- Compose Enduring Understandings that enter, reprise and exit throughout the curriculum
- Compose Essential Questions that enter, reprise and exit throughout the curriculum
- Create Perspectives-Practices-Products Infographics and Intercultural Word Clouds
- Research and Compose Intercultural Communicative Competence Inquiry Project

Chapter 3

- Design three *Turnarounds for Transfer* with existing tasks and learner 'in role' as experts
- Design a Context for your AATT

Chapter 4

- Design tasks for identifying main ideas and details using images
- Design Constructing or Posing Questions from cultural community texts
- Use the Capacities for Imaginative Learning to design for the Interpretive-Receptive mode
- Design three listening, viewing and reading Interpretive mode tasks for the AATT and Stage Two
- Develop the PASS Can-Dos from each Interpretive mode task

Chapter 5

- Use the Capacities for Imaginative Learning to design for the Interpersonal-Interactive mode
- Design three summative Interpersonal mode tasks for the AATT and Stage Two
- Develop the PASS Can Dos from each Interpersonal mode task

Chapter 6

- Use the Capacities for Imaginative Learning to design for the Presentational-Productive mode
- Design three summative Presentational tasks for the AATT and Stage Two

- Develop the PASS Can-Dos from each Presentational mode task
- Derive Intercultural Transfer Targets for your AATT set

Chapter 7

- Review, Spiral and New
- Intercultural Transfer Targets
- Turnaround formative tasks to transfer
- Unit Guide implementation tool
- Articulation: In a different place and at a different pace
- Task for Principle 1: Multimedia presentation, two concepts and key performances on articulated timeline
- Task for Principles 2 and 3
- Task for Principles 4 and 5
- Task for Principles 6 and 7
- Tool for articulation with the Seven Guiding Principles

Appendix A

Stage One and Stage Three at a Glance

Stage One	Stage Three
Enduring Understandings Essential Questions	Objective Statements Focus Questions
Concepts and Themes Recursive Use cultural perspectives to design them Last a lifetime	Skills and Facts Recall Use lesson content to design them Answerable end of class
Good health combines mind, body, spirit. *What is a healthy lifestyle?*	*Students will be able to identify healthy food choices.* *What are common breakfast foods in Mexico?*

Adapted with permission from the Northeast Conference on the Teaching of Foreign Languages and from the Editor of the NECTFL Review.

Eddy, J. (2017). Unpacking the Standards for Transfer: Intercultural Competence by Design. In Rebecca Fox (Ed.) Special Volume on Intercultural Competence for Northeast Conference on the Teaching of Foreign Languages. *NECTFL Review,* 79 (1), 53-72.

Appendix B

ITT Articulation Chart

	Enduring Understanding	Essential Question	Intercultural Transfer Target	Intercultural Transfer Target	Intercultural Transfer Target
			Novice	Intermediate	Advanced
Cuisine	Food is charged with all sorts of personal, familial and cultural symbolism.	To what extent does our lifestyle influence our diet? Why does eating together matter?	I can identify eating habits between cultures through gestures, images and phrases to someone else unfamiliar with them.	I can compare dishes served in schools from other countries to others and clarify details that may be new for someone else.	I can make dietary preferences between cultures accessible to someone unfamiliar with them and explain concerns.
Health	Health depends on many factors, including our habits, culture, diet, and lifestyle. Health is a combination of mind, body, and spirit.	What is good health? How do culture, media and lifestyle affect health?	I can identify common remedies across cultures to someone unacquainted with these products.	I can compare health practices across cultures for people unaccustomed to them.	I can explain to someone unaware of *remedios caseros* why a culture chooses some remedies and practices over others.

(Eddy, 2006a, 2007d, 2017, 2019a; Wiggins & McTighe, 2005; NCSSFL-ACTFL, 2017)

Appendix C

ICANADAPT Unit Sample
Viva la Vida

Health　　　**Spanish**

Intercultural Spiral Points
- Identify healthy lunch across cultures with infographics and school meal plans.
- Select foods based on different dietary needs.
- Explain changes in health practices for different communities with multimedia presentations.

Stage 1: What are the Desired Results? Culture Using a variety of culturally authentic materials and transfer tasks, students will examine lifestyle choices and healthy initiatives in the community.			
Enduring Understandings	**Essential Questions**	**Intercultural Transfer Targets**	**Mediation for Transfer**
* Health practices and perspectives vary across cultures. * Health depends on many factors, including our diet, culture and lifestyle. * Sociopolitical, media and environmental factors can play a role in healthcare.	? How does the media affect our health and lifestyle? ? To what extent does culture inform our health and wellness practices? ? How do we talk about our health with others in my family and community?	• I can identify and compare health practices and food products to people who may be unaware of them. • I can choose and design health conscious meal options with someone else's or the community needs in mind.	• Bridge and exchange ideas on *remedios caseros* and Western medicine. • Identify visuals to explain concepts to others. • Explain information on an infographic or chart to someone. • Compare practices and community response to wellness.

Stage 2: Determine Acceptable Evidence: Communication Intermediate Mid

Context for the Summative Performance Assessment	Summative Performance Assessment Task	
Viva la Vida is looking for episode content with a focus on healthy lifestyles.		
Interpretive (IN)	**Interpersonal (IP)**	**Presentational (PR)**
Students examine a variety of infographics and videos and commercials to categorize items with high sugar, salt, fat and carbs. Students write three questions on foods.	With a partner, come to consensus on which food items to include on a diet for people with different health needs and goals.	The *Viva La Vida!* channel is focusing one week of programming on diabetes prevention. Create a multimedia presentation outlining healthy lifestyle choices in the community.
Interpretive Can Dos	**Interpersonal Can Dos**	**Presentational Can Dos**
I can identify and compare foods and ingredients from authentic resources. I can categorize food items as healthy or not healthy. I can pose questions from information I listen to or watch.	I can come to a consensus on healthy choices to include in a presentation. I can choose proper foods with a partner depending on someone's dietary needs. I can ask questions on food choices with a partner.	I can make a presentation with facts and suggestions on a local and global health concern. I can report on community initiatives. I can compare food options in different communities.

Stage 3: Learning Experiences and Instruction: Connections-Comparisons-Communities

Formative Assessments during lessons	Mode	Performance Assessment Specific Statements I can …	Vocabulary and Grammar Review (R) same year Spiral (S) previous year New (N) for this unit.	Intercultural Transfer Targets I can …
Students watch videos on three steps to a healthy lifestyle and Mexican school initiatives. On a chart, categorize the actions mentioned in the video. Write three questions for a partner. Using the chart, ask your partner about dietary choices. Use Voicethread/Flipgrid to offer tips for a healthy lifestyle.	Interpretive Interpersonal Presentational	I can create a chart about steps to a healthy lifestyle. I can ask my partner about their healthy choices. I can write a script about healthy initiatives and diet choices.	Gain or lose weight (N) Exercise (S), Drink water (S), Walk (S), Whole grains (S) Fried (N), Carbohydrates (S) Have to (S), Starch (N) harm (N), prohibit (N), junk food (N)	I can identify some common lifestyle habits and health concerns in other cultures to someone unfamiliar with them. I can compare food and lifestyle initiatives from different cultures in the media. I can describe lifestyle choices across cultures to others.
Use a Venn diagram to compare foods served in your school and on the TL website. Write five questions about food sold in schools. Come to consensus with your partner on what foods should not be served or sold. Create a short video with an infographic on healthier choices for your school and community stores.	Interpretive Interpersonal Presentational	I can compare cafeteria food choices in my own and other countries. I can agree and disagree when planning school menus. I can create a presentation on healthy v. junk foods.	Junk food (N), Artificial flavours (N), Salt (S), Fats (R), Fast Food (R), Sugary (N), Dairy products (R), Feel Hungry (N), Feel Full (N), processed (N), packaged (N), diabetes (N), Dietary (N), mandate (N)	I can identify school foods served in different countries to others and clarify details that may be new for someone else. I can suggest healthy food choices for stores in my community. I can compare foods sold and served in a target language community with my own experience.

	Interpretive Interpersonal Presentational		
Categorize on a chart the information on diabetes affecting indigenous people of Mexico. Write three questions on this health concern. With a partner, ask questions and come to consensus on steps to make people aware of the effects of sugary drinks. Create an infographic and brochure on diabetes in the indigenous communities. Compare this health concern with communities in your country.	I can identify and organize terms and issues on diabetes and its effect on particular groups. I can pose questions on health concerns. I can decide and plan a course of action for awareness of the health crisis. I can develop materials directed towards teens on diabetes.	Junk food (R) Sugary (R), Feel Hungry (R) diabetes (R) predispositioned (N) cause of death (N) alcoholism (S)	I can outline causes and effects of diabetes for different community groups. I can facilitate conversation when others agree and disagree on issues related to health practices. I can explain information to different community groups on a health issue and how it affects them.

Adapted with permission from the Northeast Conference on the Teaching of Foreign Languages and from the Editor of the NECTFL Review. Eddy, J. (2017). Unpacking the Standards for Transfer: Intercultural Competence by Design. In Rebecca Fox (Ed.) Special Volume on Intercultural Competence for Northeast Conference on the Teaching of Foreign Languages. *NECTFL Review, 79* (1), 53–72.

Appendix D

Perspectives, Practices and Products Inventory

Styles of dress	
Ways of greeting people	
Beliefs about hospitality	
Leisure time	
Who eats first	
Paintings	
Wearing colours associated with milestone	
Literature	
Views on raising children	

Attitude about personal space and privacy	
Informality or formality	
Gestures	
Arriving late	
Holiday customs	
Dance	
Helping the host in the kitchen	
Celebrations	
Concept of fairness	

Friendship	
Ideas about clothing appropriateness	
Losing face	
Taking one portion until everyone has some	
Greetings	
Facial expressions	
Concept of self	
Work ethic	
Disagreeing openly at a meeting	

Religious rituals	
Concept of beauty	
Rules of polite behaviour	
Attitude toward age	
Giving gifts	
The role of family	
Visiting the cemetery	
Styles of dress	
Eating habits	

Add your own below:

Perspectives, Practices and Products. Cultures Standard goal areas. National Standards Collaborative Board. (2015). World-Readiness Standards for Learning Languages.

Appendix E

Bridge to Design Axe Porridge

Reflect to reveal

1 What intercultural perspectives does Ms. Kalmanson's want pupils to take away from this exemplar?

2 What is the axe porridge recipe? What do folktales teach us about culture and daily life?

3 How does the context set the scene for what will happen but not give too much away?

4 Why does Ms. Kalmanson want to take 'centuries old wisdom' and connect it to the pupil's experiences today?

5 Can you explain this element of the cultural story to someone else? Do you have an example from your own culture?

Questions for my colleagues

? How does the pupil's role as detectives facilitate inquiry and pull them into the 'story'?

? Is there a folk tale from the culture you will teach that is essential for your curriculum? Please share it.

? Share a design feature that you notice and share why with your colleague. Ask your colleague a question about this exemplar.

? What would you do differently? What would you add or otherwise change?

Re-imagine and elaborate

1 What could be other products or performances for the 'Smekalka fair'?

2 Would these tasks come before or after the ones you see in the AATT?

3 What could people do at the 'Smekalka fair' after they watch the interactive video?

4 What can other pupils do in class while they view products or presentations?

5 How might you adapt any of these tasks for your chosen curricular theme, transfer targets and cultures?

Ask the designer
What is your question for Ms. Kalmanson? What else do you want to know about this exemplar and her design thinking?

Research in the practice redux
Which design features, researchers and practitioners do you think may have guided Ms. Kalmanson in creating her exemplar? How did she design with these in mind? Explain below for each component.

1 Enduring Understandings and Essential Questions

2 Cultural symbolism

3 Context with pupils 'in role' as experts

4 Tasks which facilitate mediation with others and compare what pupils already know with new content

5 Is there a design feature that calls out to you? Share with colleagues.

Appendix F

OSEE for Intercultural Performance Assessment

Interpretive:

- Observe watch the video, listen or observe the image or object.
- State impartially and objectively what you see and hear, without giving personal opinions or assumptions. Write two questions by yourself.

What I see and hear	
Question 1	Question 2

Interpersonal:

- **Explore** possible explanations regarding the products or practices in the video, image, photo or object within your small group. Gather more information with others. Ask your two questions. Come to consensus.

Questions
Additional information
Possible explanations

Presentational:

- **Evaluate** these explanations and the perspectives responsible for the products and practices you see. Connect with new authentic text on a similar theme from the culture(s) you teach. Compare with those perspectives, practices and products. Develop and present findings. Write three intercultural transfer targets. These statements start with I can …

Perspectives-Values-Beliefs	New Material to Consider	Comparison with My Own	Intercultural Transfer Targets

Based on Berardo & Deardorff (eds.) 2012; Deardorff, 2009.

Appendix H

Layers, Lifespan and Level

How to identify recursive concepts for your curriculum	
Layers	
Does it have many layers, allowing you to deeper into cultural perspectives over time through different tasks and activities?	
Lifespan	
Could you change your mind about it and the importance of it over a lifetime?	
Level	
Do you need to know all about it to really understand it? Can it also be understood by anyone on a surface level?	

Eddy, (2010c, 2015c, 2016d, 2017)

Appendix J

Side by Side

Enduring Understandings	Essential Questions
Personal names are symbolic.	Do names portray family glory and fame? What's in a name? Who am I?
A healthy lifestyle integrates mind, body and spirit.	What is good health? To what extent do cultural practices influence diet?
Education is both formal and informal. Education is a lifelong endeavour that has no definite location.	What is school? What is the relationship between culture, education and career choices?
Milestone events are present in all cultures and their people.	Why do people talk about things that have happened before?

Eddy (2006a, 2007e, 2014b, 2015a, 2017, 2019a)

Appendix K

AATT Review Criteria and AATT Design Rubric

Articulated Assessment Transfer Task Review Criteria

> KEY TO RATINGS: 3 = *extensively* 2 = *somewhat* 1 = *not yet*

CRITERIA

1 The task assesses recurring performances at targets across levels of learner engagement for vertical articulation with increased complexity.   3 2 1

2 The task calls for transfer; applying learning flexibly, beyond knowledge to real-world, novel situations or contexts. The task is designed to solve problems and/or create products, not to simply recall or provide formulaic response.   3 2 1

3 The task requires interdisciplinary content with twenty-first-century skills: critical thinking, creativity, collaboration – not just a fact-based or rote answer.   3 2 1

4 The task is framed within an 'authentic' context: realistic purpose, a target audience and relevance beyond the classroom, applicable to community, career, civic or world readiness.   3 2 1

5 The task addresses/assesses (inter)cultural perspectives, practices, and products relevant to the cultural communities and does not simply focus on surface features of a product or performance.   3 2 1

6 The task integrates culturally authentic materials from various media across content areas for use within the modes of communication. 3 2 1

7 The task generates specific PASS Can-Do statements indicating transferable skills beyond knowledge acquisition. 3 2 1

© 2020 Jennifer Eddy. Adapted with permission from ©2013/2018 Jay McTighe **Cornerstone Tasks**

AATT Design Rubric

Criteria/Task	Exceeds Expectations	Meets Expectations	Does Not Meet Expectations
Enduring Understandings	EUs are derived from **cultural perspectives and concepts relevant to the theme and topic.** Important, transferable ideas within and across) disciplines. Students will understand that …	EUs are derived largely from **cultural practices relevant to the theme and topic.** Important, transferable ideas within (and sometimes across) disciplines. Students will understand that …	EUs are **written like objective statements** (students will be able to) or as purpose or description of task.
Essential Questions	EQs are derived from the EU and direct learners to concepts of cultural perspectives and practices. EQs extend beyond curriculum and are transdisciplinary. **Recur over time and can and are revisited again and again over curriculum.**	EQs are derived from the EU and direct learners to concepts of cultural perspectives and practices. **EQs are open-ended and do not have a single, final, and correct answer. Can be limited to one discipline or unit.**	Written as focus questions answerable by the end of the period, lesson or a few lessons. **Based on facts or recall of material.**

Context	Task is directed toward audience with relevance beyond the classroom, applicable to community, career or global readiness. **Task suggests novel deliverable to solve problem or create product.**	Task is directed toward audience with relevance beyond the classroom, applicable to community or career. **Task suggests novel deliverable to solve problem or create product.**	Task is meaningful **only within classroom or school** context.
Authentic resources	Are based on rich, culturally appropriate material. Provide real-life examples of language used in everyday situations. **Are designed for native speakers of the language. Are engaging and encourage learning beyond current proficiency level.**	Are based on culturally appropriate materials. Show real-life situations. **Are in the target language. Are engaging and appropriate for designing tasks at any level.**	Are not based on authentic cultural materials or are **pedagogically prepared.** Do not show real-life situations. **Are not in the target language, have translations. Theme is not meaningful or appropriate for students.**
Interpretive tasks	Instructions for tasks are clear. Tasks give students an opportunity to engage with material in a meaningful way with insightful evidence of **student comprehension, inference and questioning.**	Instructions for tasks are clear. Provides opportunity for evidence of student **comprehension beyond recall/ drill-mastery/ discrete items.**	Tasks are not clear and do not provide evidence of student comprehension or are mostly **recall/ drill-mastery/ discrete items.**

Interpersonal tasks	Tasks elicit spontaneous and **improvised conversation between students related to the authentic resources** in a meaningful way. No supports or scaffolds given.	Tasks elicit **scaffolded or supported conversation between students but are still spontaneous and improvised.** Are related to authentic resources in a meaningful way.	Tasks do not elicit spontaneous or improvised conversation between students. Do not relate to authentic resources and are not meaningful. **Tasks rely on practiced or memorized sentences and turn taking.**
Presentational tasks	Tasks align with all modes using authentic context/resource. **Novel** tasks engage students in meaningful representation of language to create a written or spoken product for transfer.	Presentational mode aligns with all modes using authentic context/ resource. **Novel** tasks engage students to create a written or spoken product with supports and cues for near transfer.	Presentational mode partially aligns with the other modes using authentic context/resource. **Familiar** or previously assigned tasks of written or spoken product with no transfer.
Can-Do statements	Can-Do statements align with each proficiency target, are **specific to the task** and **reflect the performance and skill** required for the tasks.	Can-Do statements align with each proficiency target, are **specific to the task** and **reflect the performance** or skill required for the tasks.	Can-Do statements are not aligned with proficiency target or **are general and not specific to the task** or do not reflect the performance or skill required for the tasks.

AATT Design Rubric developed by Dr Elaine Margarita, Queens College Methods Instructor and retired district supervisor, Dr Jennifer Eddy and QC World Language Candidates and Alumni.

Appendix N

None-Nigh-Near-Novel Stages of Transfer Assessment Inventory

Gather assessment tasks from different sources: classroom, textbook, workbooks, ancillaries, professional learning communities, etc. Using the criteria and the exemplars in the chapters, do an inventory of assessments for a given unit or scheme of work.

1 Write the task **description**.
2 Explain its designation over the four categories of Transfer with its **design** features or characteristics. Do you recognize where the task is along this continuum?
3 If you have samples of pupils' work, include that impact on learning evidence to show **implementation** results of such a task. Is there evidence of Transfer?
4 When completed, what did you **discover**? Is there a novel transfer task? Too many supports that prevent full transfer? No variation of audience? Same materials? Are there some of each?
5 If there are a majority of tasks in None or Nigh, how can you **Turnaround** these tasks to meet criteria for Near and far Novel Transfer?

None	Nigh and Nearby	Near Transfer	Novel Transfer
Drill Decontextualized Content	Familiar Task with Supports	Unfamiliar Task with Supports	Completely New Task No Supports

Appendix P

Bridge to Design Leisure in 1884 and Today

Reflect to reveal

1. What cultural perspectives does Dr Eddy want pupils to take away from this exemplar?
2. What do works of art reveal to us and our learners?
3. Why is the concept of time, how we use it and why practices change worth revisiting over a curriculum?
4. Why does Dr Eddy want learners to design interactive tasks with works of art?
5. Can you explain how time is valued within the context of 'cultural story' to someone else? Do you have an example from your own culture?

Questions for my colleagues

? How does the pupils' role to design the museum exhibit help them engage in mediation?

? Are there works of art depicting leisure and social groups from the culture you will teach that is essential for your curriculum? Please share it.

? Share a design feature that you notice and share why with your colleague. Ask your colleague a question about this exemplar.

? What would you do differently? What would you add or otherwise change?

Re-Imagine and elaborate

1 What could be other products or performances for the museum exhibit?

2 Would these tasks come before or after the ones you see in the AATT?

3 What could people do at the Seurat exhibit before or after interacting with the work of art?

4 What can other pupils do in class while they view products or presentations?

5 How might you adapt any of these tasks for your chosen curricular theme, transfer targets and cultures?

Ask the designer
What is your question for Dr Eddy? What else do you want to know about this exemplar, her design process and this work of art? What would you ask Georges Seurat? Watch *Sunday in the Park with George* (Sondheim & Lapine, 1984). What would you ask them about transfer and creative design?

Research in the practice redux
Which design features, researchers and practitioners do you think may have guided Dr Eddy in creating her exemplar? How did she design with these in mind? Explain below for each component given.

1 Develop tasks for transfer to create something new for different audience

2 Aesthetic Education, 'as if' and personal interaction with the work of art

3 Context with pupils 'in role' as experts

4 Tasks which facilitate mediation with others and compare what pupils already know with new content

5 Is there a design feature that calls out to you? Share with colleagues.

A Sunday on La Grande Jatte – 1884. Date: 1884/86. Artist: Georges Seurat. French, 1859–1891.

Appendix DD

Full Unit Sample

ICANADAPT Three Unit Sample   Chinese
School and Education Ms. LingLing Xie, Herricks High School, NY

Stage 1: What Are the Desired Results? Culture

Using a variety of culturally authentic materials and transfer tasks, students will understand the perspective of collectivism by learning about school daily life, the learning environment and values of the Chinese education system.

Enduring Understandings	Essential Questions	Intercultural Transfer Targets	Mediation for Transfer
* Education is the key channel to personal success in China. * Intense study for a good grade in the college exam can lead to a bright future. * Chinese families make every effort to send the children to a good college or to study abroad. * Chinese school curriculum and school life reflects the culture of collectivism.	? How do we define success and plan for it? ? What matters in our schools? ? What do priorities in educational systems tell us about our own culture? ? To what extent does family play a role in education? ? What do students learn and do in school?	• I can identify some elements of a school schedule, learning environment, and how they reflect the culture. • I can compare school and curricula to determine what is valued now and then in my own and other cultures.	• Bridge and exchange ideas and concepts of schooling and education between cultures. • Clarify typical visuals, signs, materials in schools. • Explain features of school procedures to others. • Share expectations of school here and abroad.

Stage 2: Determine Acceptable Evidence: Communication Nov. High, Int. Mid, Int. High

Context for the Summative Performance Assessment		Summative Performance Assessment Task
A Chinese high school is developing an international exchange student programme with a US high school. They need your help for presenting to Chinese families about school and education between two countries. The programme wants to combine the advantages of both Chinese and American education and meet the needs of both Chinese and American students. You are presenting to the Chinese audience the best school schedule, a day on a high school campus and comparison of the educational system and benefits of studying abroad.		
Interpretive (IN)	**Interpersonal (IP)**	**Presentational (PR)**
NH: Students will read an authentic school schedule and answer the questions. IM: Students will watch a vlog about a day in Chinese high school and ask and pose questions about the video. IH: Students will read an article about the road to college, taking the Chinese college examination, or studying abroad. They will pose and answer questions.	NH: Students will discuss with their partners and post their comments about different school subjects on the schedule. IM: Students will discuss with the partners about similarities and differences between Chinese and American school schedules and learning environments. IH: With a partner, students will interact with each other and talk about the different product, perspective and practice between Chinese and American school culture.	NH: Students will create a best school daily schedule which fits the needs of Chinese and American students. IM: Students will create a vlog to present about what is the best school and learning environment. IH: Students will write and post a blog about their viewpoints on Eastern and Western education and present their ideal school system.

Interpretive Can-Dos	Interpersonal Can-Dos	Presentational Can-Dos
NH: I can understand questions about a school schedule. IM: I can understand live or recorded introductions and descriptions by students from a partner school.	NH: I can exchange information about which classes are harder or easier than others and why. IL: I can exchange opinions about the length of the school day and the learning environment between different cultures.	NH: In my own and other cultures, I can identify some elements of a school schedule, and how they reflect the culture. IL: I can create a video to describe my ideal school day and learning environment.
IH: I can understand the main idea of the article about the goal of high school in various time frames.	IM: I can compare and exchange opinions about education in different cultures.	IM: I can compare school and curricula to determine what is valued now and then in my own and other cultures.

Stage 3: Learning Experiences and Instruction: Connections-Comparisons-Communities

Formative Assessments during Lessons	Mode	Performance Assessment Specific Statements I can …	Vocabulary and Grammar Review (R) same year Spiral (S) previous year New (N) for this unit.	Intercultural Transfer Targets I can …
		NOVICE HIGH		
Students will read a schedule about a Chinese school and answer the questions. With a partner, students will interact and come to a consensus on the type of subject schedule that fits their needs. Students will develop a survey for their peers about school subjects and their needs for the China high school.	Interpretive Interpersonal Presentational	I can understand the class schedules of a day at a Chinese school. I can interact and exchange information to select the type of subjects that best fits my needs. I can develop a simple survey about school subjects and schedules.	中文 (S) 'Chinese' 老师 (R) 'teacher' 学生 (R) 'student' 课 (S) 'class' 英文 (N) 'English' 数学 (N) 'Math' 体育 (N) 'Physical education' 音乐 (N) 'Music' 喜欢 (S) 'like'	I can identify some elements of a school schedule, or levels of schooling in my own and other cultures.
Students watch an interview video and fill out the chart about the typical Chinese student daily schedule. Paired with a partner, the students ask questions and create Venn diagrams to illustrate similarities and differences between their daily schedules at their school and in China. Students will present the Venn diagram and talk about the similarities and differences between Chinese and American school schedules.	Interpretive Interpersonal Presentational	I can listen and interpret the information in the video. I can compare the daily school schedule at my school and in China. I can present and compare the daily schedule between Chinese and American schools.	Numbers (R) 点 (N) 'O'clock' 分 (N) 'Minute' 刻 (N) 'Quarter' 几 (N) 早上 (R) 'Morning' 中午 (R) 'Noon' 下午 (R) 'Afternoon' 晚上 (R) 'Evening' 忙 (N) 'busy'	In my own and other cultures, I can compare school routine and curricula to determine how they reflect the culture.

	Interpretive Interpersonal Presentational		
Students will read about the courses which Chinese international high school programme offers, answer and pose the questions. With a partner, students will discuss different subjects and come to a consensus on the best subjects based on their preferences and needs. Students will write an email to the school counsellor to indicate which subjects they want to choose and why.	I can understand the descriptions about high school courses. I can exchange information about which classes are harder or easier than others and why. I can describe what I plan to do to learn and the type of subject schedule next year.	选 (S) choose 有意思 (S) interesting 有趣 (N) interesting 简单 (N) easy 容易 (N) easy 难 (N) difficult 为什么 (N) why 因为 (N) because	I can answer simple questions about my study abroad plans.

Formative Assessments during Lessons	Mode	Performance Assessment Specific Statements I can …	Vocabulary and Grammar Review (R) same year Spiral (S) previous year New (N) for this unit.	Intercultural Transfer Targets I can …
INTERMEDIATE LOW-MID				
Students will read an article about the major differences between American and Chinese school curriculum, answer and pose the questions. With a partner, students will interact and come to a consensus on the type of subject schedule that fits their needs. Students will develop a survey for their peers about school subjects and their needs for the China high school.	Interpretive Interpersonal Presentational	I can understand the description about class subjects and school curriculum. I can interact and exchange information to select the type of subjects that best fits my needs. I can develop a simple survey about school subjects and schedules.	科目 (N) subject 门 (N) mw for subjects 除了 … 以外, … Apart from …., … 课 (S) Class 选 (S) choose 生物 (N) biology 化学 (N) chemistry 汉语 (R) Mandarin 汉字 (N) Chinese characters 比如 (N) such as 对 … 好 (N) treat … well 大概 (N) about 准备 (N) prepare 或者 (N) or (in a statement) 学习 (R) study	I can meet with an advisor in the target culture to select courses that match my preferences and academic goals.

Appendix

Students will watch a video about a high school introduction, then answer and pose questions. With a partner, students will discuss their school and learning environment and compare it with the school facility in the video. Students will draw a school map with directions and describe the school environment in the video.	Interpretive Interpersonal Presentational	I can understand live or recorded introductions and descriptions by students from other schools. I can compare and contrast different school maps with partners. I can create a video to introduce and describe my school.	校园 (N) campus 教室 (R) classroom 教学楼 (N) school building 运动场 (N) sports field 停车场 (N) parking lot 体育馆 (R) gym 图书馆 (R) library 实验室 (N) lab 办公室 (N) office 礼堂 (N) auditorium 餐厅 (S) cafeteria 游泳池 (S) swimming pool 校长 (R) principal 环境 (N) environment 树 (R) tree 草 (R) grass 草坪 (N) lawn 山 (R) mountain 对面 (S) opposite side 安全 (S) safe 干净 (s) clean 安静 (N) quiet 吵 (N) noisy 参观 (S) visit 欢迎 (S) welcome	In my own and other cultures, I can compare school/ learning environments to determine what is valued.

Students will watch a video about Chinese college entrance exam 'Gaokao', write down their thoughts and pose questions. With a partner, students will interact and discuss Gaokao, then compare it with the American college exam. Students will develop a survey for their peers about their opinions on both college exams, and their plan for their exam.	Interpretive Interpersonal Presentational	I can understand the video and identify the main description and emotions in the video. I can discuss and exchange opinions about the college exams in different cultures. I can develop a simple survey about college exams and plans.	高考 (N) Chinese college exam 成绩 (R) grade, score 压力 (N) pressure 知识 (N) knowledge 选择 (N) choice, to choose 参加 (S) to participate, to attend 准备 (R) to prepare 安排 (N) to arrange 紧张 (N) nervous 家长 (R) parents	In my own and other cultures, I can identify some elements of a classroom, a school schedule, or levels of schooling and how they reflect the culture.

Formative Assessments during Lessons	**Mode**	**Performance Assessment Specific Statements I can …**	**Vocabulary and Grammar Review (R) same year Spiral (S) previous year New (N) for this unit.**	**Intercultural Transfer Targets I can …**
INTERMEDIATE HIGH				
Students will watch a video about Chinese college entrance exam 'Gaokao', write down their thoughts and pose questions.	Interpretive Interpersonal Presentational	I can understand the video and identify the main description and emotions in the video.	高考(N) Chinese college exam 成绩 (R) grade, score 压力 (N) pressure 知识 (N) knowledge 选择 (N) choice, to choose	In my own and other cultures, I can identify some elements of a classroom, a school schedule, or levels of schooling and how they reflect the culture.

With a partner, students will interact and discuss Gaokao, then compare it with the American college exam. Students will develop a survey for their peers about their opinions on both college exams, and their plan for their exam.		I can discuss and exchange opinions about the college exams in different cultures. I can develop a simple survey about college exams and plans.	参加 (S) to participate, to attend 准备 (R) to prepare 安排 (N) to arrange 紧张 (N) nervous 家长 (R) parents	
Students will read an article about the six differences between Chinese and American education and write down their thoughts and questions. With a partner, students will discuss the differences between Chinese and American educational systems. Students will write a short report about what they have learned about educational systems.	Interpretive Interpersonal Presentational	I can understand and follow an author's analysis of comparison on Chinese and American education. I can have a conversation with my peers about Chinese and American education and make a comparison. I can research and write about educational systems.	教育 (N) education 方式 (N) method 理念 (N) concept 制度 (N) system 选课 (S) course selection 死记硬背 (N) to learn by note 创造 (R) to create 合作 (N) cooperation 讨论 (R) discuss 分析 (N) analyse 课外活动 (S) Extracurricular activities	In my own and other cultures, I can compare educational systems to determine what is valued.

Students will read an article about three students' study abroad experience and how they decide to study abroad, answer and pose the questions. With a partner, students will discuss pros and cons of studying abroad and come to a consensus on their options to college. Students will write a plan to tell their parents about their options and plans to get to college.	Interpretive Interpersonal Presentational	I can understand an article about a student's study abroad experience. I can discuss the pros and cons of studying abroad. I can present a plan about my options and plans to the college.	留学 (N) study abroad 有意义(S) meaningful 交流 (N) communication 交换生 (R) exchange student 夏令营 (S) summer camp 经历 (N) experience 独立 (N) independent 申请 (N) apply 支持 (N) support 费用 (N) expense	I can identify the products, practices and perspectives between Chinese and American school culture.

Appendix HH

Axe Unit

ICANADAPT Unit

Axe Porridge

Ekaterina Kalmanson

National Identity

> Novice High › Intermediate Low › Intermediate Mid › Intermediate High › Advanced

Articulation Spiral Points
- Integrate *smekalka* and hospitality examples.
- Recreate story for modern audiences.
- Debate changes in values.
- Compose video.

Stage 1: What Are the Desired Results? Culture

The Russian cultural perspectives of *smekalka* and *khlebosolstvo* are intercultural. For the Russian people these concepts are deeply ingrained in folklore, behaviours, practices and artefacts. Using a variety of culturally authentic materials and transfer tasks, students will examine these values, beliefs and ways to demonstrate ingenuity and hospitality.

Enduring Understandings	Essential Questions	Intercultural Transfer Targets	Mediation for Transfer
* There are differences and similarities between people of different cultures in their values, beliefs and ways to show hospitality. * Thinking outside the box is intercultural quality.	? What is *hospitality*? ? How do we think 'outside the box' and handle problems creatively? ? How do we emerge from a difficult situation with no support or resources? ? Do some perspectives belong to one culture and others to many?	• I can recognize Russian culture values and beliefs. • I can identify ways Russian people show their hospitality. • I can show hospitality in a culturally appropriate manner. • I can compare Russian *smekalka* and hospitality with that of my own culture.	• Bridge and exchange ideas and concepts of hospitality and creative problem-solving. • Identify visuals and memes to explain concepts applicable to real-life context. • Explain information on an infographic or chart to someone. • Recognize words to indicate concepts in proverbs. • Compare practices and cultural norms around hospitality and problem-solving.

Appendix

Stage 2: Determine Acceptable Evidence: Communication Novice High

Context for the Summative Performance Assessment	Summative Performance Assessment Task
The first day of detective school, the new students are mystified by an anonymous letter. The letter states that Russian people have *smekalka* and every Russian can make porridge from an axe. Even though the author of this mysterious letter states that Russian people are kind and hospitable, the students are perplexed. They begin an independent investigation on this mystery of *smekalka*. To find out the axe porridge recipe, they go to the library. They learn that there is not an axe porridge recipe, but a book called *Axe Porridge*. Their chief Russian language and culture expert agrees to tell them the story. After finding out what axe porridge is, our young detectives find out more about Russian people, their values, *smekalka* and ways to show hospitality.	

Interpretive (IN)	Interpersonal (IP)	Presentational (PR)
Axe porridge is a symbol of Russian *smekalka*. Virtually investigate the Russian Artifice and Smekalka museum and find evidence of Russian *smekalka* and hospitality. On the chair, indicate if you like it and mark it with +. If you do not like it, mark it with -. Remember our school values each student's opinion. Identify evidence of Russian people's values and support your opinion with pictures. Axe Porridge – an interesting and very instructive everyday fairy tale. A resourceful and savvy soldier offered to cook up porridge from an axe. The soldier lures valuable food from the hostess, which she would never voluntarily share with the poor person. Russian Artifice and Smekalka Museum celebrating ingenuity and improvised, creative solutions.	Share your findings with classmates. What is your conclusion? Do only Russians have *smekalka*? Are they hospitable? What are their values and beliefs? Decide together on *smekalka* for Russian and other cultures.	To celebrate that smekalka is a universal quality, students organize *smekalka* Fair. Students will create a flyer about 'Russian Artifice and *smekalka* museum' or Russian hospitality traditions or axe porridge infographic recipe to hand out at the Fair.

Interpretive Can-Dos	Interpersonal Can-Dos	Presentational Can-Dos
I can identify the signs of Russian *smekalka* and hospitality with visuals. I can find information about the museum. I can differentiate between *smekalka* and artifice.	I can exchange key information on museum exhibits. I can offer opinions about Russian hospitality and *smekalka*. I can decide on key information to include about Russian people's beliefs and values.	I can design a flyer about *smekalka* with visuals. I can design an informational flyer for the museum using keywords, phrases and visuals. I can prepare an infographic recipe for axe porridge.

Stage 3: Learning Experiences and Instruction: Connections-Comparisons-Communities

Formative Assessments during lessons	Mode	Performance Assessment Specific Statements I can ...	Vocabulary and Grammar Review (R) same year Spiral (S) previous year New (N) for this unit	Intercultural Transfer Targets I can ...
IN Answer the survey questions. Record your responses. Look at the survey results from Russia. Find out if you have something in common. IP Survey other students and record their responses.	Interpretive Reading Interpersonal Speaking Presentational Writing	Answer questions about whether and why someone prefers to visit or receive guests. Survey others to identify preferences to visit or receive guests.	Я люблю/ не люблю +Infinitive (S) Я+ noun (S) Present Tense (R) Sentences with НО (BUT) (R) Cardinal numbers +Genitive case (N)	Identify how Russian people like to visit and to receive guests. Identify differences between Russian and American people and preferences to visit or receive guests.

PR Working in a group of four students, process the data and create infographics comparing answers of Russian and American people.		Present comparison data on preferences to visit or receive guests.	New vocabulary: расходы (expenses), домосед -ка (homebody), ничего не имею против (I do not mind) Ходить в гости VS принимать гостей	I can have a discussion in the culturally appropriate manner.
IN Oh, no! Someone tried to shred an article about Russian hospitality! Detectives restore the article by putting sentences in correct order. What did Russian people do to show hospitality? IP With two other students contrast and compare Russian hospitality with other cultures.	Interpretive Reading Interpersonal Speaking Presentational Speaking	Identify five main traditions of Russian hospitality. Compare and contrast Russian and my culture's hospitality traditions.	Present Tense (S) Past Tense (R) Russian proverbs about hospitality (N)	Define ways Russian people show hospitality. Compare the similarities and differences on Russian cultural practices in hospitality and my own culture.

PR Good agents are always up to any adventure! Two groups prepare and perform the scene of guests' arrival to a Russian house and home in your culture. Use at least three proverbs from the article.			Create a theatre piece and show hospitality using proverbs and behaviours.		Present common ways to show hospitality in Russia.
IN Inspect Russian memes about *smekalka* and arrange them from the least favourite to the most favourite. Write three questions about *smekalka* you see in pictures. IP Ask your classmates if they have *smekalka* or personally know people who have it. Can they prove it with pictures? How many people did you count? PR Create and present your own meme about *smekalka*.	Interpretive Reading Interpersonal Speaking Presentational Writing and Speaking		Identify evidence of *smekalka* in visuals. Ask questions about *smekalka*. Identify how people count and measure in Russian. Present memes on thinking out of the box.	Numbers (S) Ordinals (R) Cardinal numbers + Genitive case (N) смекалка	Compare intercultural qualities of thinking outside the box with memes. Participate with peers on how to get what you want with *smekalka*. Demonstrate smekalka behaviours to peers.

Appendix MM

Unit Plan Guide

Enduring Understandings

Students will understand that …

* Health depends on many factors, including our diet, culture and lifestyle.
* Health is a combination of mind, body and spirit.
* Health practices and perspectives vary across cultures.
* Healthcare systems vary between countries.
* Sociopolitical, media and environmental factors can play a role in healthcare.
* Effective communication skills enhance overall wellness and reduce health risks.

Essential Questions

? What is good health?
? To what extent does our culture and lifestyle influence our diet?
? How do I stay healthy?
? How does the media affect our health and lifestyle?
? To what extent does culture inform our health and wellness practices?
? How is the individual responsible for their own health and well-being?
? What factors influence health-related behaviours and decisions?
? How do we talk about our health with others in my family and community?
? To what extent does family play a role in shaping our values and beliefs?
? What role or purpose does spirituality serve in a culture?

Context or Scenario:

Viva la Vida channel is looking for episode content with a focus on healthy lifestyles.

PASS Can-Do Statements

I can categorize meals as healthy or not.

I can decide which meals are best for different diets.

I can identify a diet for a diabetic person.

I can compare school food choices in the target language country.

I can present my findings on meal choices in my community.

Intercultural Transfer Targets

I can write and speak about healthy food choices for stores in my community.

I can compare food and lifestyle initiatives from different cultures in the media.

I can identify some common lifestyle habits in other cultures.

I can compare food shopping in a target language community with my own experience.

I can create a multimedia presentation on healthy lifestyle choices from various countries.

Adapted with permission from the Northeast Conference on the Teaching of Foreign Languages and from the Editor of the NECTFL Review.

Eddy, J. (2017). Unpacking the Standards for Transfer: Intercultural Competence by Design. In Rebecca Fox (Ed.) Special Volume on Intercultural Competence for Northeast Conference on the Teaching of Foreign Languages. *NECTFL Review*, 79 (1), 53–72.

Appendix NN

Master List Mode Tasks

Interpretive Mode	Interpretive Mode
• Match image to listening • Drag and drop the picture that matches what is being described • Match gesture to text • Use physical objects or props • Identify, list or sequence events in order • Listen to recorded media for comprehension • Categorize with graphic organizer • Listen, read, watch and write questions • Fill in a table, chart or graph • Listen to the song melody without the lyrics • Can take notes in a list • Listening and completing graphic organizers • Note-taking from a listening passage or video • Brainstorming with mind maps • Comparing between visuals • Written responses after listening for information • Listening and checking off items you hear from a list • Interpret and draw conclusions from a recorded source • View video and take notes on organizer • Label stages of a procedure • Reconstructing texts for collaborative jigsaw readings • Summarize and synthesize information from a recorded sample • Make a simple choice or two categories	• Reading and completing graphic organizers • Note-taking from texts • Sort information into paragraphs • Read headline and summarize by choosing correct picture, or word • Match image to informational or literary text • Read song lyrics without music • View film without sound • Assign words/phrases • Interpret proverbs and quotations • Drawing and labelling maps, diagrams, etc. • Identify and summarize main points and significant details • Interpret idioms and idiomatic expressions • Recognize literary genres • Form questions after reading • Infer the purpose and intention of the speaker/writer • Read and respond to literature • Identify literary elements and techniques (e.g. tone, characterization, point of view, conflict, poetic structures) • Use of visual stimuli to make inferences • Classify information after reading • Graphic organizers • Completion of online or paper forms • Put sentences or comic strip sections in logical order • Sequence within paragraphs

• Form questions after listening • Interpret oral and written dialectical/regional registers • Listen, draw maps and graphs • Make inferences and predictions from spoken, written and auditory sources using authentic materials • Classify/categorize information after listening • List events, dates, cost, information • Draw what you hear • Circle the correct picture • Circle the correct word or phrase • Label or identify as you listen or watch • Make a list while listening or watching a video • Listen to pre-recorded author's interview • Listen for the gist – identify main idea • Guess meaning from context • Compose a title or headline • Paraphrase in native language	• Summarize short fiction and non-fiction texts • Read and respond to time-related exercises with schedules, agendas and timelines • Summarize text • Identify the topic from an article using Poll Everywhere • Mentimeter • Word Wall for sorting • Wordle or Word It Out, Taxedo for word clouds with a text • Manipulate text in correct order with Vocaroo and Flippity • Take notes from text with Evernote • Summarizing and paraphrasing texts • Say step-by-step instructions out loud after you watch • Hear instruction, mediate with word/phrase, other person does activity

Interpersonal Mode	**Interpersonal Mode**
• Paired discussions • Guided small-group discussions • Organize and define the task for collaboration and contributions • Maintain focus of planning and discussion • Information gap tasks • Negotiate who does what • Come to consensus on what, where, when, how, with whom, how much, how often, etc. • Give limitations, come to compromise/consensus • Respond to interpretive mode questions • Improvised, unscripted role play • Group discussions in response to a variety of stimuli	• Ask and/or respond to spontaneous, unscripted oral questions • Propose solutions with a classmate on issues presented in work of art • Change the time frame of the scene and improvise seconds, minutes, days or years before or after the key event occurs • Come to consensus, plan and choose with a partner • Create an on-air talk show that is spontaneous and unscripted • Find the differences in two pictures • Share details of a personal experience • Interviews with grid • Explain important event from a cultural community's past

• Word Wall for choosing and deciding and sorting together • Organize plans • Controversial topic debates	• Brainstorming lists with peers • Retell a sequence of events, real or imagined • Circumlocution tasks • Make suggestions on what to see and do • Accept or reject choices
Presentational Mode	**Presentational Mode**
Oral products • Innovate a familiar text • Write a new episode of the story • Write new verse to song • New stanza to poem • Opinion polls • Commercials • Create a new character who responds, • Animate a previously inanimate feature • Theatre production • Public service announcement • Recite poetry • Oral histories • Poetry reading • Broadcasts • Oral multimedia/video presentations • Defend ideas and points of view • Demonstration • TV or radio spot • Infomercial • Respond to critical commentary • Marketing campaigns • Radio shows • Oral presentation using graphic organizers • Rehearsed role play or skit	*Written products* • Flipgrid video • Cultural comparison • Brochure or itinerary • Letter • Commentary or brief • Social media sites • Video or podcasts • Advertisement • Agenda or Schedule • New beginning or ending of story, song • Change genre: story/art/ poem/ screenplay • Design a survey and present findings • Essays, plays • Cause and effect essays • Written response to an oral or written prompt • Narratives or descriptive writing • Storytelling • Magazine article • Clip art • Narratives • Written response to an oral presentation • Fable, myth and/or legend writing • Research paper • Titles for a play, story or article • Headlines in newspaper style • Literary journal • Informational list development • Curate museum exhibit • Written material for online magazine, TV series • Written material for public service organization • Pear Deck interactive presentation

Appendix OO

ICANADAPT Template

ICANADAPT Template

Select Title *Select Overarching Concepts in curriculum* *Select Theme for This Singular Unit*

Intercultural Spiral Points

Stage 1: What Are the Desired Results? Culture

Enduring Understandings	Essential Questions	Intercultural Transfer Targets	Mediation for Transfer
		• I can • I can • I can	

Stage 2: Determine Acceptable Evidence: Communication Performance Target Level ___

Context for the Summative Performance Assessment	Summative Performance Assessment Task	
Interpretive (IN)	Interpersonal (IP)	Presentational (PR)
Interpretive Can Dos	Interpersonal Can Dos	Presentational Can Dos
I can	I can	I can

Stage 3: Learning Experiences and Instruction:
Connections-Comparisons-Communities

Formative Assessments for Lessons Near Transfer	Mode IN IP PR	Performance Assessment Specific Statements I can ...	Vocabulary and Grammar Review (R) same year Spiral (S) previous year New (N) for this unit.	Intercultural Transfer Targets I can ...
		I can I can I can		I can I can I can

Adapted with permission from the Northeast Conference on the Teaching of Foreign Languages and from the Editor of the NECTFL Review.

Eddy, J. (2017). Unpacking the Standards for Transfer: Intercultural Competence by Design. In Rebecca Fox (Ed.) Special Volume on Intercultural Competence for Northeast Conference on the Teaching of Foreign Languages. *NECTFL Review*, 79 (1), 53–72.

Appendix PP

Tool for Articulation Using the Seven Guiding Principles for World Language Curriculum Design

Principle	Design	Implementation	Evidence	Non-Evidence
Intercultural perspectives and transdisciplinary content unfold articulated curriculum and scaffold key tasks of meaningful performance.				
Learners acquire and own language not by predictable memorization of forms but through creative, unpredictable interaction in tasks and transdisciplinary content in texts.				

Complexity differentiates tasks, not topics, themes or texts.				
Performance tasks are designed for transfer to novel contexts, situations or audiences.				
Tasks solve problems and create products relevant to college, community, work and world.				
Learners are active social agents co-constructing meaning through mediation and complex tasks across languages and cultures.				
Learners take risks to apply their repertoire flexibly but not with native-like accuracy.				

Glossary

AATT Articulated Assessment Transfer Tasks are designed across at least three performance target levels of differentiation but with a common context for deliverable product or problem solving.

Assessment for Transfer Inventory categorizes tasks within a unit from drill mastery to full transfer, enabling shifts towards performance assessment goals.

Authorship for the interpretive mode indicates texts in which intercultural perspectives and transdisciplinary concepts begin, reside and become accessible to any learner.

Autonomy is teacher as designer for transfer which enables learner autonomy and flexible, novel language use: By themselves and beyond themselves.

Aesthetic Education aligns participatory engagement with arts to performance assessment to encourage an adaptable, self-directed language learner.

Articulation in this book is intentional, collaborative curriculum and assessment design between levels via intercultural concepts and transdisciplinary performance transfer tasks or AATTs.

Articulation Spiral Points are tasks for tangible evidence of concepts, integrated perspectives, novel performances and products.

Complexity is a feature of AATTs; a shift from self to others, problem-solving, or different variables for transfer. It is not a consequence of the text but the task set designed with it.

Conception is our first contact with anything we listen to, watch, view, read and need to understand. It indicates authorship, ownership, interaction and mediation.

Consensus is a strategy between learners when they plan, choose and decide together within a task, most often in order to plan and organize the final product or deliverable within an AATT.

Context within the AATT presents a possible audience, problem to solve and deliverable. Contexts typically have value beyond the classroom or school and are relevant and applicable to community, work and world.

Creation for this book is when the language user designs or delivers something new for someone else with their needs in mind, allowing that person to see differently and move mediation forward.

Cultural Community Authentic Texts are spoken, written, signed, created or viewed media designed by cultural communities for the public to consume, use, or experience.

Glossary

Drama Pedagogy or Process Drama in this book refers to learners participating in intentional, yet improvised responses within tasks to make meaning of text, contexts and symbols for managing unpredictable places and spaces.

Enduring Understandings in this design framework are overarching, curricular and program-level concepts recursive through cultural perspectives, cultural history and transdisciplinary content.

Essential Questions in this design are overarching and recurring questions on concepts and themes derived through intercultural perspectives which are not answerable in a unit or lesson.

Far Transfer is indicated by a completely novel task not done previously in class. These tasks carry no cues or support information from the teacher on how to solve the problem or create the product.

Formative Assessment in this book are lesson level performance tasks that represent some novelty but also offer scaffolds or support strategies.

ICANADAPT Intercultural Curriculum Aligns Novel Assessment Design Articulated Performance and Transfer is the unit and curriculum framework for this book. The AATTs represent Stage Two of the unit, with one level developed to stage three lessons.

Intercultural Transfer Targets are perspectives, practices, comparisons, transdisciplinary connections and community engagement, designed for utility beyond the classroom. They enable mediation, making culture accessible to others who may be new to the culture and need a bridge to understand these elements.

Improvisation for this book is our reaction to input from a partner, group or text. Every interaction is a co-created, improvisational scene, a more accurate term than spontaneous, which has no external input.

Key Performance Catalogue is a set of performance tasks that all learners in your program will do by the time they finish your school or program. These are designed across languages and levels by teaching faculty.

Mediation for Transfer are tools within AATTs to clarify, compare, elaborate, facilitate, revise, reconstruct and collaborate with others to move both plurilingual and pluricultural space forward and place new language and cultural contexts within reach.

Near Transfer are formative performance tasks during lessons that are new but provide cues and supportive suggestions on how to do the task.

Novelty for this design is essential for transfer; learners should experience novel tasks every day, using what they learned in a different way as not to expect predictability in language use.

Ownership in the interpretive mode is when learners develop an intercultural mindset from texts which uncover enduring understandings and essential questions over time.

Performance Assessment Specific Statements (PASS) derived after task design to eliminate coverage habit to only what appears in task.

Performance is defined as language learned and demonstrated within a controlled environment such as a classroom, using familiar contexts. Performance for Transfer provides evidence that one can resolve and create something within a prepared, yet novel and unanticipated situation with someone else's needs in mind and provides a bridge to proficiency.

Proficiency refers to how well someone uses the language in an unplanned manner at any given time wherever they are, regardless of when, how or where language is acquired.

Review, Spiral, New is in stage three on the ICANADAPT template, indicating grammar and vocabulary reviewed from the same year, spiralled from a previous year, or new to this unit.

Summative Assessment in this book is the final performance assessment for the unit that indicates far transfer, problem solving and deliverables that are novel from previous tasks.

Transdisciplinary for this design emphasizes unifying concepts between subjects and facilitates new meaning making within real world themes, contexts and issues.

Transfer evidence for world language education is when we can use our knowledge and skills repertoire independently to solve novel intercultural challenges or create a product of value with no cues or instructional help.

Turnarounds for Transfer is a professional learning activity within this design where teachers revise drill/mastery tasks to become transfer performance assessments with complexity, autonomy and novelty.

References

Abugasea Heidt, M. (2021). Harnessing imagined communities: Motivating and empowering language learners. *The Language Educator*, 16 (4), 38–42.

ACTFL. (2010). Position statement on use of the target language in the classroom. Retrieved August 2020 from https://www.actfl.org/advocacy/actfl-position-statements/use-the-target-language-the-classroom.

ACTFL/CAEP. (2013). Program standards for the preparation of foreign language teachers. Retrieved from https://www.actfl.org/assessment-professional-development/program-review-services.

Adair-Hauck, B., Glisan, E., Koda, K., Swender, E., & Sandrock, P. (2006). The Integrated Performance Assessment (IPA): Connecting assessment to instruction and learning. *Foreign Language Annals*, 39(3), 359–382.

Agarwal, P. (2019). Retrieval practice & Bloom's taxonomy: Do students need fact knowledge before higher order learning? *Journal of Educational Psychology*, 111 (2), 189–209.

American Councils for International Education (2017). The National K-12 Foreign Language Enrollment Survey Report. Retrieved from https://www.americancouncils.org/sites/default/files/FLE-report-June17.pdf.

American Council on the Teaching of Foreign Languages. (2002). ACTFL/NCATE Program standards for the preparation of foreign language teachers. Retrieved from http://www.actfl.org/files/public/ACTFLNCATEStandardsRevised713.pdf

American Council on the Teaching of Foreign Languages (ACTFL). (2012). Performance descriptors for language learners.

Anderson, L.W. (Ed.), Krathwohl, D.R. (Ed.), Airasian, P.W., Cruikshank, K.A., Mayer, R.E., Pintrich, P.R., Raths, J., & Wittrock, M.C. (2001). *A taxonomy for learning, teaching, and assessing: A revision of Bloom's Taxonomy of educational objectives* (Complete edition). New York: Longman.

Armstrong, M., Connolly, A., & Saville, K. (1994). *Journeys of discovery*. Melbourne: Oxford University Press.

Baldwin, P. (2012). *With drama in mind – real learning in imagined worlds*. 2nd ed. London and New York: Continuum.

Beacco, J., Byram, M., Cavalli, M., Coste, D., Cuenat, M.E., Goullier, F., & Panthier, J. (Eds.). (2016). *Guide for the development and implementation of curricula for plurilingual and intercultural education*. Strasbourg: Council of Europe.

Bennett, M.J. (1986). A developmental approach to training intercultural sensitivity. In J. Martin (Guest Ed.), *Special Issue on Intercultural Training, International Journal of Intercultural Relations*, Vol 10, No.2. (pp. 179–186) Elmsford, NY: Pergamon Press.

Bennett, M.J. (1993). Towards ethnorelativism: A developmental model of intercultural sensitivity (revised). In R. M. Paige (Ed.), *Education for the intercultural experience* (pp. 21–71) Yarmouth, ME: Intercultural Press.

Bennett, M.J. (2004). Becoming interculturally competent. In J.S. Wurzel (Ed.), *Toward multiculturalism: A reader in multicultural education* (pp. 62–77). Newton, MA: Intercultural Resource Corporation.

Bennett, M.J. (2008). Transformative training: Designing programs for culture learning. In M. A. Moodian (Ed.), *Contemporary leadership and intercultural competence: Understanding and utilizing cultural diversity to build successful organizations* (pp. 95–110). Thousand Oaks, CA: Sage.

Benson, P. (2011). *Teaching and researching autonomy in language learning* (2nd ed.; first published, 2001). London: Pearson Education.

Berardo, K. & Deardorff, D. (Eds.) (2012). *Building cultural competence. Innovative activities and models*. Elmsford, NY: Pergamon Press.

Bloom, B.S. (1956). *Taxonomy of educational objectives, handbook I: The cognitive domain*. New York: David McKay.

Boal, A. (1982). *The theatre of the oppressed*. New York: Urizen Books, 1979. Republished by Routledge Press in New York/ London, 1982.

Boal, A. (1992). *Games for actors and non-actors*. New York: Routledge.

Bomba Estéreo, (2015, June 2). Soy yo. [Recorded by L. Saumet and S. Mejía]. On *Amanecer*. Sony Music International.

Bower, K., Coyle, D., Cross, R., & Chambers, G.N. (Eds.). (2020). *Curriculum integrated language teaching: CLIL in practice*. London: Cambridge University Press.

Brantmeier, E.J. (2013). Pedagogy of vulnerability: Definitions, assumptions, and applications. In J. Lin, R. Oxford, & E.J. Brantmeier, *Re-Envisioning Higher Education: Embodied Pathways to Wisdom and Transformation*. Information Age Publishing.

Bräuer, G. (Ed.) (2002). Body and Language. *Intercultural Learning through Drama*. Westport, CT/London: Ablex.

Britton, J., Burgess, T., Martin, N., McLeod, A., & Rosen, H. (1975). *The development of writing abilities* (11–18). London: Macmillan.

Bruner, J. (1960). *The process of education*. Cambridge, MA: Harvard University Press.

Bruner, J. (1961). The art of discovery. *Harvard Educational Review*, 31, 21–32.

Bruner, J.S. (1962). The conditions of creativity. In H. E. Gruber, G. Terrell, & M. Wertheimer (Eds.), *Contemporary approaches to creative thinking* (pp. 1–30). New York: Atherton Press.

Bruner, J. (1973). *Going beyond the information given*. New York: Norton.

Bruner, J. (1978). "The Role of Dialogue in Language Acquisition." In A. Sinclair, R. Jarvella, and W. Levelt (Eds.), *The Child's Conception of Language* NY: Springer.

Bruner, J. (1996). *The culture of education* (pp. 241–255). Cambridge, MA: Harvard University Press.

Byram, M. (1997). *Teaching and assessing intercultural communicative competence*. Clevedon: Multilingual Matters.

Byram, M. (2008). *From foreign language education to education for intercultural citizenship: Essays and reflections*. Clevedon: Multilingual Matters.

Byram, M. (2009). Intercultural competence in foreign languages – the intercultural speaker and the pedagogy of foreign language education. In D. K. Deardorff (Ed.), *The Sage handbook of intercultural competence* (pp. 321– 332). Thousand Oaks, CA: Sage.

Byram, M. (2011). Using the concept of perspective to integrate cultural, communicative, and form focused language instruction. *Foreign Language Annals*, 44(3), 525–543.

Byram, M. & Fleming, M. (Eds.) (1998). *Language learning in intercultural perspective. Approaches through drama and ethnography*. Cambridge: Cambridge University Press.

Byram, M., Gribkova, B., & Starkey, H. (2002). *Developing the intercultural dimension in language teaching: A practical introduction for teachers*. Strasbourg: Council of Europe.

Byram, M., & Wagner, M. (2018). Making a difference: Language teaching for intercultural and international dialogue. *Foreign Language Annals*, 51(1), 140–151.

Byrnes, H. (1990). Addressing curriculum articulation in the nineties: A proposal. *Foreign Language Annals*, 23(4), 281–292.

Byrnes, H. (2002). Language and culture: Shall the twain ever meet in foreign language departments? *ADFL Bulletin*, 33(2), 25–32.

Byrnes, H. (2008). Articulating a foreign language sequence through content: A look at the culture standards. *Language Teaching*, 41(1), 103–118.

Byrnes, H. (Ed.) (2010). Perspectives: Revisiting the role of culture in the foreign language curriculum. *Modern Language Journal*, 94(2), 315–336.

Chen, D., & Yang, X. (2015). Culture as the core: Challenges and possible solutions in integrating culture into foreign language teaching. *Journal of Language Teaching and Research*, 7(1), 168–177.

Cook, V.J., & Wei, L. (2016). *The Cambridge handbook of linguistic multi-competence*. Cambridge: Cambridge University Press.

Cope, B., and Kalantzis, M. (2009). A grammar of multimodality. *The International Journal of Learning*, 16(2), 361–423.

Corbett, J. (2003) An intercultural approach to English language teaching. Clevedon. New York: Multilingual Matters LTD.

Couet, R., Duncan, G., Eddy, J., Met, M., Smith, M., Still, M., Tollefson, A. (2008). *Starting with the end in mind: Planning and evaluating highly successful foreign language programs*. Boston, MA: Pearson Education, Inc.

Council of Europe (1998). *Modern languages: Learning, teaching, assessment: A Common European Framework of reference*. Strasbourg: Council of Europe, Council for Cultural Cooperation, Education committee, CC-LANG (95) 5 rev. V.

Council of Europe. (2001). *Common European framework of reference for languages: Learning, teaching, assessment*. Cambridge: Cambridge University Press. www.coe.int/t/dg4/linguistic/Source/Framework_EN.pdf

Council of Europe. (2009). *Autobiography of intercultural encounters*. Strasbourg: Council of Europe Publishing. Retrieved from www.coe.int/t/dg4/autobiography/default_en.asp

Council of Europe. (2015). *TASKs for democracy: 60 activities to learn and assess transversal attitudes, skills, and knowledge*. Strasbourg: Council of Europe.

Council of Europe. (2020). *Common European framework of reference for languages: Learning, teaching, assessment – Companion volume [First published 2018].*, Strasbourg: Council of Europe.

Coyle, D. (2007). Content and language integrated learning: Towards a connected research agenda for CLIL pedagogies. *International Journal of Bilingual Education and Bilingualism*, 10, 543–562.

Coyle, D., Bower, K., Foley, Y., & Hancock, J. (2021). Teachers as designers of learning in diverse, bilingual classrooms in England: an ADiBE case study. *International Journal of Bilingual Education and Bilingualism*, DOI: 10.1080/13670050.2021.1989373

Cunico, S. (2005). Teaching language and intercultural competence through drama: Some suggestions for a neglected resource. *Language Learning Journal*, 31(1), 21–29.

Curtain, H. & Dahlberg, C. (2016). *Languages and learners: Making the match: World language instruction in K-8 classrooms and beyond*, 5th ed. Boston: Pearson Education.

Dann, R. (2014). Assessment as learning: Blurring the boundaries of assessment and learning for theory, policy and practice. *Assessment in Education: Principles, Policy & Practice*, 21 (20), 149–166.

Davies, A. (2003). The native speaker. *Myth and reality*. Clevedon, UK: Multilingual Matters.

Dawson, K., Cawthon, S., & Baker, S. (2011). Drama for schools: Teacher change in an applied theatre professional development model. *Research in Drama Education: The Journal of Applied Theatre and Performance*, 16(3), 313–335.

Dawson, K., & Lee, B.K. (2018). *Drama-based pedagogy: Activating learning across the curriculum*. London: Intellect.

Deardorff, D.K. (2006). Identification and assessment of intercultural competence as a student outcome of internationalization. *Journal Studies in International Education*, 10(3), 241–266.

Deardorff, D.K. (2008). Intercultural competence: A definition, model and implications for education abroad. In V. Savicki (Ed.), *Developing intercultural competence and transformation: theory, research, and application in international education*, (pp. 32–52). Sterling, VA: Stylus.

Deardorff, D.K. (2009). Implementing intercultural competence assessment. In D.K. Deardorff (Ed.), *The SAGE handbook of intercultural competence* (pp. 477–491). Thousand Oaks, CA: SAGE.

Deardorff, D.K. (2011). Intercultural competence in foreign language classrooms: A framework and implications for educators. In *Witten Harden's intercultural competence: Concepts, challenges, evaluations, ISFLL Vol. 10* Peter Lang International Academic Publishers.

Department for Education (2013). *Languages programmes of study: Key stage 3*. National curriculum in England.

References

Dérose, A. (1987). *Chanson Pour Haiti*. [Yole et Ansy Dérose] Les Producteurs Artistiques.

Dewey, J. (1938). *Experience and education*. New York: Macmillan.

Diamantidaki, F. (2019). Teaching poetry in modern foreign languages. In F. Diamantidaki (Ed.), *Teaching literature in modern foreign languages* (pp. 97–112). London: Bloomsbury Academic.

DICE Consortium (2010). The DICE has been cast: Research findings and recommendations on educational theatre and drama. DICE: Drama Improves Lisbon Key Competencies. Retrieved from http://www.dramanetwork.eu/file/Policy%20Paper%20long.pdf.

Earl, L.M. (2003). *Assessment as learning using classroom assessment to maximise student learning*. Thousand Oaks, CA: Corwin Press.

Eddy, J. (2005). From the classroom: Transfer. Big ideas. *Journal of Authentic Education*. Winter.

Eddy, J. (Writer), & Couet, R. (Director). (2006a). What is performance assessment? [Television series episode]. In *South Carolina Department of Education (Producer), teaching and language learning collaborative*. Columbia, SC: ETV.

Eddy, J. (2006b). *Sonidos, sabores, y palabras*. Boston, MA: ThomsonHeinle.

Eddy, J. (2006c). *Unpacking the New York LOTE standards with backward design*. Saratoga Springs, NY: New York State Association of Foreign Language Teachers.

Eddy, J. (2007a). Children and art: Uncovering cultural practices and perspectives through works of art in world language performance assessment. *Learning Languages*, 12(2), 19–23.

Eddy, J. (2007b). Uncovering content, designing for performance. *Academic Exchange Quarterly*, Spring, 233–237.

Eddy, J. (2007c). Discover languages through song: Designing performance assessment. *Hispania*, Spring, 142–146.

Eddy, J. (2007d). Coverage without pity: World Language Assessment exposed in the light of backward design. In R. Fry (Ed.), *Languages: Connecting students with the world*. Annual Series, No. 23. New York State Association of Foreign Languages. Buffalo: NYSAFLT.

Eddy, J. (2007e). Unpacking the standards: Informing instruction through performance assessment. *The NCLRC Language Resource*. 11(5). Washington, DC: National Capital Language Resource Center.

Eddy, J. (2007f). *Through a cultural lens darkly: Teacher candidate revelations on cross cultural adaptability*. Pembroke College, Oxford, England.

Eddy, J. (2007g). Unpacking the standards with backward design: World language assessment uncovered. Hawaii International Conference on Education. Honolulu, HI.

Eddy, J. (2008). *Unpacking the standards with backward design: Curriculum and performance assessment design for world languages*. [Conference Presentation]. Sturbridge, MA: Annual Meeting of the Massachusetts Foreign Language Association.

Eddy, J. (2009a). *Developing teacher expertise in backward design and performance assessment*. [Conference Presentation]. Sixth International Conference on Language Teacher Education. Washington, DC: Georgetown University, George Washington University and the Center for Applied Linguistics.

Eddy, J. (2009b). *Unpacking the standards with backward design*. [Conference Presentation]. San Diego, CA: American Council on the Teaching of Foreign Languages (ACTFL).

Eddy, J. (2010a). Becoming designers: Paradigm shifts for performance and transfer. In Davis, (Ed.), *World language teacher education: transitions and challenges in the twenty- first century* (pp. 97–102). Charlotte, NC: Information Age.

Eddy, J. (2010b). *Planning for performance with backward design*. Seattle Public Schools STARTALK [Conference Presentation]. Seattle: WA.

Eddy, J. (2010c). *Unpacking the standards with backward design: performance assessment and transfer. National council on less commonly taught languages* [Conference Presentation]. Madison, WI.

Eddy, J. (2010d). backward design and standards-based instruction: making the essentials come alive. National capital language resource center [Conference Presentation]. Georgetown University and George Washington University. Washington, DC.

Eddy, J. (2011). *Unpacking the standards with backward design I: Uncovering culture*. Baltimore, MD: Northeast Conference on the Teaching of Foreign Languages.

Eddy, J. (2012a). assessment planning for performance and transfer. Professional development series on assessment. [Conference Presentation]. Foreign Language Educators of New Jersey.

Eddy, J. (2012b). *Backward design: Curriculum planning for teacher programs*. STARTALK. [Conference Presentation]. Atlanta, GA.

Eddy, J. (2013a). *Performance assessment down pat*. STARTALK Spring Conference. [Conference Presentation]. Orlando, FL.

Eddy, J. (2013b). *Designing your PAL: Program in African languages. leadership institute in African languages. National African language resource center*. Indiana University, Bloomington, IN.

Eddy, J. (2014a). Turnarounds to transfer: Design beyond the modes. *Learning Languages, Spring/Summer, XIX*(2), 16–18.

Eddy, J. (2014b). *Designing your PAL: Program in African languages. Leadership institute in African languages. National African language resource center*. Indiana University, Bloomington, IN.

Eddy, J. (2015a). *Curriculum design with culture at the core*. Sturbridge, MA: Massachusetts Foreign Language Association.

Eddy, J. (2015b). *Unfolding curriculum with backward design*. Sturbridge, MA: Massachusetts Foreign Language Association.

Eddy, J. (2015c). Uncovering curriculum: Language performance through culture by design. *Journal of the National Council of Less Commonly Taught Languages, XVI*, 1–22.

Eddy, J. (2015d). *Planning for performance: A leadership program for developing high quality programs in African languages*. National African Language Resource Center, Indiana University. Bloomington, IN.

Eddy, J. (2016a). (Re) Imagining learning: Releasing creativity for transfer. [Conference Keynote Address]. Annual Conference. Foreign Language Educators of New Jersey.

Eddy, J. (2016b). Uncovering Curriculum: Designing for Intercultural Competence and Transfer. American Council on the Teaching of Foreign Languages [Conference Presentation]. Boston, MA.

Eddy, J. (2016c). Intercultural competence and transfer by design. New York State Association of Foreign Language Teaching [Conference Presentation]. Syracuse, NY.

Eddy, J. (2016d). Uncovering curriculum: Intercultural competence by design. Northeast Conference on the Teaching of Foreign Languages [Conference Presentation]. New York, NY.

Eddy, J. (2017). Unpacking the standards for transfer: Intercultural competence by design. In Rebecca Fox (Ed.), Special Volume on Intercultural Competence for Northeast Conference on the Teaching of Foreign Languages. *NECTFL Review*, 79(1), 53–72.

Eddy, J. (2019a). Preparing teachers of critical languages for articulated performance assessment task design. *Journal of the National Council on Less Commonly Taught Languages*, 25(1).

Eddy, J. (2019b). Literature and drama for transfer. In F. Diamantidaki (Ed.), *Teaching literature in modern foreign languages* (pp. 45–62). London: Bloomsbury Academic.

Eddy, J. & Bustamante, C. (2020). Closing the pre and in-service gap: Perceptions and implementation of the IPA during student teaching. *Foreign Language Annals*, 53, 634–656.

Edmiston, B. (2003). What's my position?: Role, frame and positioning when using process drama. *Research in Drama Education: The Journal of Applied Theatre and Performance*, 8(2), 221–229.

Egan, K. (1989). *Teaching as storytelling*. Chicago: University of Chicago Press.

Egan, K. (1992). *Imagination in teaching and learning*. Chicago: University of Chicago Press.

Egan, K. (2005). *An imaginative approach to teaching*. San Francisco: Jossey-Bass.

Eisner, E. (2002). *The arts and the creation of mind*. New Haven: Yale University Press.

Ellis, R. (2009). Task-based language teaching: Sorting out the misunderstandings. *International Journal of Applied Linguistics*, 19(3), 221–246.

Erickson, H. (2007). *Concept-based curriculum and instruction for the thinking classroom*. Thousand Oaks, CA: Corwin.

Even, S. (2008). Moving in(to) imaginary worlds: Drama pedagogy for foreign language teaching and learning. *Unterrichtspraxis/Teaching German*, 41(2), 161–170.

Even, S. (2016). Nothing moves if you don't let go. Performative teacher training. In Mentz, Olivier & Fleiner, Micha (Eds.), *The Arts in Language Teaching. International Perspectives: Performative – Aesthetic – Transversal*. Berlin et al., LIT Verlag.

Fantini, A., & Tirmizi, A., (2006). Exploring and assessing intercultural competence. *World Learning Publications*. Paper 1. Retrieved from http://digitalcollections.sit.edu/worldlearning_publications/1

Farmer, D. (2007). *101 Drama games and activities*. Norwich: DramaResource.

Feldhendler, D. (2007). *Playback theatre: A method for intercultural dialogue*. Scenario.

Fels, L. & McGivern, L. (2002). Intercultural recognition through performative inquiry. In Bräuer, Gerd (Ed.) *Body and language: Intercultural learning through drama*. (pp. 19–33). Westport: Ablex Publishing.

Frey, N., & Fisher, D. (2006). *Language arts workshop: Purposeful reading and writing instruction*. Upper Saddle River, NJ: Merrill Education.

Fisher, D., Frey, N., & Hattie, J. (2016). Visible *learning for literacy, grades K-12: Implementing the practices that work best to accelerate student learning*. Corwin Literacy.

Fisher, R. (2005). What is creativity? In R. Fisher & M. Williams (Eds.), *Unlocking creativity: Teaching across the curriculum* (pp. 6–20). New York: Routledge.

Fox, J. (2003). *Acts of service: Spontaneity, commitment, tradition in the nonscripted theatre*. New Paltz, NY: Tusitala.

Freire, P. (2018). *Pedagogy of the oppressed: 50th anniversary edition*, London: Bloomsbury.

Gagnon, G.W. and Collay, M. (2001). *Designing for learning: Six elements in constructivist classrooms*. Thousand Oaks, CA: Corwin Press, Inc.

Gagnon, G.W. and Collay, M. (2006). *Constructivist learning design: Key questions for teaching to standards*. California: Corwin Press.

Galloway, V. (1998). Constructing cultural realities: "Facts" and frameworks of association. In J. Harper, M. Lively, & M. Williams (Eds.), *The coming of age of the profession* (pp. 129–140). Boston: Heinle and Heinle.

Galton, M. (2008). *Creative practitioners in schools and classrooms*. Cambridge: University of Cambridge Faculty of Education.

Garcia, O., & Wei, L. (2014). *Translanguaging: Language, bilingualism and education*. New York: Palgrave Macmillan.

Gardner, H. (1999). *The disciplined mind: What all students should understand*. New York: Simon and Schuster.

Gardner, H. (2006). *Five minds for the future*. Boston: Harvard Business School Press.

Gee, J. P. (2012). *Situated language and learning: A critique of traditional schooling*. London: Routledge.

Gilmore, A. (2004). A comparison of textbook and authentic interactions. *ELT Journal*, 58 (4), 360–374.

Gilmore, A. (2007). Authentic materials and authenticity in foreign language learning. *Language Teaching*, (40), 97–118.

Gingerich, W. (1987) Heidegger and the Aztecs: The poetics of knowing in pre-Hispanic Nahuatl poetry. In B. Swann and A. Krupat (Eds.), *Recovering the word: Essays on Native American literature* (pp. 85–112). University of California Press. Berkeley.

C.A. Glisan, E.W., Adair-Hauck, B., Koda, K., Sandrock, S.P., & Swender, E. (2003). *ACTFL integrated performance assessment*. Yonkers, NY: ACTFL.

Glisan, E.W. & Donato, R. (2017). *Enacting the work of language instruction: High-leverage teaching practices*. Alexandria, VA: ACTFL.

Glisan, E.W., Uribe, D., & Adair-Hauck, B. (2007). Research on integrated performance assessment at the post-secondary level: Student performance across the modes of communication. *Canadian Modern Language Review*, 64(1), 39–67.

Goldstein, D. (1965). The Wounded Lion. In *Hebrew poems from Spain* (pp. 59–60). Oxford; Portland, Oregon: Liverpool University Press.

Grandin, T. (2006). *Thinking in pictures, expanded edition,* New York: Vintage Press, Random House.

Greene, M. (1995). *Releasing the imagination: Essays on education, the arts, and social change*. San Francisco: Jossey-Bass.

Greene, M. (2001). *Variations on a Blue Guitar: The Lincoln Center Institute lectures on aesthetic education*. New York: Teachers College Press.

Guariento, W. & Morley, J. (2001). Text and task authenticity in the EFL classroom. *ELT Journal*, 55(4), 347–353.

Hagger-Vaughn, L. (2016). Towards 'languages for all' in England: The state of the debate. *The Language Learning Journal*, 44(3), 358–375.

Hall, E.T. (1976). *Beyond culture*. Garden City, NY: Anchor Press.

Hall, J.K. (2002). *Methods for teaching foreign languages: Creating a community of learners in the classroom*. Upper Saddle River, NJ: Prentice Hall.

Halpern, D. F. (1998). Teaching critical thinking for transfer across domains: Dispositions, skills, structure training, and metacognitive monitoring. *American Psychologist*, 53(4), 449–455.

Haseman, B. & O'Toole, J. (1987). *Dramawise*. Melbourne: Heinemann.

Hattie, J. (2012). *Visible learning for teachers*. Abingdon, UK: Routledge.

Heathcote, D. & Bolton, G. (1994). Drama for learning: Dorothy Heathcote's mantle of the expert approach to education. *Dimensions of Drama Series*.

Heathcote, D. & Bolton, G. (1995). *Drama for learning: Dorothy Heathcote's mantle of the expert approach to education*. Portsmouth, NH: Heinemann Press.

Heathcote, D. & Herbert, P. (1985). A drama of learning: Mantle of the expert, theory into practice. *Educating through Drama*, 24 (Summer), 173–180.

Holec, H. (1988). *Autonomy and self-directed learning: Present fields of application*. Strasbourg: The Council of Europe.

Holliday, A. (2006). Native-speakerism. *ELT Journal*, 60, 385–387.

Holzer, M. (2005). *Aesthetic education philosophy and practice: Education traditions*. New York: Lincoln Center Institute.

Holzer, M. (2007). *Aesthetic education, inquiry and the imagination. Lincoln Center for the Performing Arts*. New York: Lincoln Center Institute.

Holzer, M., & Noppe-Brandon, S. (Eds.). (2005). *Community in the making: Lincoln Center Institute, the Arts, and Teacher Education*. New York: Teachers College Press.

Housen A. (2002). Aesthetic thought, critical thinking and transfer. *Arts Learning Journal*, 18(1), 99–132.

Hyun, J. (1924). One Lucky Day. Translated by K. O'Rourke in *A Lucky Day (2014)*, Bi-lingual Edition Modern Korean Literature, Vol. 87, Asia Publishers.

Johnstone, K. (2012). *Impro: Improvisation and the theatre*. London: Routledge.

Johnstone, R. (1997). Research on Language Learning and Teaching: 1995. *Language Teaching*, 29(3), 145–160.

Jourdain, S. (2008). Building connections to culture: A student-centered approach. *Foreign Language Annals*, 31(3), 439–50.

Kao, S.M. (1995). From script to impromptu: Learning a second language through process drama. In Taylor, P. and Hoepper, C. (Eds.), *Selected reading in drama and theatre education: The IDEA '95 Papers (2nd, Brisbane, Australia, July 1995)*. NA DIE Research Monograph Series, 3. Brisbane: IDEA Publications.

Kao, S.M. & O'Neill, C. (1998). *Words into worlds: Learning a second language through process drama*. Stanford: Ablex Publishing.

Kearney, E. (2010). Cultural immersion in the foreign language classroom: Some narrative possibilities. *The Modern Language Journal*, 94(2), 332.

Kingsbury-Brunetto, K. (2015). *Performing the art of language learning: Deepening the language learning experience through theatre and drama*. Blue Mounds, WI: Deep University Press.

Kolb, D. A. (2014). *Experiential learning. Experience as the source of learning and development*. 2nd ed. Upper Saddle River, NJ: Pearson Education.

Kramsch, C. (1993). *Context and culture in language teaching*. Oxford: Oxford University Press.

Kramsch, C. (1994). Foreign languages for a global age. *ADFL Bulletin*, 25(1), 5–12.

Kramsch, C. (1995). The cultural component of language teaching. *Language, Culture and Curriculum* 8 (12): 83–92.

Kramsch, C. (2006) From communicative competence to symbolic competence. *The Modern Language Journal*, 90: 249–252.

Kramsch, C. (2008). Ecological perspectives on Foreign Language education. *Language Teaching*, 41(3), 389.

Kramsch, C. (2009). *The multilingual subject*. Oxford, UK: Oxford University Press.

Kramsch, C. (2011). The symbolic dimensions of the intercultural. *Language Teaching*, 44, 354–367.

Kramsch, C. (2013). *Teaching culture and intercultural competence*. Hoboken, NJ: Blackwell Publishing.

Lado, R. (1961). *Language testing*. London: Longman.

Lamb, T.E. (2000). Finding a voice: Learner autonomy and teacher education in an urban context. In Sinclair, B., McGrath, I. & Lamb, T. (Eds.), *Learner autonomy, teacher autonomy: Future directions*. (pp. 118–127). London: Addison Wesley Longman.

Lamb, T.E. (2001). Language policy in multilingual UK. *Language Learning Journal*. (23).

Lamb, T. & Reinders, H. (2005). Learner independence in language teaching: A concept of change. In: Cunningham, D. & Hatoss, A. *An international perspective on language policies, practices and proficiencies*. Belgrave: FIPLV.

Lamb, T.E. (2008). Learner and teacher autonomy: synthesizing an agenda. In Lamb, T.E. and Reinders, H. (Eds.) *Learner and teacher autonomy: Concepts, realities and responses*. Amsterdam: John Benjamins: pp. 269–284.

Lamb, T.E. (2017). Knowledge about language and learner autonomy. In Cenoz, J. & Gorter, D. (Eds.), *Language awareness and multilingualism*. (pp. 173–186). Switzerland: Springer International Publishing.

Lange, D. (1982). The Problem of articulation. In Theodore V. Higgs, (Ed.) *Curriculum, competence, and the foreign language teacher* (pp. 113–137). Lincolnwood, IL: ACTFL Foreign Language Education series, vol. 13. National Textbook Company.

Lange, D. (1988). Articulation: A resolvable problem. In Lalande, John F. II, (Ed.), *Shaping the future of language education: FLES, articulation, and proficiency* (pp. 11–31). Report of Central States Conference on the Teaching of Foreign Language.

Lange, D. (1999). Planning for using the new national culture standards. In J. Phillips & R. M. Terry (Eds.), *Foreign language standards: Linking research, theories, and practices* (pp. 57–120). Lincolnwood, IL: National Textbook & American Council on the Teaching of Foreign Languages.

Lange, D. & Paige M. (Eds.). (2000). Culture as the core: Perspectives on culture in second language learning. *A Volume in Research in Second Language Learning*. Charlotte, NC: Information Age Publishing.

Lantolf, J., & Appel, G. (1994). *Vygotskian approaches to second language research*. New Jersey: Ablex Publishing.

Lapkin, S., & Swain, M. (2004). What underlies immersion students' production: The case of avoir besoin de. *Foreign Language Annals*, 37, 349–355.

Léon -Portilla, M. (1963). *Aztec thought and culture*. (Jack E. Davis, Trans.). Norman: University of Oklahoma Press.

Liddicoat, A., Papademetre, L., Scarino, A., & Kohler, M. (2003). *Report on intercultural language learning*, DEST, Canberra: Commonwealth of Australia.

Liddicoat, A. & Scarino, A. (2010). Eliciting the intercultural in foreign language education. In L. Sercu & A. Paran (Eds.), *Testing the untestable in language and education*, (pp. 52–73). Clevedon: Multilingual Matters.

Liddicoat, A.J. (2002). Static and dynamic views of culture and intercultural language acquisition. *Babel* 36(3): 4–11, 37.

Liddicoat, A.J. & Scarino, A. (2013). *Intercultural language teaching and learning*. Malden, MA: Wiley-Blackwell.

Linklater, K. (2006). *Freeing the natural voice: Imagery and art in the practice of voice and language*. Revised and Expanded, London: Nick Hern Books.

National Literacy Trust. (2020). Disciplinary Literacy. Accessed January 2022. https://literacytrust.org.uk/resources/disciplinary-literacy/.

Little, D. (1995). Learning as dialogue: The dependence of learner autonomy on teacher autonomy. *System*, 23(2), 175–182.

Little, D. (Ed.) (2003). *The European language portfolio in use: Nine examples*. Strasbourg, France: Council of Europe. Available from www.coe.int/portfolio.

Little, D. (2007). Language learning autonomy: Some fundamental considerations Revisited. *Innovation in Language Learning and Teaching*, 1(1), 14–29. https://doi.org/10.2167/illt040.0

Little, D. (2009a). *The European language portfolio: Where pedagogy and assessment meet*. Strasbourg: Council of Europe.

Little, D. (2009b). Language learner autonomy and the European language portfolio: Two L2 English examples. *Language Teaching*, 42(2), 222–233.

Little, D. (2011). The common European framework of reference for languages, the European language portfolio, and language learning in higher education. *Language Learning in Higher Education* 1/1, 1–21.

Little, D. (2012). The common European framework of reference for languages and the European language portfolio: Some history, a view of language learner autonomy, and some implications for language learning in higher education. *Language Learning in Higher Education*, 2(1), 1–16.

Little, D., Goullier, F., & Hughes, G. (2011). *The European language portfolio: The story so far (1991-2011)*. Strasbourg, France: Council of Europe. Available from www.coe.int

Little, D. (2020). Language learner autonomy: Rethinking language teaching. *Language Teaching*, 1–10.

Little, D. & Perclová, R. (2001). *The European language portfolio. Guide for Teachers and Teacher Trainers*. Strasbourg: Council of Europe.

Liu, J. (2002). Process drama in second language and foreign language classrooms. In G. Brauer (Ed.), *Body and language: Intercultural Learning Through Drama* (pp. 52–70). Westport: Ablex Publishing.

Looney, D. & Lusin, N. (2018). Enrollments in languages other than English in United States institutions of higher education, Summer 2016 and Fall 2016: Preliminary Report. Modern Language Association of America. Retrieved: https://www.mla.org/Resources/Research/Surveys-Reports-and-Other-Documents/Teaching-Enrollments-and-Programs/Enrollments-in-Languages-Other-Than-English-in-United-States-Institutions-of-Higher-Education.

Magnan, S. (2008). Reexamining the priorities of the national standards for foreign language education. *Language Teaching*, 41(3), 349–366.

Maley, A. & Duff, A. (2005). *Drama techniques: A resource book of communication activities for language teachers*. 3rd ed. 4th print. Cambridge: Cambridge University Press.

Manuel J., Hughes J., Anderson, M., & Arnold, R. (Eds.) (2008) *Drama and English teaching: Imagination, action and engagement*. Oxford: Oxford University Press.

Mayer, R.E. (2001). Cognitive, metacognitive, and motivational aspects of problem solving. In H.J. Hartman (Ed.), *Metacognition in learning and instruction*, (pp. 87–101). Kluwer Academic Publishers.

McKeough, A., Lupart J., & Marini, Q. (Eds.). (1995). *Teaching for transfer: Fostering generalizations in learning*. Mahwah, NJ: Lawrence Erlbaum Associates.

McNeill, D. (2000). Introduction. In D. McNeill (Ed.) *Language and gesture*, pp. 1–10. Cambridge University Press.

McTighe, J. (2014). Transfer goals. Retrieved from http://jaymctighe.com/wordpress/wpcontent/uploads/2013/04/Long-term-Transfer-Goals.pdf

McTighe, J. & Silver, H. F. (2020). *Teaching for deeper learning: Tools to engage students in meaning making*. Alexandria, VA: ASCD.

McTighe, J. & Wiggins, G. (2004). *Understanding by design professional development workbook*. Alexandria, VA: ASCD.

McTighe, J. & Wiggins, G. (2013). *Essential questions: Opening doors to student understanding*. Alexandria, VA: ASCD

Mishan, F. (2005). *Designing authenticity into language learning materials*. Great Britain: Intellect Ltd.

Moeller, A., Theiler, J., & Wu, C. (2012). Goal setting and student achievement: A longitudinal study. *The Modern Language Journal*, 96, 153–169.

Moeller, A. & Nugent, K. (2014). Building intercultural competence in the language classroom. *Unlock the gateway to communication*. In Dhonau, S. (Ed.). *Central States Conference Report* (pp. 1–18) Eau Claire, WI: Crown Prints.

Morain, G. (1997). A perspective on cultural perspectives. In M. H. Rosenbusch (Ed.), *Bringing the Standards into the classroom: A teacher's guide* (2nd ed., pp. 35–37). Ames: Iowa State University.

National Council of State Supervisors of Foreign Language. (2017). *NCSSFL-ACTFL can-do statements*. Alexandria, VA: author.

National Research Council (2000). *How people learn: Brain, mind, experience, and school*. Expanded ed. Washington, DC: National Academies Press.

National Standards Collaborative Board. (2015). *World-readiness standards for learning languages*. 4th ed. Alexandria, VA: Author.

National Standards in Foreign Language Education Project. (2006). *Standards for foreign language learning in the 21st century*. Lawrence, KS: Allen Press. (Original work published 1999).

North, B. (1992). European language portfolio: Some options for a working approach to design scales for proficiency, in Schärer, R. & North, B. (Eds.), *Towards a common European framework for reporting language competency*, (pp. 158–172). Washington, DC: NFLC Occasional Paper, National Foreign Language Center.

North, B. (2000). *The development of a common framework scale of language proficiency*, New York: Peter Lang.

North, B. & Piccardo, E. (2016). Developing illustrative descriptors of aspects of mediation for the Common European Framework of Reference (CEFR). *Research report*. Strasbourg: Council of Europe, Language Policy Unit.

Omaggio-Hadley, A. (2001). *Teaching language in context*. 3rd ed. Boston: Heinle & Heinle.

O'Neill, C. (1995). *Drama worlds: A framework for process drama*. Portsmouth: Heinemann.

Ornstein A.C. & Hunkins, F.P. (2004). *Curriculum foundations, principles and issues*. (3rd ed). Boston: Allyn and Bacon.

Ortega, L. (2019). SLA and the study of equitable multilingualism. *The Modern Language Journal*, *103*, 23–38.

O'Toole, J. (1992). The *process of drama: Negotiating art and meaning*. London: Routledge.
Pearson, P. D. & Gallagher, M. C. (1983). The instruction of reading comprehension. *Contemporary Educational Psychology*, 8, 317–344.
Perkins, D.N. & Salomon, G. (1992). *Transfer of learning*. International Encyclopedia of Education. 2nd ed. Oxford, England: Pergamon Press.
Perkins, D. N. & Salomon, G. (1988). Teaching for transfer. *Educational Leadership*, 46, 22–32.
Perkins, D.N. & Salomon, G. (2012). Knowledge to go: A motivational and dispositional view of transfer. *Educational Psychologist*, 47(3). 248–258.
Pesola, C. A. (1988). Articulation for elementary school foreign language programs: Challenges and opportunities. In *Shaping the future of foreign language. Report of central states conference on the teaching of foreign languages*. Lincolnwood, IL: National Textbook Co. (ERIC Document Reproduction Service No. ED 292 333).
Piazzoli, E. (2010). Process drama and intercultural language learning: An experience of contemporary Italy. *RiDE: The Journal of Applied Theatre and Performance,* 15(3), 385–402.
Piazzoli, E. (2011). Process drama: The use of affective space to reduce language anxiety in theadditional language learning classroom. *Research in Drama Education* (16)4, 557–574.
Piazzoli, E. (2012). Film and drama aesthetics for additional language teaching. In J. Winston (Ed.), *Second language learning through drama: Practical techniques and applications* (pp. 134–148). London/New York: Routledge.
Piazzoli, E. (2014). Engagement as perception-in-action in process drama for teaching and learning Italian as a second language. *International Journal for Language Studies*, 8(2), pp. 91–116.
Piazzoli, E. (2018). Embodying language in action. *The Artistry of Process Drama in Second Language Education*. London: Palgrave Macmillan.
Piazzoli, E. & Kubiak, J. (2019). The only learning I'm going to get: Students with intellectual disabilities learning a second language through performative pedagogy. Https://doi.org/10.33178/scenario.13.1.2
Piccardo, E. (2013). Plurilingualism and curriculum design: Towards a synergic vision. *TESOL Quarterly*, 47(3), 600–614.
Piccardo, E., & North, B. (2019). *The action-oriented approach: A dynamic vision of language education*. Bristol: Multilingual Matters.
Pink, D. (2006). *A whole new mind: Why right-brainers will rule the future*. New York, NY: Riverhead Books.
Pinker, S. (2003). *The blank slate: The modern denial of human nature*, p. 283, Penguin.
Raphael, T. E., & Au, K. H. (2005). QAR: Enhancing comprehension and test taking across grades and content areas. *Reading Teacher*, 59, 206–221.
Risager, K. (2007). *Language and culture pedagogy. From a national to a transnational paradigm*. Clevedon, UK: Multilingual Matters.
Robinson, K. (2006). Do schools kill creativity? [video]. *TED Conferences*. https://www.ted.com/talks/sir_ken_robinson_do_schools_kill_creativity

Robinson-Stuart, G., & Nocon, H. (1996). Second culture acquisition: Ethnography in the foreign language classroom. Modern Language Journal, 80, 431–449.

Rothwell, J. (2011). Bodies and language: Process drama and intercultural language learning in a beginner language classroom. *Research in Drama Education: The Journal of Applied Theatre and Performance*, 16(4), 575–594.

Sahlberg, P. (2007). Education policies for raising student learning: The Finnish approach, *Journal of Education Policy*, 22(2), 147–171.

Salas, J. (1996). *Improvising real life: Personal story in playback theatre*. New Paltz, NY: Tusitala.

Salas, J. (2006). Doing playback theatre in a foreign language: Learning language, learning culture, learning identity. *Playback Leadership*. New Paltz, NY: Centre for Playback Theatre.

Sandrock, P. (2014). *The keys to assessing language performance*. Alexandria, VA. ACTFL.

Sawyer, R.K. (2003). Improvised lessons: Collaborative discussion in the constructivist classroom. *Teaching Education*, 15(2), 189–201.

Scarino, A. (2010). Assessing intercultural capability in learning languages: A renewed understanding of language, culture, learning, and the nature of assessment. *The Modern Language Journal*, 94(2), 324–329.

Scarino, A. (2014). Learning as reciprocal, interpretive meaning-making. A view from collaborative research into the professional learning of teachers of languages. *The Modern Language Journal*, 98(1), 386–401.

Scarino, A. & Liddicoat, A. (2016). Reconceptualising learning in transdisciplinary languages education. *L2 Journal*, 8(4), 20–35.

Schewe, M. (2013). Taking stock and looking ahead: Drama pedagogy as a gateway to a performative teaching and learning culture. *Scenario*, 7(1), 5–27.

Schewe, M. & Shaw, P. (Eds.) (1993). *Towards drama as a method in the foreign language classroom*. Frankfurt: Peter Lang.

Schleppegrell, M.J., & Bowman, B. (1995). Problem-posing: A tool for EFL curriculum renewal. *ELT Journal*, 49(4), 297–307.

Sercu, L. (2006). The foreign language and intercultural competence teacher: The acquisition of a new professional identity. *Intercultural Education*, 17(1), 55–72. DOI: 10.1080/14675980500502321

Seurat, G. (1884/86). *A Sunday on La Grande Jatte – 1884*. [Painting]. The Art Institute of Chicago. Chicago, IL.

Shrum, J.L. & Glisan, E.W. (2016). *Teacher's handbook: Contextualized language instruction*. (5th ed). Boston, MA: Heinle.

Shulman, L.S. (1999). What is learning and what does it look like when it doesn't go well? *Change*, 31(4), 0–17.

Sinicrope, C., Norris, J., & Watanabe, Y. (2007). Understanding and assessing intercultural competence: A summary of theory, research, and practice. *Second Language Studies*, 26(1), Fall, 1–58.

Sondheim, S., & Lapine, J. (1984). *Sunday in the park with George*. New York: Dodd, Mead & Co. Applause Theatre Books.

Sparks, R. L. (2009). If you don't know where you're going, you'll wind up somewhere else: The case of 'Foreign Language Learning Disability.' *Foreign Language Annals*, 42(1), 7–26.

Stam, G., & McCafferty, S.G. (2008). Gesture studies and second language acquisition: A review. In S. G. McCafferty & G. Stam (Eds.), *Gesture: Second language acquisition and classroom research* (pp. 3–24). New York, NY: Routledge.

Stanford Center for Assessment, Learning and Equity (SCALE). (2019). *Ed TPA world language assessment handbook*. Palo Alto, CA: Author.

Stoller, F. (1994). The diffusion of innovations in intensive ESL programs. *Applied Linguistics*, 15, 300–327.

Stoller, F. (2006). Establishing a theoretical foundation for project-based learning in second and foreign language contexts. In G. H. Beckett, & P. C. Miller, (Eds.), *Project-based second and foreign language education: Past, present, and future* (pp. 19–40). Greenwich, CT: Information Age.

Stoller, F. (2009). Innovation as the hallmark of effective leadership. In M. Christison & D. Murray (Eds.), *Leadership in English language education: Theoretical foundations and practical skills for changing times* (pp. 73–84). New York, NY: Routledge.

Swaffar, J. (2006). Terminology and its discontents: Some caveats about communicative competence. *Modern Language Journal*, 90(2), 246–249.

Swaffar, J., & Arens K. (2005). *Remapping the foreign language curriculum: An approach through multiple literacies*. New York: Modern Language Association.

Swain, M., Kinnear, P. and Steinman, L. (2015). *Sociocultural theory in second language education: An introduction through narratives* (2nd edn). Bristol: Multilingual Matters.

Tang, Y. (2006). Beyond behavior: Goals of cultural learning in the second language classroom. *The Modern Language Journal*, 90(1), 86–99.

Taylor, F., & Mardsen, E. (2014). Perceptions, attitudes, and choosing to study foreign languages in England: An experimental intervention. *The Modern Language Journal*, 98(4), 902–920.

Todd, M. E. (1937). *The thinking body*, New York: Dance Horizons.

Tschirner, E. & Bärenfänger, O. (2012). Bridging frameworks for assessment and learning: The ACTFL Guidelines and the CEFR. *Paper presented at the 34th Language Testing Research Colloquium (LTRC)*, Princeton, NJ, 3–5 Apr 2012.

Van Lier, L. (2010). Agency, Self, and Identity in Language Learning. In B. O'Rourke & L. Carson (Eds.), *Language learner autonomy: Policy, curriculum, classroom* (pp. 9–19). Oxford: Peter Lang.

VanPatten, B. (2003). *From input to output: A teacher's guide to second language acquisition*. New York: McGraw-Hill.

VanPatten, B. (2004). Input processing in SLA. In B. VanPatten (Ed.), *Processing instruction: Theory, research, and commentary* (pp. 5–31). Mahwah, NJ: Lawrence Erlbaum Associates.

VanPatten, B. (2010). The two faces of SLA: Mental representation and skill. *International Journal of English Studies*, 10(1), 1–18.

VanPatten (2017). *While we're on the topic*. Alexandria: ACTFL.

VanPatten, B., & Benati, A. (2015). *Key terms in second language acquisition*. 2nd edition. London: Bloomsbury.

VanPatten, B., Collopy, E., Price, J., Borst, E., & Qualin, A. (2013). Explicit information, grammatical sensitivity, and the rst-noun principle: A cross-linguistic study in processing instruction. *Modern Language Journal*, 97, 506–527.

VanPatten, B., & Rothman, J. (2015). Against "Rules". In A. Benati, C. Lavale, & M. Arche (Eds.), *The grammar dimension in instructed second language acquisition* (pp. 15–35). London: Bloomsbury Publishing.

Verhoeven, L., & Perfetti, C. (2008). Advances in text comprehension: Model, process and development. *Applied Cognitive Psychology*, 22, 293–30.

Vygotsky, L.S. (1962). *Thought and language* (E. Hanfmann & G. Vakar, Eds. & Trans.). Cambridge, MA: MIT Press. (Original work published 1934).

Vygotsky, L.S. (1978). *Mind in society: The development of higher psychological processes*. Cambridge, MA: Harvard University Press.

Vygotsky, L. (1986). *Thought and language*. Cambridge, MA: MIT Press.

Vygotsky, L.S. (1997). *Educational psychology* (R. Silverman, Trans.). Boca Raton, FL: St. Lucie Press.

Wagner, J. (2002). Understanding drama-based education. in Brauer, G. (Ed.) *Body and language. Intercultural learning through drama*. (p. 2). London: Ablex Publishing.

Wagner, M., & Byram, M. (2015). Gaining intercultural communicative competence. *The Language Educator*, 10(3), 28–30.

Wagner, M., Perugini, D., Byram, M. (Eds.). (2018). *Teaching intercultural competence across the age range: From theory to practice*. Bristol, UK: Multilingual Matters.

Wiggins, G. (1998). *Educative assessment: Designing assessments to inform and improve student practice*. San Francisco: Jossey-Bass.

Wiggins, G., & McTighe, J. (2005). *Understanding by design*. 2nd ed. Alexandria, VA: Association for Supervision and Curriculum Development.

Wiggins, G., & McTighe, J. (2007). *Schooling by design: Mission, action, and achievement*. Alexandria, VA: Association for Supervision and Curriculum Development.

Wiggins, G., & McTighe, J. (2011). *The understanding by design guide to creating high-quality units*. Alexandria, VA: Association for Supervision and Curriculum Development.

Wolfe, J. L. & Neuwirth, C. M. (2001). From the margins to the center: The future of annotation. *Journal of Business and Technical Communication*, 15(3): 333–371.

Wight, M.C.S. (2015). Students with learning disabilities in the Foreign Language learning environment and the practice of exemption. *Foreign Language Annals*, 38(1), 39–55.

Yenawine, P. (2013). *Visual thinking strategies: Using art to deepen learning across school disciplines*. Cambridge, MA: Harvard Education Press.

Index

Abugasea Heidt, M. 96
Adair-Hauck, B. 11, 83, 123
aesthetic education 19, 26, 54, 131–5, 170–1, 173
Agarwal, P. 82
American Association of Teachers of German (AATG) 211. See also Creating a Safe Space (AATG initiative)
American Council on the Teaching of Foreign Languages (ACTFL) 21, 27, 79, 83, 87, 99, 123, 134, 170, 178, 246
American Councils for International Education (ACIE) 6
Anderson, L. W. 82
Anderson, M. 170
Appel, G. 125
Arens, K. 19, 59
Arirang (Korean song, Soojin Choi Kim) 147–50, 173
Armstrong, M. 47
Arnold, R. 170
Aroeste, S., *El Leon Ferido* and *Mi Monastir* (Ladino) 89–95
Articulated Assessment Transfer Task (AATT) 8, 15, 17, 21, 23, 56, 79, 84, 96, 98–9, 125, 160, 244, 264
   Arirang (Soojin Choi Kim) 148–50
   Axe Porridge (Kalmanson) 49–53, 258–62
   bullying, human rights and racism (Lennon) 182–5
   Capoeira (Bianconi) 63–6
   Chanson pour Haiti (Douce) 191–3
   child labour (Durand) 152–4
   context 86, 264
   design rubric 290–2
   DIE Imbissstadt (Garcia & McCloskey) 219–23
   Eid celebration (Kureishy) 186–8
   El Leon Ferido and *Mi Monastir* (Aroeste) 91–5
   Familienstrukturen in der deutschsprachigen Welt (Garcia & McCloskey) 214–18
   flexible, bespoke curriculum 263
   gender-based violence (D'Ugo) 225–9
   home and lifestyle (Hanna-Wicht) 253–6
   inside-outside spaces (Kuo-Flynn) 56–9
   interpersonal-interactive mode 168–9
   interpretive mode 123
   Leisure in 1884 and Today 112–13
   Lockdown Yoga (Singh) 99–103
   Made in Italy (Bonanno) 106–9
   mediation strategies for 22
   mode 121, 167, 200
   One Lucky Day (Hyun Jin-geon) 174–7
   The Paper Boy (Ilieva) 138–40
   review criteria 289–90
   Sana, Sana (Gilbert) 32–4
   school and education (Xie) 247–50
   statements for 14
   as summative/formative assessments 13, 27
   Takiwātanga (Opai) 143–6
   tasks 27
   template 12
   tips to articulated design 264–5
   use of language 18
   Viva la Vida (Eddy) 28–30
   in xochitl, in cuicatl (Sánchez) 232–4
   Yorùbá wedding celebration (Sanuth) 208–10
articulation 16, 79
   AATT (see Articulated Assessment Transfer Task (AATT))
   chart (ITT) 14, 274

Index

collaboration for 15, 48, 87, 151, 185, 205, 266-7
horizontal 16
implementation for 263-4
and transfer 84 (see also transfer)
vertical 9, 13, 16-17, 40, 71, 86, 208
world language curriculum design principles 316-17
Articulation Spiral Points 18, 43, 59, 79, 201, 241, 244
assessment
design 160
as instruction 242, 246
performance (see performance assessment)
for transfer inventory 286
Au, K. H. 134, 158
authentic communication transaction 79-80
authentic community texts 55-6, 60-1, 72, 84, 122, 127-8, 130-1, 137, 151. See also cultural community authentic texts
authorship 122. See also ownership
autonomy 5-6, 13, 23-4, 47, 71, 82, 96-7, 160
Axe Porridge (*smekalka*, Kalmanson) 48-53, 258-62, 281-2, 303-8

Backward Design 9, 13
stages 67
Baker, S. 170
Baldwin, P. 133, 171
Bärenfänger, O. 21
Beacco, J. 42
Bennett, M. J. 41
Benson, P. 96
Berardo, K. 54-5
Bianconi, C. 61
Capoeira (resistance) 61-6
Bloom, B. S. 82
Boal, A. 172
Bolton, G. 23, 88, 133, 169, 205
Bomba Estéreo 181
Bonanno, A. 105
Made in Italy 106-9
Bower, K. 17-18, 44
Brantmeier, E. J. 26
Bräuer, G. 23

Bruner, J. 17, 21
creativity 109
bullying (Lennon) 180-5
Bustamante, C. 22, 84, 123-4
Byram, M. 14, 23, 26, 41-4, 89. See also intercultural competence (IC)
Byrnes, H. 6, 16, 41

Capacities of Imaginative Learning 19, 131, 171, 203
interpersonal mode 171-2
interpretive mode 132-3
presentational mode 203
Capoeira (Brazil culture, Bianconi) 61-6
Cavalli, M. 42
Cawthon, S. 170
Chambers, G. N. 18
Chanson pour Haiti (Douce) 190-3
Chen, D. 44
child labour 137
Durand 151-4
Children and Art (Eddy) 111
classrooms 11-12, 17, 25-6, 41, 85
in Ayurvedic and Yogic lifestyle 98
culture, currency and challenge 127-8
foreign language acquisition process 62
multi-level learners 12, 86, 242
performances 18, 79
risk taking culture 170
second language, learning 44
co-creation 59, 87-8, 167, 170, 172
collaboration sampler 189
Collay, M. 126
The Common European Framework of Reference for Languages: Learning, Teaching, Assessment (CEFR) 14, 41, 83, 121, 160, 170
Companion Volume 22, 41
communication
languages and cultures 41
modes of 11, 19, 22, 54, 83-4, 121-3, 166, 199-200 (see also specific modes of communication)
transaction, authentic 79-80
Companion Volume 14, 22, 41
complexity 18, 20, 27, 43, 48, 71, 95-7, 128, 136, 225, 268

conception 83–5
  interpretation as 132
  interpretive-receptive mode as 121–5
Concept Map 67, 114, 142, 159, 195, 211, 257
Connolly, A. 47
consensus 83–5, 199, 206
  interpersonal-interactive mode as 166–9
  plan, choose, come to 88, 152, 177–9
Constructivist Learning Design 126
context 12–13, 17, 20, 22, 42–3, 71, 88, 129, 224
  AATT 86, 264
  framing 86–7
  summative performance assessment 86, 114
Cook, V. J. 178
Cope, B. 203
Corbett, J. 78
Coste, D. 42
Couet, R. 16
Council for the Accreditation of Educator Preparation (CAEP, U.S.) 123
Council of Europe (COE) 12, 14, 21, 42–3, 45–6, 79, 83, 121, 124, 160, 170, 178
  Guide for the Development and Implementation of Curricula for Plurilingual and Intercultural Education 42
COVID-19 pandemic 212–13
  Lockdown Yoga 98–9
Coyle, D. 17–18, 43–4
Creating a Safe Space (AATG initiative) 211
  DIE Imbissstadt (THE Food City) 219–23
  Familienstrukturen in der deutschsprachigen Welt 214–18
creation 83–5
  presentational-productive mode as 200–2
creative transfer 109–10, 203, 205
  play 112
  songs 89
  understanding begins with 82–3
Cross, R. 18
Cuenat, M. E. 42
cultural community authentic texts 88, 96, 127, 131–2, 136

cultural perspectives/practices/products 10, 13, 20, 31, 40, 43–4, 46, 68, 127, 273
  Arirang (Soojin Choi Kim) 147–50
  Axe Porridge (Kalmanson) 48–53, 258–62
  Capoeira (Bianconi) 61–6
  Chanson pour Haiti (Douce) 190–3
  child labour (Durand) 151–4
  concepts through images 54
  cuisine 105
  curriculum 47
  DIE Imbissstadt (Garcia & McCloskey) 211, 219–23
  Eid celebration (Kureishy) 185–8
  El Leon Ferido and Mi Monastir (Aroeste) 89–95
  Familienstrukturen in der deutschsprachigen Welt (Garcia & McCloskey) 211–18
  gender-based violence (D'Ugo) 224–9
  home and lifestyle (Hanna-Wicht) 252–6
  inside-outside spaces (Kuo-Flynn) 55–9
  inventory 279–80
  leisure time 60
  Lockdown Yoga (Singh) 98–103
  Made in Italy (Bonanno) 106–9
  on margin of curriculum 44–5
  One Lucky Day (Hyun Jin-geon) 173–7
  painting 111
  The Paper Boy (Ilieva) 137–40
  remedios caseros 27–8, 31
  Sana, Sana (Gilbert) 31–4
  school and education (Xie) 246–50
  social justice (Lennon) 180–5
  A Sunday on La Grande Jatte (Seurat) 112–13
  Takiwātanga (Opai) 142–6
  from transmit to transform 45–6
  in xochitl, in cuicatl (Sánchez) 230–4
  Yogic principles and practices 98–9
  Yorùbá wedding celebration (Sanuth) 207–10
cultural texts 126–8
cultures standard. See cultural perspectives/practices/products
Cunico, S. 171

Index

curriculum design framework (African languages and cultures) 206
Curtain, H. 133

Dahlberg, C. 133
Dann, R. 12, 87, 242
Davies, A. 178
Dawson, K. 88, 170, 172
Deardorff, D. K. 44, 54–5
 Process Model of Intercultural Competence 42
Department for Education (DfE) 14, 42
design, facets 88–9
Dewey, J., flexible purposing 110
Diamantidaki, F. 130
DICE Consortium 23
DIE Imbissstadt. See THE Food City (Garcia & McCloskey)
Dignity for All Students Act (DASA, New York) 181
Diverse Families in the German-speaking world (Garcia & McCloskey) 211–18
Donato, R. 122
Douce, E. 190
 Chanson pour Haiti 191–3
drama pedagogy 22–3, 26, 48, 131–5, 169–70
Duff, A. 132
D'Ugo, I., gender-based violence (GBV) 224–9
Durand, G., child labour 151–4

Earl, L. M. 12, 87, 242
Eddy, J. 7–8, 12, 20, 23, 28, 41, 43, 59–60, 68, 78–81, 84–5, 88–9, 110–12, 122–4, 131–2, 134, 151, 160, 171, 203, 206, 244, 246, 263, 273, 274
Edmiston, B. 88, 205
edTPA (teacher performance assessment) 124
Egan, K. 61
 learner development 47
Eid celebration (Kureishy) 185–8
Eisner, E. 170
elementary students 123
El Leon Ferido and *Mi Monastir* (Aroeste) 89–95
embodying language 132
 three-phase structure 133

Endangered Language Alliance (ELA, New York City) 230
enduring understandings (EUs) 10, 12–13, 20, 27–8, 47, 285
 and essential questions (EQs) 67, 70–1, 87
 intercultural transferable goals 264
 and objective statements 69–70, 273
 routes to transfer 68–9
essential questions (EQs) 10, 12–13, 27–8, 47, 70, 72, 273, 285
 enduring understandings (EUs) and 67, 70–1, 87
 intercultural transferable goals 264
 kinds of 71
European Language Portfolio (ELP) 14, 160
Even, S. 169
expressive products 203

Familienstrukturen in der deutschsprachigen Welt. See Diverse Families in the German-speaking world (Garcia & McCloskey)
Fantini, A. 41
Farmer, D. 172
far transfer 104, 109
Feldhendler, D. 172
Fels, L. 23
Fisher, D. 141
Fisher, R. 110
five Cs (Communication, Cultures, Connections, Comparisons and Communities) 9
Fleming, M. 23, 26, 89
flexible purposing 110
Foley, Y. 17
THE Food City (Garcia & McCloskey) 211, 219–23
foreign language, learning 9, 42, 62
Foreign Language Learners (FLL) 98
formative assessment 13, 27, 86–7, 104, 224, 242–4, 258
Fox, J. 172
Freire, P., *Pedagogy of the Oppressed* 5
Frey, N. 141

Gagnon, G. W. 126
Galloway, V., authentic texts 127

Galton, M. 170
Garcia, O. 22
Garcia, P. 212
DIE Imbissstadt 211, 219–23
   Familienstrukturen in der deutschsprachigen Welt 211–18
Gardner, H. 17
Gee, J. P. 124
gender-based violence (GBV, D'Ugo) 224–9
Gilbert, V. 31
   Sana, Sana 31–4
Gingerich, W. 230
Glisan, E. W. 11, 21, 54, 83, 122–3
Goldstein, D. 89
Goullier, F. 42, 160
grammar and vocabulary 6, 13, 42, 60, 137, 152, 181, 206, 241, 246, 263
   forms and syntax 25
   four skills 11
Grandin, T., *Thinking in Pictures* 54
Greene, M. 19, 54, 111, 131, 171, 173, 203
Gribkova, B. 41, 43, 89
Guariento, W. 128

Hagger-Vaughn, L. 6
Hall, E. T., *Beyond Culture* 43
Hall, K. 203
Halpern, D. F. 78, 82
Ha-Nagid, S., *El Leon Ferido/The Wounded Lion* 89–90
Hancock, J. 17
Hanna-Wicht, S., home and lifestyle (Arabic) 252–6
Haseman, B. 23
Hattie, J. 13, 141
Heathcote, D. 23, 88, 133, 169, 205
Herbert, P. 88, 205
Heritage Language Learners (HLL) 98
higher-order thinking skills (HOTS) 82
Holec, H. 5, 96
Holliday, A. 178
Holzer, M. 19, 26, 54, 111, 131, 171, 203
home and lifestyle (Arabic, Hanna-Wicht) 252–6
HomeTV 87
horizontal articulation 16
Housen, A. 127
Hughes, G. 160

Hughes, J. 170
human rights (Lennon) 180–5
Hyun, J., *One Lucky Day* 132, 173–7

ideokinesis 132
Ilieva, G. N., *The Paper Boy* 137–40
improvisation 23, 26, 88, 167–8
   for inevitable unexpected 130, 169–71
inside-outside spaces (Japanese culture, Kuo-Flynn) 55–9
integrated performance assessment (IPA) 11, 83–4, 123
intentional curriculum design 42
intercultural communicative competence (ICC) 32, 41–2, 81, 111, 169, 246
   inquiry project 73
   transferable goals for 42–4, 46
Intercultural Competence Can-Do Statements 44
intercultural competence (IC) 7, 20, 25, 31, 40–2, 47, 56, 89, 120, 190, 207, 247
   in Ayurvedic and Yogic lifestyle 98
   Hindi language proficiency and 99
Intercultural Curriculum Aligns Novel Assessment Design Articulated Performance and Transfer (ICANADAPT) 8–9, 15, 21, 84, 98–9, 125, 160, 206, 241–2, 246, 262–3
   Axe Porridge (Kalmanson) 303–8
   Concept Map 67, 142, 211, 257
   connections-comparisons-communities 246, 251, 277–8, 296–302
   fillable template 314–15
   flexible, bespoke curriculum 263
   full unit sample 293–302
   interpersonal-interactive mode 168–9
   mode 121, 167, 200
   stage 242
   statements for 14
   template stages 10–14
   tips to articulated design 264–5
   unit sample Viva la Vida 275–8
intercultural language 5, 59
InterCultural Performance Assessment (ICPA), OSEE 54–5, 283
intercultural perspectives 16, 60–1, 68, 72, 78, 122, 267

intercultural transferable goals 9, 42–3, 55, 59–60, 68, 263–4
intercultural transfer targets 14, 55, 246, 262, 264, 283, 310
interpersonal-interactive mode
  characteristics 168–9
  as consensus 166–8
interpersonal mode (communication) 11, 22, 55, 83–4, 88, 123, 134, 166, 168, 177–9, 199, 201, 283, 312–13
  design tips for tasks 193–4
  exhibiting empathy 171–2
  goal of 173
  improvisation 169–71
  living with ambiguity 172
  making connections 172
  sampler 179–80
interpretive-interactive mode 121
interpretive mode (communication) 11, 22, 55, 83–4, 121–4, 128–9, 141, 170, 172, 178–9, 199, 201, 224, 283, 311–12
  aesthetic education and drama pedagogy 131–5
  design tips for tasks 155–6
  embodying 132–3
  identifying patterns 133
  listening with visuals 157
  noticing deeply 132
  questioning 133–5
  sampler across three levels 156, 159
interpretive-receptive mode
  characteristics 125
  as conception 121–5
intrapersonal 125
in xochitl, in cuicatl (Nahua culture, Sánchez) 230–4
ITT articulation chart 14, 274

Johnstone, K. 169
Johnstone, R. 20
Jourdain, S. 43

Kalantzis, M. 203
Kalmanson, E., Axe Porridge (*smekalka*) 48–53, 59, 61, 258–62, 281–2, 303–8
Kao, S-M. 23, 169

key performance catalogue/tasks 16, 20, 43, 201, 206, 241–2, 244–5, 263, 270–2
key performance transfer tasks 205
Kingsbury-Brunetto, K. 172
Kinnear, P. 22
K-12 instruction 24, 124
knowledge 5, 17, 21, 31, 47, 82, 124–5, 170, 203
  collaborative problem-solving 87
  language-like 104
  and skills 10, 13, 18, 20, 78, 85, 237, 242–3, 257, 263
  through drama 170–2
Koda, K. 11, 83, 123
Kohler, M. 41
Kramsch, C. 19, 22, 41, 44, 127
Krathwohl, D. R. 82
Kubiak, J. 133
Kuo-Flynn, S. 55
  inside-outside spaces (*uchi/soto*) 55–9, 61
Kureishy, R., Eid celebration 185–8

Lado, R. 11
Lamb, T. E. 5, 23, 47, 82, 96, 126, 160
Lange, D. 16, 41
language 12, 18, 26, 59, 78–80, 84, 126, 142, 208, 231
  accessible and perspectives visible 171–3
  acquisition 25, 133
  assessment transfer, stages 104–5
  competence and facility 14
  and culture 7, 12, 18, 24, 27, 41–2, 46, 60, 62, 83, 127, 133, 186, 206, 212–13
  embodying 132–3
  knowledge of 21, 166
  learners 86, 96, 99, 129, 130, 178
  mediation 22, 110
  ownership 122
  programmes, relevance and applicability 6
  through music 89
Lantolf, J. 125
Lapine, J., *Sunday in the Park with George* 112
layers, lifespan, level 60–1, 122, 284

learner engagement, levels 12, 27, 105, 159, 195
  interpretive mode task 156
  listening with visuals 157
learners. *See* teachers and learners
Lee, B. K. 88, 170, 172
leisure (1884 and today) 112, 287–8
Leitmotiv 214
Lennon, P., bullying, human rights and racism 180–5
Leon-Portilla, M. 230
Liddicoat, A. 10, 16, 18, 25, 41
Lincoln Center Education (Capacities for Imaginative Learning) 19, 131
Linklater, K. 132
Little, D. 5, 14, 23, 82, 160
Liu, J. 23
Lockdown Yoga (Singh) 98–103
Looney, D. 6
Lupart, J. 78
Lusin, N. 6

Made in Italy (Bonanno) 106–9
Magnan, S. 44
Maley, A. 132
The Mantle of the Expert from Process Drama 88, 205
Manuel, J. 170
Mardsen, E. 24
Marini, Q. 78
McCafferty, S. G. 132
McCloskey, M. 212
  DIE Imbissstadt 211, 219–23
  Familienstrukturen in der deutschsprachigen Welt 211–18
McGivern, L. 23
McKeough, A. 78
McNeill, D. 132
McTighe, J. 9–10, 13, 20, 43, 67–8, 71, 79, 87, 122, 160
mediation 14, 21–3, 27, 47, 80, 85, 87, 96, 123–5, 133, 167, 173, 178, 201, 246
  complexity, autonomy, novelty for 97
  practice at 242–3
  symbols 141–2, 211
Mediation for Transfer 12, 22–3, 180
Menchú, R. 180–1

Mishan, F. 127, 151
mobbing 180
Modern Foreign Languages (MFL)/World Languages (WL) 5, 20, 46, 70, 80–1, 178, 212
  curriculum design, principles (*see* world language curriculum design, principles)
  performance assessment 83–5
  transfer goal for 20
Moeller, A. 41, 44, 160
Morain, G. 54
Morley, J. 128

Nahua culture 230
  Chili uan Xocolatl 231
  tōcāyoh 232
  in xochitl, in cuicatl 230–4
National African Language Resource Center (NALRC) 206–8
National Council for Accreditation of Teacher Education (NCATE). *See* Council for the Accreditation of Educator Preparation (CAEP, U.S.)
National Council of State Supervisors of Foreign Language (NCSSFL) 14, 79, 83, 160, 178, 246
National Council on Less Commonly Taught Languages 206
National Curriculum for Languages 42
National Curriculum of England 14
National Literacy Trust 59
National Research Council 243
National Standards Collaborative Board 9, 42, 46, 121, 166, 200, 246, 258
National Standards in Foreign Language Education Project 9, 42, 123
NCSSFL-ACTFL 42, 44
NCSSFL-ACTFL can-do statements 14, 41, 160
near transfer 109, 242
negotiation of meaning 16, 26, 168, 170–2
Neuwirth, C. M. 141
Nin, A. 18
none, nigh, near, novel transfer 104, 245, 286
Noppe-Brandon, S. 26
Norris, J. 41

North, B. 14, 22
novelty 7, 20, 22, 24, 47, 79, 83, 97–8, 110, 120, 128, 170–1, 242
Nugent, K. 41, 44

Omaggio-Hadley, A. 44
O'Neill, C. 23, 169
One Lucky Day (Hyun Jin-geon) 132, 173–7
Opai, K., *Takiwātanga* (Te Reo Māori) 142–6
O'Rourke, K. 174
Ortega, L. 178
OSEE (ICPA) 54–5, 283
O'Toole, J. 23, 169–72
ownership 80, 122, 166

Paige, M. 41
Panthier, J. 42
Papademetre, L. 41
The Paper Boy (Ilieva) 136–40
PASS Can-Dos 160, 237, 246, 264
PASS can-do statements 160–1, 310
Perclová, R. 14
Perfetti, C. 134
performance(s) 13, 18, 26–7, 32, 43, 104, 244
  culture-based 59
  and proficiency 79
  for transfer 79, 84
performance assessment 12, 14, 124, 160, 166, 185, 190, 206
  summative/formative 13, 27, 86–7, 104, 201, 224, 242–4, 246, 258
  transdisciplinary 16
  transfer and practice at mediation 242–3
  world language 83–5
performance assessment specific statements (PASS) 14, 160
Perkins, D. N. 79, 104
personification 230–2
Perugini, D. 44
Pesola, C. A. 16
Piazzoli, E. 132–3
Piccardo, E. 14, 22, 124
Pink, D. 47
Pinker, S. 168
plurilingual/pluricultural competence 12, 14, 22, 41, 130, 141, 172, 225

poetic 203
pointillism 112
Poster Dialogue 88, 172
post-secondary learners 123
presentational mode (communication) 11, 22, 55, 83–4, 123, 166, 168, 172, 180, 199–201, 205, 224, 237, 241, 283, 313
  creating meaning 203
  design tips for tasks 235
  expressive 203
  reflecting/assessing 203
  sampler 204–5
  taking action 203
  task products 204
  transactional 203
presentational-productive mode
  characteristics 202
  as creation 200–1
Process Drama 169–71
profession, dissonance in 5–7
proficiency 16, 20–2, 62, 79, 99, 128, 134, 151, 160, 178–9, 252

Queens College
  aesthetic education 19
  Capacities of Imaginative Learning 131
  goals at 26
  intercultural communicative competence inquiry project 73
  spiral curriculum 68
question answer relationship technique 134
questioning (interpretive mode) 133–5, 177

racism (Lennon) 180–5
Raphael, T. E. 134, 158
receptive mode 121. *See also* interpretive-receptive mode
reinvention 8–15
remedios caseros (Viva la Vida) 27–8, 31
review, spiral, new 13, 246
risk taking culture 26, 89, 110–11, 169–70
Robinson, K. 110
rote memorization/knowledge 98, 124
Rothman, J. 18, 178
Rothwell, J. 169

Salas, J. 172
Salomon, G. 79, 104
Sana, Sana (Gilbert) 31–4
Sánchez, I. 230
   Chili uan Xocolatl 231
   in xochitl, in cuicatl (Nahua culture) 230–4
Sandrock, P. 11, 83–4, 123
Sanuth, K. K., Yorùbá wedding celebration 207–10
Saville, K. 47
Sawyer, R. K. 169
Scarino, A. 10, 18, 41
Schewe, M. 23
school and education (Chinese curriculum, Xie) 246–50, 293–302
Sercu, L. 41
Seurat, G., *A Sunday on La Grande Jatte* 112–13
Shaw, P. 23
Shrum, J. L. 21, 122
Shulman, L. S. 80
Singh, B., Lockdown Yoga 98–103
Sinicrope, C. 41
smekalka (Russian culture). See Axe Porridge (*smekalka*, Kalmanson)
social justice (Lennon) 180–5
Sondheim, S., *Sunday in the Park with George* 112
Soojin Choi Kim, Arirang (Korean song) 147–50, 173
Soy yo (Bomba Estéreo) 181
Sparks, R. 132
spiral curriculum 20–1, 68, 99, 105, 151
   Key Performances 242
   themes for 180
spontaneous/spontaneity 84, 88, 166–7
stage one and three 273
Stam, G. 132
Standards for Foreign Language Learning 9, 42
Stanford Center for Assessment, Learning and Equity (SCALE) 124
Starkey, H. 41, 43, 89
Steinman, L. 22
Stoller, F. 6, 84
   the zone of innovation 22, 123
summative assessment 13, 27, 86–7, 104, 201, 224, 242–4, 246, 263

Swaffar, J. 18, 59
Swain, M. 22
Swender, E. 11, 83, 123

Takiwātanga (Te Reo Māori, Opai) 142–6
Taylor, F. 24
teacher as designer 5, 13, 40
   Arirang (Soojin Choi Kim) 147–50
   Axe Porridge (Kalmanson) 48–53, 258–62
   bullying, human rights and racism (Lennon) 180–5
   Capoeira (Bianconi) 61–6
   Chanson pour Haiti (Douce) 190–3
   child labour (Durand) 151–4
   DIE Imbissstadt (Garcia & McCloskey) 211, 219–23
   Eid celebration (Kureishy) 185–8
   El Leon Ferido and *Mi Monastir* (Aroeste) 89–95
   Familienstrukturen in der deutschsprachigen Welt (Garcia & McCloskey) 211–18
   food 105
   gender-based violence (D'Ugo) 224–9
   health perspectives and practices 27
   home and lifestyle (Hanna-Wicht) 252–6
   inside-outside spaces (Kuo-Flynn) 55–9
   Lockdown Yoga (Singh) 98–103
   Made in Italy (Bonanno) 106–9
   music 89
   One Lucky Day (Hyun Jin-geon) 173–7
   painting 111
   The Paper Boy (Ilieva) 136–40
   Sana, Sana (Gilbert) 31–4
   school and education (Xie) 246–50
   A Sunday on La Grande Jatte (Seurat) 112–13
   Takiwātanga (Opai) 142–6
   Viva la Vida (Eddy) 28–30
   in xochitl, in cuicatl (Sánchez) 230–4
   Yorùbá wedding celebration (Sanuth) 207–10
teachers and learners 5–6, 10, 12, 17–18, 21, 24–5, 44, 54, 71, 123–4, 132, 174, 243
   annotation benefits 141

autonomy (see autonomy)
certification programmes 124
claim and capture 128–9
culture-based performances 59
development 47
as experts 88, 105, 205, 230
formative/summative assessments 13, 86–7
health perspectives and practices 27, 31
horizontal articulation 16
for inevitable unexpected 78–9
interpersonal-interactive mode 167
language 86, 96, 99, 129, 130, 133, 178
as mediator 124
in novel situations 43
novel tasks 83
objectives and focus questions 13, 71, 273
presentational-productive mode 200–1
space, concept 55
variations 85, 87
texts, defining 127. See also authentic community texts
Theiler, J. 160
Thoreau, H. D. 89
Tirmizi, A. 41
Todd, M. E. 132
tolerance of ambiguity 7, 23, 111, 128
traditional and articulated curriculum 8
transactional products 203
transdisciplinary 10, 13, 16, 18–20, 24, 47, 88, 105, 111, 122, 128, 171, 246, 266–7
transfer 20, 59–60, 78, 104. See also Mediation for Transfer
assessment inventory 286
authentic communication transaction 79–80
complexity, autonomy, novelty for 97
creative 82–3, 89, 109–10, 112, 203, 205
drill/mastery tasks 80–2
far 104, 109
near 109, 242
none, nigh, near, novel 104, 245, 286
performance for 79, 84
and practice at mediation, performance assessment 242–3

reality of 81
routes for (EUs) 68–9
spiral curriculum 151
stages of language assessment 104–5
symbols 141–2, 211
tasks 79, 82, 88–9
turnarounds for 84–5, 114
Tschirner, E. 21
turnarounds for transfer 84–5, 114

uchi and *soto* (Kuo-Flynn). See inside-outside spaces (Japanese culture, Kuo-Flynn)
Uncovering Content: Assessment Design aligning Performance and Transfer (UC:ADAPT) 8–9, 206
unit guide 263, 309–10
Uribe, D. 123

Van Lier, L. 23, 169
VanPatten, B. 18, 25, 124, 178
Verhoeven, L. 134
vertical articulation 9, 13, 16–17, 40, 71, 86, 208
visual literacy 127
visual thinking 54, 127
Viva la Vida (Spanish culture, Eddy) 28–30, 257, 275–6
Vygotsky, L. S. 19, 125–6, 134

Wagner, J. 169
Wagner, M. 14, 41, 44
Watanabe, Y. 41
Wei, L. 22, 178
Wiggins, G. 9–10, 13, 20, 43, 67–8, 71, 79, 87, 122, 160
Wolfe, J. L. 141
world language curriculum design, principles 15–26, 266–7
articulated curriculum and key tasks 15–18
communicating with self-reliance/poise 25–6
learners and language 18–19
mediation and complex tasks 21–3
problem solving and products (tasks) 23–4
spiral curriculum 20–1

tool for articulation 316–17
transfer 20
world language performance assessment 83–5
World Readiness Standards for Learning Languages 9, 41–2, 44
Wu, C. 160

Xie, L., school and education (Chinese curriculum) 246–50, 293–302

Yang, X. 44
Yenawine, P. 54, 127
Yorùbá wedding celebration (Sanuth) 207–10